THE GODS OF ANCIENT EGYPT

THE GODS OF
ANCIENT EGYPT

Barbara Watterson

Facts On File Publications
New York • Oxford

For Juan and Juana

The Gods of Ancient Egypt
Copyright © Barbara Watterson 1984

Reprinted 1988

Library of Congress Cataloging in Publication Data
Watterson, Barbara.
    The gods of ancient Egypt.
    1. Gods, Egyptian.   2. Egypt — Religion.   I. Title.
BL2450.G6W37 1985   299'.31   84-13630

ISBN 0-8160-1111-7

Printed in Great Britain

10 9 8 7 6 5 4 3

4

Contents

Chronological table

It is customary to arrange Egyptian history into Dynasties of kings, following the system first used by Manetho, who wrote a history of Egypt in Greek in the third century BC, and to add two Dynasties to the end of his original list to cover the years after his death. The thirty-two Dynasties thus arrived at are divided into periods known as 'Old Kingdom', 'Middle Kingdom' and 'New Kingdom', interspersed with so-called 'Intermediate Periods'. The term 'Kingdom' is historical rather than geographical and refers to the times in Egyptian history when the country was a unified state ruled by one king. The Intermediate Periods were times when there was no strong central government.

Since we are not certain how Ancient Egyptian was pronounced, many scholars prefer to use the Greek form of royal names taken from Manetho. In the following table, both Greek and Egyptian forms are given where appropriate; in the book, the Egyptian form is used, so that it can be seen clearly which kings are named after gods.

PREHISTORY i.e. Predynastic Egypt

Palaeolithic cultures *c.* 7000–5000 BC	Lower Egypt: type sites: Fayum, Merimde	(no absolute dates known)
Neolithic cultures *c.* 5000–3100 BC	Upper Egypt: type sites: Badari, Naqada	(no absolute dates known)

HISTORY i.e. Dynastic Egypt

BC	Selected Kings Named in Book	Developments in Religion and History
Archaic Period		
Dynasty 1 *c.* 3100–2890	Scorpion (predynastic?) Menes/Narmer Hor-aha	Union of Upper and Lower Egypt Capital city: Memphis

6

HISTORY i.e. Dynastic Egypt *Continued*

Dynasty II *c.* 2890–2686	Sekhemib/Peribsen Khasekemwy Sendji	Kings buried in *mastabas* at Sakkara Beginning of writing Important gods: Horus and Seth

Old Kingdom

Dynasty III *c.* 2686–2613	Djoser	Development of step-pyramid Important god: Atum
Dynasty IV *c.* 2613–2494	Khufu (Cheops) Khafre (Chephren) Menkaure (Mycerinus)	Peak of Old Kingdom achievements in art and architecture Kings buried in first true pyramids at Giza Royal power at peak Important gods: Atum and Re
Dynasty V *c.* 2494–2345	Unas	Decline of royal power Increase in power of Heliopolitan priesthood
Dynasty VI *c.* 2345–2181	Pepi I and II	Spread of Osiris cult Kings buried in small pyramids at Sakkara and Abusir Pyramid Texts

First Intermediate period

Dynasties VII, VIII *c.* 2181–2160		Early Coffin Texts
Dynasties IX, X *c.* 2160–2040		

Middle Kingdom

Dynasty XI 2134–1991	Mentuhotep III (2010–1998) Mentuhotep IV (1998–1991)	State reunited Capital city: Thebes
Dynasty XII 1991–1786	Amenemhat (Amenemmes) I (1991–1962)	Capital city: Lisht Kings buried in pyramids at Lisht, Lahun,

HISTORY i.e. **Dynastic Egypt** *Continued*

	Senwosret (Sesostris) III (1878–1843)	Dahshur etc. Important god: Amun

Second Intermediate Period
Dynasties XIII–XVII   Hyksos invasion
1786–1551

New Kingdom

Dynasty XVIII 1551–1310	Ahmose (Amosis) (1551–1526) Thothmes (Tuthmosis) II (1493–1490) Thothmes (Tuthmosis) III (1490–1436) Hatshepsut (1490–1468) Thothmes (Tuthmosis) IV (1412–1402) Amenhotep (Amenophis) III (1402–1364) Amenhotep IV/ Akhenaten (1374–1358?) Smenkare (1359–1357) Tutankhamun (1357–1348) Ay (1347–1343) Horemheb (1343–1315)	Expulsion of Hyksos State reunited Capital city: Thebes Kings of Dynasties xviii–xx buried in rock-cut tombs at Thebes Egypt becomes Imperial power and richest state in world Amun at height of power Aten rebellion
Dynasty XIX 1310–1198	Ramesses I (1315–1314) Seti (Sethos) I (1314–1304) Ramesses II (1304–1238)	Amun restored Renewed interest in Empire
Dynasty XX 1198–1087	Ramesses III (1198–1166)	Invasion of Sea Peoples From Ramesses III, decline

8

HISTORY i.e. Dynastic Egypt *Continued*

	Ramesses IV (1166–1160) Ramesses V (1160–1156) Ramesses XI (1113–1085)	in Egyptian power

Third Intermediate Period

Dynasty XXI 1087–945	Psusennes II (959–945)	Capital city: Tanis Kings buried in sunken tombs at Tanis High Priests of Amun rule Upper Egypt from Thebes
Dynasty XXII 945–715	Shoshenq I (945–924)	Capital city: Tanis and Bubastis Kings buried at Tanis?
Dynasty XXIII 819–720		Capital city: Leontopolis
Dynasty XXIV 728–715	Tefnakhte (728–720)	Capital city: Sais

Late Period

Dynasty XXV 716–664	Shabaka (716–702)	Egypt under Kushite (Sudanese) rule Capitals at Memphis, Thebes and Napata (Sudan) Kings buried at Kurru (Sudan)
Dynasty XXVI 664–525	Psammetichus I (664–610)	Capital city: Sais Kings buried in Temple of Neit at Sais
Dynasty XXVII 525–404	Egypt under Persian rule	Capital city: Susa or Babylon
Dynasty XXVIII 404–399	Native kings	Capital city: Sais

9

HISTORY i.e. Dynastic Egypt *Continued*

Dynasty XXIX
399–380

Native kings

Capital city: Mendes or
Memphis

Dynasty XXX
380–343

Last native kings
Nectanebo I
(380–362)
Nectanebo II
(360–343)

Capital city: Sebennytos

Dynasty XXXI
343–332

Egypt once more under
Persian rule

Capital city: Susa or
Babylon

332

Alexander the Great
conquers Egypt

Greek Period
Dynasty XXXII
332–30

Alexander
(332–323)
Ptolemy V Epiphanes
(205–180)
Cleopatra VII
(51–30)
Caesarion
(44–30)

The Ptolemaic era: Egypt
ruled by the descendants
of Ptolemy Lagides,
Alexander's general
Capital city: Alexandria

Roman Period
30 BC–AD 395

Egypt under Roman
rule: Roman
Emperors:
Augustus
(30 BC–AD 14)
Tiberius (14–37)
Claudius (41–54)
Vespasian (69–79)
Domitian (81–96)
Caracalla (198–217)
Decius (249–251)
Diocletian (284–305)

Byzantine Period
AD 395–640

Byzantine Emperors

State religion of Egypt:
Christianity (Coptic)

Arab Conquest
AD 640

Arab, Syrian and
Turkish pashas

State religion of Egypt:
Islam

Map of religious centres

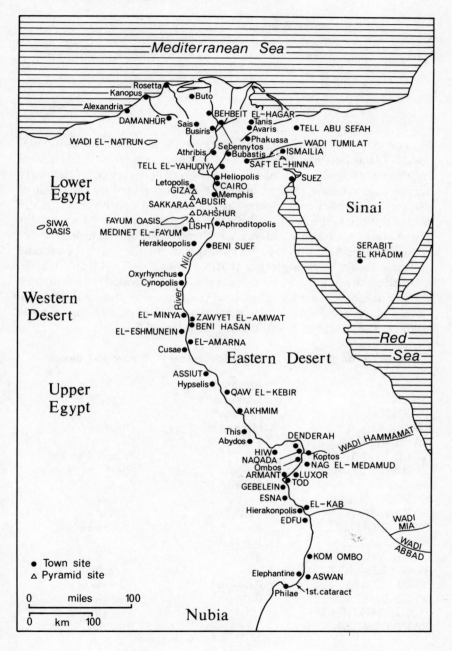

Mediterranean Sea

Rosetta
Kanopus
Buto
Alexandria
BEHBEIT EL-HAGAR
DAMANHÛR
Sais   Tanis
Busiris   Avaris   TELL ABU SEFAH
WADI EL-NATRUN   Phakussa
                              WADI TUMILAT
Athribis   Sebennytos
TELL EL-YAHUDIYA   Bubastis   ISMAILIA
                    SAFT EL-HINNA

Lower Egypt

Letopolis   Heliopolis   SUEZ
              CAIRO
GIZA △   Memphis
SAKKARA △ ABUSIR   **Sinai**
        △ DAHSHUR
FAYUM OASIS △ LISHT
SIWA OASIS   Aphroditopolis
MEDINET EL-FAYUM
Herakleopolis   BENI SUEF

Western Desert

Oxyrhynchus
Cynopolis

River Nile

EL-MINYA   ZAWYET EL-AMWAT
EL-ESHMUNEIN   BENI HASAN
            EL-AMARNA
Cusae   **Eastern Desert**

SERABIT
EL KHÂDIM

Red Sea

Upper Egypt

ASSIUT
Hypselis   QAW EL-KEBIR
                AKHMIM

This
Abydos   DENDERAH
            HIW   WADI HAMMAMAT
        NAQADA   Koptos
            Ombos   NAG EL-MEDAMUD
        ARMANT   LUXOR
        GEBELEIN   TOD
            ESNA
        Hierakonpolis   EL-KAB
                EDFU   WADI MIA
                                WADI ABBAD

            KOM OMBO

Elephantine   ASWAN
Philae   1st.cataract

• Town site
△ Pyramid site

0   miles   100
0   km   100

Nubia

Egyptian Place Names

On the map on p. 11 the place names are those most commonly used today. It has become the custom for scholars to refer to many places by their Graeco-Roman names, following the practice of the early Egyptologists whose interest in Egypt was stimulated by the classical authors; this practice, however, is not followed consistently. In the text of this book, the Ancient Egyptian name has been used, except for particularly well-known places which have become familiar under their Greek or Arabic names: for example, Edfu, for which it would be perverse to use anything other than the name derived from Arabic.

In the following table, place names are listed under 1) the modern Arabic name; 2) the name by which the place was known during the period of Graeco-Roman rule; 3) the Ancient Egyptian name. Names used on the map are marked with an asterisk *.

Modern name	Classical name	Ancient name
	Alexandria*	
ABUKIR	Kanopus*	
RASHID	Rosetta*	
DAMANHÛR*	Hermopolis Parva	*Demit-en-Hor*
SA EL-HAGAR	Sais*	*Sau*
TELL EL-FARA'UN	Buto*	*Pe* and *Dep*
BEHBEIT EL-HAGAR*	Iseum	*Hebyt*
ABUSIR	Busiris*	*Djedu*
SAMANNUD	Sebennytos*	*Tjebnutjer*
SAN EL-HAGAR	Tanis*	*Dja'net*
TELL EL-DAB'A	Avaris*	*Pi-Ramessu*
FAQUS	Phakussa*	
TELL ABU SEFAH*	Sile	*Tjel*
WADI EL-NATRUN*		
TELL ATRIB	Athribis*	*Kem-wer*
TELL BASTA	Bubastis*	*Bast*
WADI TUMILAT*		
SAFT EL-HINNA*		*Per-Soped*

Modern name	Classical name	Ancient name
ISMAILIA*		
TELL EL-YAHUDIYA*	Leontopolis	*Nay-ta-hut*
	Heliopolis*	*Iunu (On)*
CAIRO*		
AUSIM		
GIZA*	Letopolis*	*Khem*
ABUSIR*		
SAKKARA*		
DAHSHUR*		
LISHT*		
MIT RAHINA	Memphis*	*Ineb-hedj*
FAYUM OASIS*	Moeris	*She-resy* (later *Mer-wer*)
MEDINET EL-FAYUM*	Krocodilopolis	
ATFIH	Aphroditopolis*	
IHNASYA EL-MEDINA	Herakleopolis*	*Henen-nesut*
BENI SUEF*		
EL-BAHNASA	Oxyrhynchus*	*Per-medjed*
EL-QEIS	Cynopolis*	
EL-MINYA*		
ZAWYET EL-AMWAT*		*Hebenu*
BENI HASAN*		
EL-AMARNA*		*Akhetaten*
EL-ESHMUNEIN*	Hermopolis Magna	*Khemenu*
EL-QUSIYA	Cusae*	*Qis*
ASSIUT*	Lykopolis	*Zawty*
SHUTB	Hypselis*	*Sha-sehetep*
QAW EL-KEBIR*	Antaeopolis	*Djew-Qa*
AKHMIM*	Panopolis	*Khent-Min*
GIRGA	This*	*Tjeny*
	Abydos*	*Aabdju*
DENDERAH*	Tentyris	*Iunet*
HIW*	Diospolis Parva	*Hoot-sekhem*
TUKH	Ombos*	*Nebet*
QIFT	Koptos*	*Gebtu*
WADI HAMMAMAT*		
NAQADA*		
LUXOR*	Diospolis Magna (Thebes)	*Waset*
NAG EL-MEDAMUD*		*Madu*
ARMANT*	Hermonthis	*Iuny*
TOD*	Tuphium	*Djerty*
GEBELEIN*	Aphroditopolis	*Per-Hathor*
ESNA*	Latopolis	*Ta-sny*

Modern name	Classical name	Ancient name
EL-KAB*	Eleithiapolis	*Nekheb*
KOM EL-AHMAR	Hierakonpolis*	*Nekhen*
EDFU*	Apollinopolis Magna	*Wetjeset-Hor*
WADI MIA*		
WADI ABBAD*		
KOM OMBO*	Ombos	*Nebet*
ASWAN*	Syene	
	Elephantine*	*Abu*
	Philae*	*Pi-lak*

Principal Cult-Centres of Ancient Egypt

The list below gives the principal cult-centres of the major deities discussed in this book, using the names by which places are most likely to be referred to in other books.

Buto: Edjo
Sais: Neit
Sebennytos: Onuris
Tanis: Seth
Busiris: Osiris
Bubastis: Bastet
Leontopolis: Shu, Tefnut
Heliopolis: Atum, Re, Geb, Nut, Khepri
Memphis: Ptah, Sokar, Sekhmet
Cynopolis: Anubis
Hermopolis: Thoth

AMARNA: Aten
Abydos: Osiris
DENDERAH: Hathor
Koptos: Min
Ombos: Seth
Thebes: Amun, Mut, Khonsu
ARMANT: Montu
ESNA: Khnum
EL-KAB: Nekhbet
Hierakonpolis: Horus the Elder
EDFU: Horus
Elephantine: Khnum
Philae: Isis

Glossary

ankh-sign	amulet shaped like the Egyptian hieroglyph ⚲ which means 'life'
barque (or bark)	a ship (usually mythological, e.g. the Barque of Re) or a portable shrine shaped like a ship
cartouche	elongated version ⬭ of the hieroglyphic sign ⊙ *shen* which means 'to encircle'. Two of a king's five names were written inside a cartouche to indicate that he ruled over everything that the sun encircled
Coffin Texts	magical spells painted on inside of coffins belonging to commoners
Copt, Coptic	originally native Egyptians of Graeco-Roman period onwards, eventually came to mean Christian Egyptians
crook	hooked-staff or sceptre carried as symbol of authority by King of Egypt
cultus temple	temple dedicated to the worship of one or more deities
decans	the (Greek) name given to the period of time (10 days) during which the Egyptians observed that certain constellations were visible on the horizon. There were 36 decans in the Egyptian year of 360 days, and tables were drawn up recording them so that the Egyptians were able to tell the time at night: a given constellation would be at a particular point in the sky depending on what hour it was
demotic	script used on business documents etc. from about 700 BC onwards. By the Graeco-Roman period it had become the ordinary writing of everyday life. Word derived from Greek *demoticos* meaning popular
dynasty	the divisions into which Egyptian history was divided by the scholar-priest Manetho in third century BC. Dynasties are roughly families of kings
ennead	group of nine deities e.g. the Ennead of Heliopolis (from Greek for 'nine')
epagomenal days	the five days added on to the Egyptian year of twelve months of thirty days to bring it up to 365 days (from Greek *epagomenal* or 'added')

faience	quartz sand heated in crucible with soda until quartz melts then solidifies into glaze. Many colours but most popular was green or turquoise made by adding copper filings before heating. Substitute for lapis lazuli which had to be obtained from Afghanistan
fetish	inanimate object thought to be endowed with magical and mystical powers
fetishism	worship of such an object
flail	sometimes called flagellum. Symbol of royal authority
hieratic	cursive script derived from hieroglyphs
hieroglyphs	picture-writing of Ancient Egypt. Word derived from Greek *hieros* (sacred) *glupho* (sculptures). Hieratic comes from Greek *hieratikos* (priestly)
mastaba	private tomb of the Old Kingdom. Rectangular in shape with slightly battened sides; reminiscent of the bench found outside village houses in Egypt and called in Arabic *mastaba*: hence the name for the tomb
menat-collar	bead necklace with counterpoise to hang down back of wearer
mortuary temple	temple dedicated to worship of dead king
necropolis	cemetery (from Greek *nekros*: corpse, *polis*: city)
nome	word first used by Greeks to describe the administrative districts of Egypt (42 in all)
obelisk	shaft of stone (usually granite) with pointed top (e.g. Cleopatra's Needle); word comes from Greek *obeliskoi*: little spits
ogdoad	group of eight gods
papyrus	plant (*Cyperus papyrus L.*) which used to grow prolifically in Egypt, especially in Delta marshes. Used for making boats, ropes, baskets, sandals, etc. Pith used to make writing material. Papyrus-paper made in 'pages' which could be stuck together to make a roll (standard roll had 20 pages). Pages seldom more than 43cm wide (but note the Greenfield Papyrus, No. 10554 in British Museum which is 49.5cm wide); and 48cm high. Longest known Roll is the Great Harris Papyrus (No. 9999 in British Museum) which is 41 metres long. Subject matter on papyrus rolls could be administrative, medical, mathematical, literary, religious (e.g. The Book of the Dead or What is in the Underworld)
predynastic	period of Egyptian history that predates writing and unification of Egypt into one state. The prehistoric period before 3100 BC
pyramid	royal tomb in use in Egypt from Dynasty III to Dynasty XVII
pyramidion	pyramid-shaped tip of obelisk (see above), or capstone of pyramid

Pyramid Texts	spells and magical inscriptions found inside pyramids from end of Dynasty v to Dynasty vi
sarcophagus	stone coffin (from Greek *sarco*: flesh, *phag*: eat, swallow)
stele (or stela)	rectangular in shape with curved top, decorated with relief and inscription
syncretism	absorption of one god into the cult or persona of another
theogamy	process by which the supreme god of the time took on the form of the reigning king in order to beget a child upon the queen, the child being destined to become King of Egypt
Tuthmoside	period during which kings named Thothmes ruled Egypt
The Two Lands	Egypt i.e. Upper Egypt (South) and Lower Egypt (North)
waas-sceptre	staff with straight shaft split into two at bottom and topped by the head of an animal. Symbol of royal authority
wadi	Arabic word meaning dried-up river-bed

See also general index

List of illustrations

NOTE

The letters and numbers in brackets refer (i) to the museums in which the objects are housed and (ii) to the numbers given to them in the collection. Abbreviations been used as follows:

Ash. Ashmolean Museum, Oxford
B.M. British Museum, London
E.L. Egyptology Department Museum, School of Archaeology and Oriental Studies, University of Liverpool
E.M. Egyptian Museum, Cairo
G.I. Griffith Institute, Ashmolean Museum, Oxford

The objects appearing in plates 11, 17, 20, 27, 28, 39 and 41 were photographed *in situ* during the clearing of Tutankhamun's tomb, that is, from 1922 onwards, by Harry Burton, who was seconded from the Metropolitan Museum, New York, at the request of Howard Carter. The photographs are now in the Griffith Institute.

A Note on Transliteration

As was explained in the introduction to the Chronological Table, the Greek forms of the names of kings are often used by Egyptologists because the pronunciation of Ancient Egyptian is not known with a sufficient degree of certainty.

From about 3100 BC, the Egyptian language was written in hieroglyphic script, a decorative and complex picture-writing that remained in use for over 3,000 years, until, in 30 BC, Egypt came under Roman rule. The Romans abolished the institution of monarchy in Egypt, and the dissolution of what had been the linch-pin of Egyptian society, combined with the advent of Christianity, to which most of Egypt had been converted by the fourth century AD, meant that the use of hieroglyphs fast deteriorated, to be replaced by Greek.

The Egyptian language, as expressed in hieroglyphs, hieratic and demotic (see Glossary), was lost for centuries until, in AD 1822, Champollion became the first man of modern times to decipher hieroglyphs correctly.

In order for an English-speaker to be able to read what the hieroglyphic script says, the pictures it uses have to be turned into an approximation of the English alphabet: this is called transliteration. Unfortunately, the Egyptians only used consonants in their hieroglyphic script: their language must have had vowels in it, but where these vowels came in Egyptian-language words is not made clear in hieroglyphic script.

It should perhaps be mentioned here that the official language of Egypt today is Arabic, and has been since the Arab Conquest of AD 640; and that Arabic is not the same language as Ancient Egyptian, although the script of both has one thing in common: in neither language are the vowels written.

Thus, there are schools of transliteration for both languages with different traditions for inserting vowels: some write Idfu where we write Edfu (Arabic place-name); some write Ra where we write Re (name of Ancient Egyptian Sun God), and so on. As a general rule of thumb, English-speaking Egyptologists tend to put an 'e' into Egyptian words wherever it would otherwise be difficult to pronounce a string of consonants.

Preface

The artefacts of the Ancient Egyptian civilization, from the largest temples to the smallest amulets, have been much admired for their beauty and workmanship. Admiration soon leads to curiosity about the purpose or significance of recurring themes or designs. Representations of gods in many guises constitute ever recurring themes, and some knowledge of the more commonly represented gods allows the admirer to understand something of the purpose and motives which directed the skills of the Egyptian artisans.

In assembling this 'gazetteer' of the gods of Ancient Egypt, I have aimed at introducing only the thirty or so more important members of a tribe numbered in hundreds, and in addition to more factual details of form, time and place have related the sometimes elaborate mythology pertaining to each. These mythologies are the Egyptian version of the folklore and fairy stories which all societies produce. This book is not a study of Egyptian religion as such, and the only purpose of the brief introductory chapters is to allow the reader to appreciate the theological context in which the gods were worshipped. No attempt has been made to make comparisons with the gods or beliefs of other cultures, although any description of a culture different from our own, especially one so far removed from us in time, inevitably incorporates implicit and sometimes very subjective comparisons with our own twentieth century European tribal customs and beliefs.

Representations of the gods chosen for inclusion can be found in any illustrated book on almost any aspect of Ancient Egyptian civilization. However, there is a tendency for some of the better known artefacts to be illustrated time and again. I have therefore attempted wherever possible to use, as illustrations of points in the text of the present book, objects which have not previously been seen by the general public. In particular I have made extensive use of exhibits from the excellent collection of Egyptian antiquities in the Department of Egyptology, University of Liverpool.

The glossary found on pages 15–17 includes explanations of specialised words in the text; and an explanation of the way in which Egyptian words (proper nouns, place names, kings' names, etc.) have been written is given on p. 20.

Acknowledgements

I should like to thank the following for their invaluable help in the production of this book: Mr J. Lynch for drawing the map on page 11. Mr D. Smart for his photographic help in the production of line drawings. Mr R. Dickinson for photographing the objects in the Museum in the School of Archaeology and Oriental Studies, Liverpool University; Professor A.F. Shore for allowing the objects in the collection to be photographed; and Miss P. Winker for being ever-ready to assist, both in her capacity as Secretary in the Department and as photographer's assistant. My daughter, Juana, for drawing the figures; and, above all, my husband, Juan, for his advice and encouragement.

Acknowledgements for photographs
The photographs of objects in the British Museum are reproduced by kind permission of the Trustees of the Museum. The copyright on the photograph on Plate 53 is owned by the Ashmolean Museum and on the Harry Burton photographs by the Griffith Institute. All other photographs were taken by the author, including those on Plates 16, 27 and 41, which were photographed from the 4-volume Mackenzie edition (c. 1862) of Francis Frith's photographs.

PART I

Introduction

Religion can be thought of as the recognition by human beings of a superhuman power that controls the universe and everything that is, was or shall be in it. Each individual human being can consider that the superhuman controlling power is a deity worthy of being loved; or capable of inspiring awe, obedience, and even fear. The effect of these feelings on individuals can lead to the setting-up of a system of worship of the deity; and to a drawing-up of a code of beliefs and conduct inspired by their religious faith.

Three of the major religions of the modern world—Judaism, Islam and Christianity—recognize a single god. Each is a revelation of one basic truth; its message, which in the case of Christianity and Islam, must be preached to the unconverted, is contained in a holy book: and the Torah, the Koran and the Gospels can all be used to teach the dogma of their Faith. In Ancient Egypt, religion was not like this. The Egyptians recognized many gods; they did not have one universal system of religious belief. They had no sacred books analogous to the Bible or the Koran; there were no theological commentaries or treatises, neither was there any dogma.

The polytheism of the Ancient Egyptians led to tolerance. Apart from two brief periods in their history when there was an attempt to promote a solar monotheism, the Egyptians never suffered from persecutions carried out in the name of religion: there were no Egyptian saints, no martyrs. The Egyptians were a gentle people for whom the family was important, and their religion was based on family life: the gods were given wives, goddesses given husbands; both had children.

Temples continued the domestic theme, being called 'Houses' or 'Mansions' of the god, and architecturally they were based on the house form, with rooms in them for eating and sleeping. The innermost sanctuary was regarded as the bedroom of the god; and it was surrounded by 'guest bedrooms' for visiting deities. The daily ritual of the temple was domestic in form: the morning ritual gave the god his breakfast; the evening ritual gave him his dinner. Egyptian religion did not indulge in bloodbaths with animal or human

25

sacrifices. Instead, each god lived in peace in his home, the temple, very often as part of a trinity of deities, a holy family consisting of father, mother and child.

For much of their history, the Egyptians were accommodating of other people's gods and always ready to receive additions to their pantheon. They received but they did not feel any great need to give: hence there was no real attempt to persuade non-Egyptians to worship Egyptian gods.

In Ancient Egypt, the basis of religion was not belief but cult, particularly the local cult which meant more to the individual. Thus, many deities flourished simultaneously and the Egyptian was seemingly ever-ready to adopt a new god or to change his views about the old. The predominant characteristics of much of Egyptian religion were animism, fetishism and magic. There was also the belief that certain animals possessed divine powers—the cow, for example, represented fertility, the bull virility—which led to the cult of sacred animals, birds and reptiles, each of which was considered to be the manifestation on earth of a divine being.

It was this aspect of Egyptian religion more than any other that the Greeks found curious and the Romans horrifying. Both Greeks and Romans were happy about the polytheism, being polytheistic themselves. However, their own gods, although they were celestial, immortal beings, were nevertheless recognisably human: they had human shapes, and were possessed of human emotions and frailties.

But the Egyptian gods! The most cursory look at reliefs carved on temple walls showing representations of gods revealed one with the body of a man and the head of a hawk; another with the body of a man and the head of a jackal; yet another man seemed to have a beetle in place of a head. While the woman standing next to him had the head of a lioness. They were all gods; and so were the vultures and cobras hovering in attendance on them.

Inside those temples, the Egyptians kept real live cats, bulls, ibises, hawks, and worshipped them as gods; and when they died, mummified them and buried them as they did their kings.

Who does not know, Volusius, what monsters are revered by demented Egyptians? One part worships the crocodile; another goes in awe of the ibis that feeds on serpents. Elsewhere there shines the golden effigy of the sacred long-tailed monkey.

Juvenal would perhaps have been even more scornful had he realised the number and diversity of the gods worshipped by Egyptians, who had created hundreds of deities, probably more than any people before or since.

If the Greeks and Romans found Egyptian religion difficult to comprehend, many modern Europeans have found it impossible. In the nineteenth century, several Egyptologists, themselves brought up in the Judaeo-Christian tradition, sought to prove that although Egyptian beliefs were complex, their religion was really monotheistic.

Two of the greatest of the early Egyptologists were Jean-François Champollion (1790–1832) and Emmanuel de Rougé (1811–1872). Champollion was the Founder of Egyptology who deciphered the hieroglyphic script; de Rougé was the Founder of Egyptian Philology, the first man to lay down correct rules for reading and translating hieroglyphic texts. As Maspero, another great Egyptologist, said: 'Champollion deciphered the texts . . . de Rougé gave us the method which allowed us to utilize and bring to perfection the discovery of Champollion.' Without the work of Champollion and de Rougé, we would not know as much as we do, insufficient as that is, about Egyptian religion. The two men, however, read Egyptian texts and came to the conclusion that the Egyptians were monotheists.

Champollion wrote: 'the Egyptian religion is a pure monotheism which manifested itself externally by a symbolic polytheism.' And de Rougé, in the introduction to his edition of a hieratic text of the Book of the Dead, seemed to indicate that in his opinion the Egyptians believed in One supreme, eternal, almighty God, who had much in common with the God of both Hebrews and Christians. Some years later, Wallis Budge, the doyen of British Egyptology, enlarged on the theories of the two Frenchmen by explaining that the Egyptians were monotheists, but different from Christian monotheists. The Egyptians had One God—the Sun God—and all other gods were but forms of Him.

Thus it can be seen that some modern men have been reluctant to accept that the Egyptians, regarded as being advanced, intelligent and much to be admired in many ways, could have been primitive enough to worship so many gods let alone so many peculiar gods.

Yet the desire to imagine the object of worship in tangible form is common to many men: god tends to be visualised in man's image. The Christian God as depicted, for example, by Michelangelo, is a venerable old man with a beard; and Christian iconography reflects the conventions of the time in which the work was painted or sculpted. One supposes that the Ancient Egyptians looked to their own surroundings for manifestations of divinity, as did other peoples in the early stages of development of their society. Seen objectively, the Egyptians' worship of a falcon-god is surely no more strange a manifestation of religious belief than was the Angel Gabriel with his halo and enormous wings. And the Egyptians could daily watch the sweep of a falcon across the sky, whereas the number of people who have beheld the Angel Gabriel is not large.

I The land of Egypt: its influence upon the religion of the Ancient Egyptians

It is a truism that the activities of people everywhere are influenced by the conditions under which they live, and religious thought is no exception to this. Before the days of mass communication, an Eskimo, living in a cold climate, had no experience of any great heat generated by the sun. His idea of hell, therefore, was of a place of extreme cold. Conversely, a man living in a hot climate can only visualise hell as an even hotter place than any with which he has ever had acquaintance.

The Egyptians lived in a river valley, 1,200km long from Egypt's southern border at Aswan to her northern boundary on the Mediterranean, hemmed in by ancient river terraces. The only naturally verdant land was that watered by the great river which flowed through the valley, the Nile: the rest was desert. In some places, the green strip of land was just over 1km wide; in others, its width stretched up to 21km. For the final 160km or so, the Nile fanned out into the Delta, a triangular, flat area of tributaries, marshes and fields some 240km wide.

The land in which the Egyptians lived was 'the gift of the River', according to the Greek traveller, Herodotus, who visited Egypt in the middle of the fifth century BC. Every year, the Nile, swollen by the torrential rain that fell in Uganda and Ethiopia, where the river had its twin sources, and by the melting snows of the Ethiopian mountains, flooded its banks. Herodotus noted that 'when the Nile inundates the land all of Egypt becomes a sea, and only the towns remain above water, looking rather like the islands of the Aegean'.

The Inundation which came annually to Egypt was only halted at the end of the nineteenth century AD with the building of a dam at Aswan. After completion of this, the Old Aswan Dam, in 1902, the flood waters which had caused the Inundation were held back in a great 230km-long reservoir behind the dam and only allowed through its 180 sluices in a regulated flow.

The annual flood not only irrigated the narrow river valley of Egypt but it also had another inestimable benefit. When the flood waters receded, they left behind them a rich alluvial silt, scoured from the soil of Uganda and Ethiopia as the White and Blue Niles flowed through their respective countries before joining together at Khartoum in the Sudan. This silt enabled the Egyptians to become an agricultural society rather than desert-dwelling nomads. The Nile brought prosperity to Egypt: the desert that bounded the area covered by the Inundation gave her security, for it was an effective barrier against attack from other countries.

The desert also isolated Egypt against outside influences. This, and the narrowness of the land in which they lived, meant that the Egyptians had limited horizons, both physically and metaphorically. They were an intensely inward-looking people, distrustful of foreigners. Indeed, they looked upon non-Egyptians as less than human: their word for mankind was the same as that for Egyptians. Whenever they spoke of the inhabitants of other countries, they usually appended a derogatory epithet—'that vile Kush' or 'the wretched Beduin'. The phenomenon is not unknown to other peoples isolated from outside contacts: the Eskimoes call themselves Inuit, 'the men', meaning human-beings; to the Chinese, the term for 'foreign' and 'non-human' is the same.

The regularity of the Inundation and the security afforded by the desert not only moulded the mental attitudes of the Egyptians; they also determined the way in which they lived. Life in Egypt depended upon the vagaries of the Nile. If the annual flood were too high, havoc ensued. If the flood were too low, a smaller area of land was rendered fit for the sowing of crops and less food could be grown. If a low flood was repeated over several consecutive years, shortage of food was the inevitable outcome, sometimes reaching famine proportions.

At an early date, the Egyptians recognized how important the Nile was to them. Over 5,000 years ago, the many separate tribes which then inhabited Egypt began to cooperate with each other. They banded together to make the best use of the Nile by harnessing and conserving the water, by building dykes, irrigation ditches and canals. In so doing, they developed a unified society ruled by a central authority which was responsible for directing the control of the water, building and maintaining dykes and canals and storing the agricultural produce of the nation. They became, in fact, one of the earliest civilizations; and their conservatism, allied with their isolation behind natural barriers, enabled them to enjoy that civilization for over 3,000 years.

Many aspects of life in Ancient Egypt were influenced by the Nile. The seasons of the year were determined by the behaviour of the River; there were three of them: Inundation (*akhet*, which means

29

'flooded')—the four months (July–October, when the lunar and solar calendars were in step: see p. 49) during which the land was covered by the flood waters of the Nile; Winter (*peret*, which means 'coming forth')—the four months (November–February) during which the fields emerged from the water and seed was sown; and Summer (*shomu*, which perhaps means 'deficiency of water')—the four months (March–June) during which the harvest was gathered.

The Nile determined property values. Land in Egypt was divided into (1) that which always received the benefit of the Inundation; (2) that which sometimes did; and (3) that which never did. Taxes were assessed accordingly. Even Justice was influenced by the Nile. There were incessant wrangles over rights to use water, or over boundaries that had been blurred by the Inundation, and many of these cases came to Court. The importance of the Nile and its water was reflected in the accounts men gave of themselves in the Afterlife; or left as their records for posterity. The declaration that a man had not 'held up the water in its season' or 'built a dam against running water' or 'diverted his neighbour's water for his own use' was held to be of equal importance with the avowal of never having committed murder or robbery.

The Nile, which the Egyptians called the River (*iteroo*), came, or so they thought, from the place where the world began. Accordingly, they metaphorically oriented themselves with respect to the south and towards the cavern at Aswan where the Nile had its mythological source (p. 80). The mythological cause of the Inundation was the goddess, Isis, weeping copious tears into the Nile in commemoration of her dear, dead husband, Osiris; and every year the Egyptians celebrated the event at the great festival that marked the beginning of the Inundation, the festival called the Night of Clouds (*Gerekh-en-Haty*); an event that modern Egyptians celebrated before the building of the Aswan Dam as the Night of the Tear Drop (Leilet el Nuktah: June 18).

Considering that the Nile was so vital to the Egyptians, it is perhaps surprising to discover that this great river was not elevated to the position of most important god in the land. In fact, the Nile as such was not deified at all. Instead, it was represented by Hapy, the Spirit or Essence of the Nile. Many are the figures of Hapy that can be seen in temples, carved on the dadoes that run along the bases of walls within the temple: he is depicted as a man with a pendulous belly (always a sign of a prosperous and well-fed man to the Ancient Egyptians, a man to be respected) and the breasts of a woman, wearing on his head clusters of Nile plants.

Thus, the characteristics peculiar to the land of Egypt—a long,

The land of Egypt: its influence upon the religion of the Ancient Egyptians
narrow valley surrounded and protected by desert, a river which
ensured a plentiful supply of water and fertile soil, a climate which
had little rainfall and no snow or fog, a land on which the sun shone
constantly but which was prevented from turning into an arid waste
by that plentiful supply of water—combined to make the Ancient
Egyptians into a highly conservative, parochial, even complacent,
society. They lived in a land that was productive but nevertheless
demanded constant hard work, and encouraged its inhabitants to be
practical. The Egyptians tended to be people of little imagination,
who did not indulge in any great flights of fancy. They were
parochial: their eyes were turned on their own neighbourhood no
matter how confined that neighbourhood might be. The Ancient
Egyptians had no real sense of nationalism; they certainly did not
have a sense of internationalism.

In spite of their narrow, inward-looking way of life, many
Egyptians must have posed the eternal, universal questions: who
created the world? and the sun and the stars? who created life on
earth, both animal and human? what happens to a man when he dies?
is there life after death? They found acceptable answers to their
questions by conceiving gods and a religion that were developed
directly from their own experience of life as they lived it in the land of
Egypt.

II Forms of religion in Ancient Egypt

The earliest Egyptians, in common with many primitive peoples, probably worshipped simple things such as oddly-shaped stones and hills. Such worship is termed *animism*, that is, the attribution of a living soul to inanimate objects and natural phenomena. Whereas a 'rational' man, having stubbed his toe against a stone, would regard it as an accident, an animist may believe that the stone has attacked him and consider it to be something unfriendly or even malevolent, and, if sufficiently in awe of it, may even turn the stone into an object of worship.

Animists believe that the souls attached to inanimate objects can detach themselves and become 'spirits', which are able to take any form they choose and which pose a threat to men, for they are always looking for an opportunity to enter the bodies of men and animals. Once a spirit gains entrance to a man's body, it changes the behaviour of its host and can even bring about his death through madness or disease. Animists also believe that spirits can be disembodied and cause disasters and calamities, although, on the other hand, some spirits are thought to be beneficial and kindly; and they believe that dead men possess souls and must be propitiated by the living in case they try to do harm: hence, animists are often practitioners of ancestor-worship.

The early Egyptians, like other animists, identified certain animals, birds, trees or stones as homes of spirits, both good and bad. Even geographical features could be venerated: thus the highest peak in the Theban area was worshipped as *Ta-Dehenet* (the Mountain Top) and became the goddess of the Theban necropolis. Gradually, the good spirits became 'gods' and were served by magicians who claimed to have power to influence their actions on behalf of men, and to be able to avert the malevolence of the evil spirits. Eventually, theories were developed that turned magic into religion. The Egyptians, however, never entirely lost their primitive instincts and remained a very superstitious people in whose lives and religious practices and beliefs magic always played an important part.

The early Egyptians were also fetishists. *Fetishism* endows an object with magical and mystical power, but not with a living soul. A wide variety of objects were worshipped as fetishes, each in its own locality, and amongst the known fetishes are fossil belemnites, a shield and arrows and a sceptre. Reasons for the choice of an object as a fetish are often difficult to guess at, but chance likeness to parts of the human body, or a particular association with a district, seems to account for some of them, in much the same way as heraldic devices are chosen in the composition of coats of arms.

The Egyptians often chose objects of worship from amongst the animals and birds with which they were in daily contact. An animal was first venerated, perhaps, because of some particular quality it possessed—strength, beauty, virility, grace, swiftness; and worshipped because of the admiration or fear it engendered. Animal worship was localized so that the exemplar of virility, for instance, might in one place be a ram, in another a bull and in yet another a goose. Reasons for the particular choice are, of course, impossible for us to determine with any certainty, although especial rarity or abundance of a species in a locality may have influenced the choice.

The Egyptians of the prehistoric era eventually began to give human form to their sacred animals and objects. There are inherent difficulties in having purely inanimate or animal gods: inanimate gods, for instance, are unable to speak and make their wishes known. Anthropomorphism solves some of these difficulties. To us, it might seem that the obvious way to anthropomorphise these deities would have been to give them human heads and tongues. Why the Egyptians chose not to do so we do not know: they chose, instead, to retain the animal heads but to equip them with human bodies. A further development was to represent the god in fully human form, but to link him with an animal, often the animal that had been sacred in that locality since prehistoric times. The sacred animal was then considered to be imbued with the spirit of the god or to be his manifestation upon earth.

The fourth type of deity worshipped by the Ancient Egyptians was the cosmic god—moon, storm, wind and, especially, the sun—who represented a more advanced form of divine being whose comprehension and worship demanded a greater intellectual effort than was necessary with the more tangible fetish and animal gods of earlier times. Cosmic gods were not fully developed until the historic era (post 3000 BC), when the sun in particular became a universal god, worshipped throughout the land and, around 2500 BC, elevated to the position of state god.

The characteristics of the land in which the Egyptians lived influenced their religion by diversifying it. Until about 3000 BC Egypt was divided into two distinct halves, each inhabited by tribes of different ethnic groups. The northern half, usually called Lower Egypt because the lower reaches of the Nile run through it, was inhabited by people of semitic origins. It was cut in all directions by arms of the Nile, marshes and canals. The southern half, or Upper Egypt, lay in the narrowest, least fertile, part of the Nile Valley, where the river often runs between high cliffs, thus denying the Inundation access to the land. It was inhabited by people of African origin. Communication between the two halves of the country, and even within the two halves, was extremely difficult: the Nile was the only highway. Thus Egypt fell easily into provinces, each with differences in speech, ways of life, customs and religion. In the historic period, these provinces were called *separt*, later renamed Nomes by the Greeks, the term that is now generally used when referring to the administrative districts of Ancient Egypt. There were forty-two Nomes, established early in Egyptian history: twenty-two in Upper Egypt and twenty in Lower Egypt. Their boundaries were shifted from time to time, but their number remained constant since forty-two was considered to be a magic number by the Egyptians.

Within each Nome, towns and villages tended to be cut off from each other. The Nomes themselves had characteristics of their own since each was probably based on what had been a tribal area. Each Nome had a capital city; a special deity which was given the name of the Nome and could be impersonated by a human-being during great national ceremonies in temples; and a Nome standard which carried a representation of the chief god or fetish worshipped in the Nome. Thus in each province, town and village in Egypt, religion took on forms peculiar to that province, town and so on. Each locality had its own local god who was often worshipped in a way that was special to him and equipped with myths and legends of his own.

During periods of unrest, or when there was a weak central government, religious differences were intensified but the process was reversed when the country was united. The principal deity of the town or city which was the seat of the official royal residence—this varied from time to time according to the vicissitudes of history—became the state god. His temple was visited from all parts of the country, its god recognised by all, and the fame that providing the state god for the country brought to his home town caused other towns to wish for a god of such distinction. And so they either introduced his worship into their own temple; or they 'discovered' that he was in reality one and the same god as their own local deity: and the two would be blended into one—for example, Amen-Re (p. 141). As a uniform way of life developed in Egypt, this process of merging gods, called syncretism, should have led inexorably to one god with a very long name made up of the syllables of the names of all the gods of Egypt. This 'happy state' was never attained!

Thus, throughout Egyptian history, there was a great number of gods in Egypt. How many is impossible to establish, since some are merely names mentioned in hieroglyphic texts, and with each discovery or translation of a new text, more gods may be revealed. The number is enlarged, some estimate to over two thousand, because many gods have female counterparts; and because the hieroglyph denoting 'god', ⍓ or ⍟ , is often added to the name of any unusual creature. Many gods, therefore, have more in common with fairies, pixies, goblins, demons and similar creatures than with anything that is generally accepted as a true deity.

The myriad gods worshipped by the Ancient Egyptians fell into three main categories:

1 Local gods, which were the inanimate objects (fetishes) or animals, birds and other living creatures associated with a particular locality: the earliest type of deity worshipped by the Egyptians, whose outward form, be it bull, ibis, monkey or whatever, was worshipped at many different places but whose name differed from town to town.

2 Universal gods, the cosmic deities who represented the forces of nature—the sun, the moon, the stars, wind and storm—the gods who were made the subjects of the great myths of Egypt, whose temples were great cult centres.

3 Personal gods, the objects or creatures chosen by individuals to receive their allegiance. Anything might be chosen as a personal god—the snake that lived in a hole near the door to a man's house; the fox that came down from the desert to scavenge amidst his refuse; any object or creature that inspired awe through superstition or fear of its potential for harm.

Sometimes, the distinction between a local god and a personal god is not clear. For example, the people of Deir el Medina, the village where the workers in the Theban necropolis lived from Dynasty XVIII to Dynasty XX, worshipped a local cobra-goddess, Mertseger, the 'Lover of Silence', but the ever-present danger of being bitten by the cobra that lurked in the rocks amongst which the people of Deir el Medina lived and worked made the veneration of Mertseger a very personal affair!

Personal gods were important to the Egyptians. Because the ordinary man had no admittance to temples, and never saw the deities who were supposed to reside in the statues kept there except when those statues were brought out of the temple for sacred festivals, he had his own beliefs, his own private god or gods to whom he could turn for aid and comfort. Whereas the Egyptians erected official temples for local and universal gods, the private individual was happy to construct with his own hands a small shrine near his house for his personal god.

Meanwhile, the official state religion of Egypt concerned itself with promoting the well-being of the gods, which they reciprocated by maintaining the established order of the world. The vehicle through which the gods received favour, and in turn dispensed it, was the King, aided by a hierarchy of priests. One of the most important aspects of Egyptian religion was the fact that the King was regarded as a god. Tradition stated that in the beginning, Kingship came to earth in the person of the god-king, Re, who brought his daughter, Maat, the embodiment of Truth and Justice, with him. Thus the beginning of the earth was simultaneous with the beginning of kingship and social order.

The kings of Egypt legitimised their claim to the throne in ways that were influenced by religious beliefs. The god-king, Horus, was the son of Osiris who had been king; and so every new king of Egypt became a Horus to his predecessor's Osiris. By acting as Horus had towards Osiris, in other words, by burying his predecessor, each new king made legal his claim to the throne (p. 103). The device of theogamy was also used for this purpose. Here, the principal god of the time was said to have assumed the form of the reigning king in order to beget a child on his queen: that child later claimed to be the offspring of both his earthly and his heavenly father; and the earthly father was quite content to be cuckolded by the god (pp. 132, 141).

The king was the unifying factor in Egyptian religious life. In theory, he was chief priest in every temple; the only person entitled to officiate in the temple rituals, the only person entitled to enter the holy of holies within the temple. Obviously, this was a fiction: the king could not be in every temple at once. However, the fiction was maintained in the reliefs carved on the walls of temples, which always show the king making offerings to the gods. He was the embodiment of the connection between the world of men and the world of gods, the linchpin of Egyptian society. It was his task to make the world go on functioning; it was his task to make the sun rise and set, the Nile to flood and ebb, the grain to grow: all of which could only be achieved by the performance of the proper rituals within the temples.

For Egyptians the term 'temple' meant something very different from what it means to people today. Egyptian temples symbolised the earth: thus they were made of the most enduring materials that the Egyptians were capable of handling at any given period. The earliest temples were built of reeds and mud; during the Old Kingdom, most were constructed of mud-brick, only the lintels of their doors and windows, and the bases of columns, being made of stone. By the end of the Old Kingdom, the Egyptians had the ability to build their temples entirely in stone, although not many of these structures can be seen today, due to the fact that it was the custom never to build a 'new' temple on a virgin site, but to 'renew' it on a site that had been in use since time immemorial. Thus, the great stone structures that can still be seen at Thebes, for instance, or at Edfu, have been built over much older temples. Inside, the ceilings of the temples were painted with stars to represent the firmament, and the walls decorated at the base with carvings of the marsh plants and reeds that grew on the banks of the Nile.

The Egyptians believed that the earth was constantly threatened by the forces of chaos that had existed before the world was created: they had been overcome but were an ever-present danger. Only the gods could keep them at bay. These gods appeared in different guises in different places all over Egypt, where they had to be equipped with homes—temples, the houses or mansions of the gods. Inside these houses, the gods could be protected and nourished so that they could perform their divine tasks.

From the beginning of the historical period, there were two distinct types of temple in Egypt: the mortuary or funerary temple, dedicated to the worship of a dead king; and the cultus temple, dedicated to the worship of one or more of the many gods of Egypt. Each type of temple owned property and estates, often in many parts of the country, and sometimes outside it, which not only rendered it self-supporting but also produced extra revenue so that temples could become owners of great wealth.

The cultus temple especially played an important part in the life of the community. For the ordinary man, however, its role was not that of a place of worship. The Egyptian temple was nothing like a church, mosque or synagogue. It was not a place to which a man might go for spiritual comfort, to praise god, to discuss theological points and be instructed in religious matters. In fact, the ordinary man was not allowed to set foot inside the temple.

The Egyptian temple was a land-owner: the ordinary Egyptian could and did rent land from it. It was the repository for legal documents, the place where births and marriages were registered and contracts drawn up. Schools were centred on temples: scribes, artists and doctors were trained there. Most Egyptians were illiterate; temple scribes were therefore employed to draw up documents and write such letters as were necessary. The doctor-priests tended the ailments of the Egyptians, and some temples even had rudimentary hospitals within their precincts where the sick could receive treatment, which often used magical as well as medical methods.

Temples were big business: the only chance the ordinary Egyptian was given to worship the gods housed in them came when the cultus statue of the god, in which the spirit of the deity was thought to reside, and which was normally kept in the innermost sanctuary of the temple, was brought out of its shrine on the occasion of one of the great feasts which took place at certain times of the year, and carried in procession around the town for the edification of the populace.

Just as the Egyptian temple was unlike anything modern man understands by the word 'temple', so an Egyptian 'priest' was not like the spiritual leader that is the modern concept of a Christian priest or a Muslim imam; neither was he a recognised authority on religious law as for instance is a Jewish rabbi.

The priests of Ancient Egypt were not spiritual leaders or preachers; they did not have parishioners. They were not inspiring deliverers of sermons because congregations of worshippers did not feature in the life of an Egyptian temple. They were not expected to be authorities on general religious doctrine, for there was none. There was no central system of religious belief or organisation; each town had its own, and so the priesthood of any temple followed the customs and practices peculiar to that temple.

In theory, the king appointed all priests; and in every temple in the land they served as his surrogates. To become a priest, a man did not have to have any special calling or gift for religion. His task was that of administrator of temple property, estates and revenues; and within the temple his function was to act as a domestic servant to the god and minister to his daily needs. This was the case whether the god was a living animal or bird kept in the temple as the representative on earth of a god; or a golden effigy of the deity.

The one stipulation for entry to the temple was that a man, or a woman, be pure. Several days before entering a temple, a priest (or priestess) had to purify himself by chewing natron and fumigating himself with incense; on the day that he entered the temple, he had to wash himself, cut his finger and toe nails, and, in the case of a priest, be shaved and depilated of all body hair. Priests also had to be circumcised. Neither priests nor priestesses were required to lead celibate lives outside the temple. But they had to be prepared to observe the prohibitions observed by their particular temple—a taboo on eating fish, perhaps, or on certain gestures.

Although the priestly office was usually hereditary, it was possible to be appointed priest by the king as a mark of favour, especially if he wanted to place his own man in office; or to purchase that office. Anyone prepared to make the sacrifice of, for instance, being circumcised, or refraining from sexual intercourse during his time of service, could be a priest: the essential qualification was purity rather than a talent for the priesthood.

The number of priests serving in a temple depended upon the size and importance of that temple, which in turn depended upon the importance of its god or of the town in which it was situated. A majority of the priests in any temple were part-time laymen who, after their period of temple-service, went back to their homes to carry on normal life. These priests were divided into 'gangs'; there were four gangs to each temple, and each served one lunar month in four during their years of service in the temple.

Certain categories of priest were permanent members of the temple staff: the High Priest of the temple, whom the Egyptians called the First Servant of the God, was one such. The career structure that led to this position is well illustrated by one Bakenkhons, who served in the Temple of Amun at Thebes at the beginning of Dynasty XIX. Bakenkhons entered the service of the god when he was fifteen years old, and served as a 'pure-priest'—the lowest category of priest—for four years. When he was nearly twenty years old, he was promoted to the rank of 'Father of the God', a second rank priest. At thirty-two, he was made third 'Servant of the God'; at forty-seven, he became second 'Servant of the God'. Then, when he was fifty-nine years old, he became First Servant of the God—in other words, High Priest of Amun, one of the most powerful men in the land at that time, a position he held for twenty-seven years until his death at the age of eighty-six.

The advantages of being a priest were many. Each priest received a share of the income from temple estates, and of the offerings which came into the temple every day, the share being greater or lesser according to the size of the temple and the rank of the priest. The wives and daughters of priests were entitled to certain allowances from temple revenue, and the priests themselves were exempted from certain taxes. They were often granted immunity from having to undertake state labour such as work on dykes and canals; and in certain temples, the priesthood was granted immunity from all such labour by special royal decree.

There was no rigid division between the sacred and the secular world in Egypt. The secular world viewed the temples that were to be found in every sizeable town more or less as places of business; whereas the priests of those temples all worked, in their different ways and according to the beliefs and customs of their own temples, to maintain the equilibrium between the world of the gods and the world of men. The worship of gods therefore was just one of the many activities undertaken by the temple bureaucracy, which was also responsible for many of the functions that nowadays would come within the province of local government.

The worship of gods was, however, the chief *raison d'être* for the existence of the temples. In some ways, this worship bore a resemblance to, say, Christian worship, in that hymns of praise were sung to the gods. Other forms of extolling god, such as dancing and clapping, were also employed. The most obvious difference between Egyptian and Christian worship can be seen in the prayers made to the god of each temple. Christian prayers tend to be supplications to the Almighty either for the general good or for the well-being of a person other than the supplicant. Christians are taught that it is not an acceptable way of praying to ask for things directly for oneself.

The Egyptians adopted a much more business-like approach: their 'prayers', as we know from the texts carved on the walls of their temples, are made in the spirit of *quid pro quo*. The priest/king makes an offering to the god: and the god reciprocates in kind. Thus, for example, if the king offers the god wine, the god in turn rewards the king with the gift of the vineyards that produce the wine; if the royal offering is incense, the god promises the king that he shall have dominion over the land from whence the incense came. All this makes Egyptian religion sound less than spiritual. In many ways, it was. On the other hand, there is evidence from texts which exhort priests to live in accordance with high moral principles that spiritual ideals were not entirely absent from Egyptian religious life.

The number of gods worshipped in Ancient Egypt meant that there was no one version of the answers posed at the end of Chapter I. For us, Egyptian religion seems to consist of many conflicting beliefs. One of the reasons for this is that the Egyptians, conservative as they were, never discarded any of their old beliefs in favour of new ones: they simply assimilated them. They were quite content to have several different explanations for the same thing, for each explanation might serve in different contexts. There were, for instance, several variations on the theme of the creation of the world, for the great creator-gods such as Atum, Re, Ptah and Thoth each had his own version. But whichever deity performed the act of creation, there was one underlying image: in the beginning, water covered the earth and all was dark and void. This primordial water was called the Nun, and it is a natural image for the Egyptians to have conjured up. They must have seen their land covered by water during the Inundation, and have seen, when the flood water began to recede, little islands of land begin to emerge. Just so did the first piece of Earth emerge from the primaeval waters of the Nun.

There were many ideas of what the Universe was. The sky was visualised as a cow whose feet rested on the earth (Hathor); or as a woman who supported herself with hands and feet on the earth (Nut). Or the sky was said to be a sheet of water on which the stars sailed in boats, just as the Egyptians themselves sailed on the Nile. Or the sky rested on four fabulous mountains situated at the four corners of the earth—the pillars of heaven. The sun was said to be the right eye of a great god whose left eye was the moon (Atum; Re). It was born every morning as the calf of the celestial cow (see above); or as the child of the sky goddess. It was rolled across the sky by a beetle (Khepri) until in the evening it became an old man (Atum). The sun, the moon and the stars were said to sail in ships over the heavenly ocean. There was said to be a second heaven under the earth; through this heaven a river ran just as the Nile runs through Egypt. Every night, the sun descended under the earth, where it traversed the underworld Nile. And every morning, it ascended to earth again through two whirlpools at Elephantine (Aswan).

The great gods were accompanied by their own retinues of lesser deities: thus, at Heliopolis (p. 50), Re is the head of a group of nine gods known to the Egyptians as the *pesdjet* and to us as the Great Ennead (from the Greek word 'ennead' meaning 'group of nine'); at Hermopolis (p. 179), Thoth is the head of a group of eight gods, now known by the Greek term Ogdoad. When other towns wished to possess an ennead of their own, they displaced one of the original gods and inserted their own deity in his place. Sometimes, they simply added their own local god to the ennead, not a whit abashed that in so doing they made their 'group of nine (ennead)' into a group containing ten members!

The Egyptians had a very relaxed attitude towards their gods, whether they were great state gods or lesser divinities. The stories told about Egyptian gods, often by their own adherents, show that the Egyptians regarded these deities as a class of being much like themselves: they had the same need for food and drink; they could suffer pain, age or death; they had the same vices and virtues, they were just as apt to commit acts of folly, treachery or trickery as a fallible human-being. Their lapses, however, did not earn them scorn from their worshippers: instead, they merely moved the Egyptians to treat their gods in a tolerantly amused way. In spite of this, the gods of

Ancient Egypt were beings to be respected, for it was only through their beneficence and good-will that Egypt prospered, as she undoubtedly did, for over 3,000 years!

The beliefs associated with some of the more important of these deities, their origins and chief places of worship, are set out in the following chapters, which are arranged more or less according to the importance of the gods discussed in them rather than in any historical or geographical order.

PART II

The Major Gods of Egypt

THE SUN GOD

The Ancient Egyptians undoubtedly recognised that life was dependent upon the sun. In a land such as Egypt, where the sun shines every day undimmed by rain or fog, winter and summer alike, it was perhaps inevitable that it should become an object of worship, reverenced for its beneficial qualities and at the same time feared for its potential for destruction.

The sun was worshipped in different forms, under several names. The most important sun-gods were: Re, who was the sun's disk itself, the noon-day sun; Khepri, who was thought of as a beetle (*Scarabaeus sacer*) and denoted the rising sun; Atum, who was thought of as an old man leaning on a stick and represented the setting sun; Horus, who usually took the form of a falcon; Horakhty, another falcon-god, whose name means 'Horus-of-the-Horizon', and who, when coalesced with Re as Re-Horakhty, became identified with the sun; Aten, who became especially popular during the reign of Amenhotep IV–Akhenaten (the Amarna Period) and was represented as the sun's disk with rays which terminated in hands.

The cult of the sun was established, probably long before Dynastic times, at Iunu or On in Lower Egypt, where it was worshipped in the forms of Atum, Khepri, Horakhty and, above all, Re. After the Unification of Egypt into one kingdom, an event which took place around 3100 BC, Memphis was established as the capital of Egypt. The priesthood of On, however, continued to exert great influence, and this influence probably extended to the new Rulers of all Egypt.

The Greeks later named On Heliopolis (the City of the Sun). Today, the site of the city which was once the spiritual centre of Egypt lies under the suburb of Matarieh on the north-east side of Cairo.

ATUM

Atum, whose name means 'the Complete One', was one of the great creator-gods, possibly the oldest deity to be worshipped at Heliopolis, where, coalesced with Re to form Re-Atum, he became a sun-god.

The ichneumon or Egyptian mongoose, which the Egyptians today call Kutt Fara'un (Pharaoh's Cat), is the great destroyer of snakes and crocodile eggs and was thought to be the incarnation of Atum. One legend says that the god was once attacked by a snake and had to transform himself into an ichneumon in order to destroy it. Atum, however, is never depicted as an ichneumon but always as a man with a man's head.

Atum was held to be a self-created god who made the whole of creation out of himself. He first took shape as a serpent which came into being in the Primaeval Waters of the Nun. Although eventually he took on human form, the Egyptians believed that at the end of the world, Atum would revert to his serpent form and return to the Nun with which the earth would once more be covered.

The earliest written doctrine of Atum as procreator was set down about 2350 BC. At this time, the last king of Dynasty V, Unas, built a pyramid-tomb at Sakkara. Here, for the first time, inscriptions were carved inside a pyramid, in the burial chamber and its antechamber. These inscriptions are known as the Pyramid Texts. The Texts, which are found also inside many of the Dynasty VI pyramids, are a collection of so-called 'spells', arranged haphazardly and differing from pyramid to pyramid: Unas' selection, for example, has 228 spells out of a possible total of over 700. They tell of the creation of the world according to Heliopolitan doctrine; they give the dead king all the information needed concerning the Afterlife and how to reach it; and provide the magical means with which to ensure the well-being of the deceased.

By the end of Dynasty VI, exclusive royal power had waned. One result of this was the adaptation of the Pyramid Texts for use by those commoners who were accorded burial in a tomb. These commoners were not buried in pyramids, a type of tomb used only by kings of certain periods and, sometimes, their queens. Thus, instead of decorating the walls of pyramids with these magical texts, commoners had them painted on the wooden coffins in which they were buried. Hence, the Pyramid Texts became the Coffin Texts.

One Coffin Text makes Atum speak about the Beginning:

> 'I [Atum] was still alone in the Waters, in a state of inertness. I had not yet found anywhere to stand or sit, Heliopolis had not yet been founded that I might be therein.'

Before Atum arose from the Primaeval Waters, he created the first creatures: Shu, male, and Tefnut, female.

There are two versions of the act by which 'he who had been one became three'. One is told in Pyramid Text 527, which says that:

> Atum was creative in that he proceeded to masturbate himself in Heliopolis. He took his penis in his hand so that he might obtain the pleasure of orgasm thereby. And brother and sister were born— that is, Shu and Tefnut.

This is obviously a late, Heliopolis-oriented version of the myth— several other Texts say that the masturbation took place not in Heliopolis but in the Primaeval Waters.

Other myths concerning the creation of Shu and Tefnut maintain that Atum spat them forth from his mouth. This concept makes use of plays on two words which both mean 'to spit' or 'to expectorate'— *ishesh*, which has a sound similar to Shu; and *tef*, which forms the first syllable of the name Tefnut. The version of the birth of Shu and Tefnut through spitting from Atum's mouth rather than through the more crude but perhaps more logical method of masturbation is the forerunner of the idea that the world was created through God's word.

Atum's mouth contained spittle and the breath of life. Tefnut was formed from the spittle and therefore became the goddess of moisture. Shu, being formed from Atum's breath, became the god of air; and, because air is essentially the breath of life, he became Life itself. After their birth, the two newly-formed deities became separated from their father, Atum, and were lost in the dark immensity of the Nun. Atum sent his Eye to look for them. When they were found, he named his son, Shu, as Life, and his daughter, Tefnut, as Order, the personification of what we would call the forces of Nature; and lay entwined with them in the Nun, keeping them safe.

Spell 80 of the Coffin Texts tells us what happened next. Atum, tired of lying inert in the Nun, asks how he can create a resting place for himself. Nun tells him:

'Kiss your daughter, Order, put her to your nose; so will your heart live. Never let her leave you, let Order, who is your daughter, be with your son, Shu, who is Life.'

Atum then asks Shu to support him while he holds Tefnut to his nose, or kisses her. And so Heliopolis came into being as the first mound which rose out of the waters of the Nun. And Atum was able to rest upon it. According to Pyramid Text 600, Atum *was* this mound, which was called the High Hill in Heliopolis. Only when Atum appeared as or on the Hill did light break over the hitherto dark Nun.

Other accounts of the first dawn tell of a heron, known to the Egyptians as the Benu Bird, skimming over the waters of the Nun until it came to rest on a rock. As it did so, it opened its beak and a cry broke over the unutterable silence of the Nun. The world was filled with 'that which it had not known'; the cry of the Benu Bird 'determined what is and is not to be'. Thus, the Benu Bird as an aspect of Atum, the god who created himself, brought light and life to the world.

The rocky perch upon which the Benu Bird alighted was worshipped at Heliopolis in the form of the Benben Stone, a pillar topped by a pyramid-shaped stone, the *pyramidion*, the sides of which reflected the sun's light at dawn. This Stone was the most sacred fetish worshipped at Heliopolis. The capstone of every pyramid, if not the pyramid itself, was thought to be a representation of the Benben and the dead king buried under it was thought to be under the direct protection of the Sun God himself.

The Benu Bird's cry began the cycles of time which the Egyptians believed to be divinely appointed: the twenty-four hour day with twelve hours allotted to daytime and twelve to night-time; the cycle of ten days which made up the Egyptian week; the thirty-day month; the year of twelve months but 365 days (p. 49); the periods of 1,460 years during which the civil and astronomical calendars diverged and then coincided again due to the fact that the astronomical year has $365\frac{1}{4}$ days. The Benu Bird became the deity connected with the division of time; and its temple at Heliopolis, where the chief title of its High Priest was 'Overseer of Observers', was primarily concerned with the regulation of the calendar by solar and astral means. Herodotus reported that the priests of Heliopolis were the most learned of all.

Herodotus recounted the legend of the Benu Bird, which the Greeks called the *phoinix*, as follows:

I have not seen a phoenix myself, except in paintings, for it is very rare and visits the country (so at least they say in Heliopolis) only at intervals of 500 years, on the occasion of the death of the parent bird. To judge by the paintings, its plumage is partly golden, partly red, and in shape and size it is exactly like an eagle. There is a story about the phoenix: it brings its parent in a lump of myrrh all the way from Arabia and buries the body in the Temple of the Sun. To perform this feat, the bird first shapes some myrrh into a sort of egg as big as it finds, by testing, that it can carry; then it hollows the lump out, puts its father inside and smears some more myrrh over the hole. The egg-shaped lump is then just of the same weight as it was originally. Finally, it is carried by the bird to the Temple of the Sun in Egypt. I give the story as it was told to me—but I don't believe it.[1]

Herodotus did not believe the story: but other Greeks did and enlarged upon the myth until eventually the phoenix became a fabulous bird which consumed itself in flames only to be reborn from the ashes. The Greeks believed the phoenix to be a herald of important events, whilst to the Egyptians, a heron flying out of the sunlight was a sign of joy and hope.

The Benu Bird depicted in Egyptian paintings, or on the papyrus rolls placed in the coffins of the dead to help them find their way to the Afterlife, is undoubtedly a gigantic heron, usually said to be an enlarged version of the grey heron, *Ardea cinerea*, which is common in Egypt, although there is a possibility that it is based on the Goliath heron, *Ardea goliath*, now found, amongst other places, on the coast of the Red Sea but which may have been more widespread in ancient times.

Recent excavations at Umm an-Nar (Trucial Oman) have uncovered bird bones which, when reconstructed, prove to be from a species of heron much larger than any now living. It seems certain that a heron considerably larger than the Goliath heron lived in the region of the Persian Gulf some 5,000 years ago.

Accordingly, Ella Hoch[2] has proposed that a new species be erected for this heron under the name *Ardea bennuides*, the Benu-bird heron. She points out that although many thousands of ibises, baboons, cats and other creatures have been found mummified in Egypt, no example of a mummified heron has yet come to light; and she makes out a very persuasive case for the Egyptians having seen her *Ardea bennuides* only as an extremely rare visitor to Egypt. The Benu Bird may, in fact, be based on travellers' tales of the enormous heron seen on their trading expeditions to the Arabian Seas.

In the Heliopolitan myths, Shu and Tefnut produced two children, Geb, the earth, and Nut, the sky. Thus Atum had created step by step air and moisture, earth and sky. Only when these elements were put together did the physical world come into being—an intellectual concept of the Creation.

In Egyptian representations of the universe, Shu is depicted standing with arms upraised supporting above his head the out-stretched body of a woman wearing a long dress, with a man lying prone at his feet. The woman is Nut; the man is Geb; and thus was earth separated from sky by air. How this separation came about is a problem which exercised the minds of many early cultures. The Egyptians' version of the solution to the problem is lost, and can only be guessed at through allusions in the Pyramid Texts, and in inscriptions and pictures on coffins dating from the New Kingdom.

It seems that even in the womb Nut was at odds with her mother, Tefnut, and freed herself violently. She married her brother, Geb, and they lay together, Nut, the sky, lying directly above Geb, the earth. But when Nut became pregnant by Geb, her father, Shu, was jealous. He tore them apart and, placing one foot on Geb, held Nut aloft in his arms. Thus Earth became separated from Sky by Air.

Nut eventually gave birth to Geb's children—they became the sun, the stars and the planets and were placed on Nut's belly. According to a legend retold by Plutarch, Shu was so enraged by his beloved daughter bearing these children to Geb that he cursed her with a peculiar form of barrenness. He declared that she should be delivered of a child in no month in no year.

Nut determined to evade her father's curse. She had a lover, the god of time, Thoth, whom she challenged to a game of dice; and she succeeded in winning from him five days. The Egyptians used this myth to account for the five extra or epagomenal days which they had to add on to their regular calendar of 360 days, divided into twelve thirty-day months, in an attempt to bring lunar and solar time into balance. They never made allowance for the extra quarter of a day which is now accounted for in our Leap Year; hence the astronomical

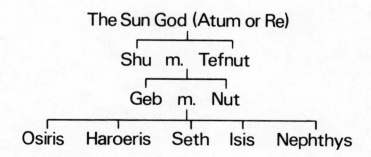

The Sun God (Atum or Re)
Shu m. Tefnut
Geb m. Nut
Osiris   Haroeris   Seth   Isis   Nephthys

year gradually fell behind the civil calendar, so that the real winter fell in the summer of the civil calendar.

Nut used the five extra days to bring forth children—as these days lay outside the normal year, the curse of her father, Shu, did not apply to them. On the first day, her son, Osiris, was born; on the second, her son, Horus, later known as Haroeris or Horus the Elder; on the third, her son, Seth; on the fourth, her daughter, Isis; and on the fifth, her daughter, Nephthys.

Later, Osiris married Isis and Seth married Nephthys. They, together with their parents, Geb and Nut, their grandparents, Shu and Tefnut, and their brother, Haroeris, formed the group of gods which, with Atum at its head, was the Great Ennead of Heliopolis.

SHU

Shu, the son of Atum, was one of the oldest cosmic deities: the god of air and light. Since these were qualities difficult to portray, he was usually represented as a man wearing on his head the feather which is the hieroglyphic symbol for his name ⸕ . His main function was to support the heavens, which he accomplished by kneeling on the earth with his arms raised above his head holding up the sky goddess, Nut. Apart from the feather, his other symbol was ⵍⵍⵍⵍ, which depicts the four supports of heaven which supposedly stood at the four corners of the earth and helped Shu with his task.

Shu's chief sanctuary, which he shared with Tefnut, was some 20km to the north-east of Heliopolis, at *Nay-ta-hut*, now known as Tell el-Yahudiya (The Mound of the Jews). The Greeks named the city as Leontopolis (The City of the Lion), since here Shu was worshipped in the form of a lion and Tefnut in the form of a lioness. The explanation for this is to be found in the local version of the Heliopolitan creation legend which says that Shu and Tefnut first took shape as a pair of lion cubs who grew into the Two Lions who guard the eastern and western horizons. It is easy to understand why lions should be connected with the sun on the horizon: they lived in the deserts where the Egyptians thought that the sun died each evening and was born again each morning; and they were also thought to be able to see as well in the dark as in the light. Hence, the Lion of the Western Horizon guarded the sun by night whilst the Lion of the Eastern Horizon supervised the rising of the sun each morning.

The belief that man needed to be guarded while he slept at night so that he might rise like the sun next day led the Egyptians to decorate their beds with lion motifs. Such was the purpose of the lion-headed funerary couch found in the tomb of Tutankhamun. Headrests were decorated in similar fashion: Tutankhamun had a charming lion-headed example which could be folded for travelling.

Legend says that Shu once reigned as King of Egypt for many years. A late version of his story was inscribed during the Ptolemaic period on a black granite shrine[3] which was erected in Phakussa (Faqus), the capital of the 20th Nome of Lower Egypt. In the nineteenth century AD, this shrine was removed to nearby Ismailia, where it was placed in the Museum of the Suez Canal Company.

According to the Phakussa inscription, Shu was a good king who reigned upon the throne of his father—Re-Harmarkis in the Phakussa version of the legend—in his palace at Memphis. His son, Geb, when he asked the gods what his father, Shu, had accomplished during his reign, was told that Shu had slain all the enemies of Atum and Re, and had irrigated the towns, the settlements and the nomes of Egypt, erected walls to protect her, and built temples throughout the Two Lands (i.e. Egypt).

After many years of unchallenged rule, Shu became weak in body and diseased in his eyes. His followers quarrelled amongst themselves. Even his son, Geb, was disaffected, partly because he was envious of his father's position as king and partly because of Shu's action in separating him from Nut (p. 49). At last, Shu went up into heaven together with his followers. Darkness fell upon the land and the wind howled. For nine days neither god nor man could see the face of his fellow. And then, the wind died down, the darkness receded and Geb appeared upon the throne of his father with all those who were in the palace making obeisance to him. Geb became King of Egypt whilst Shu took a place in the Company of Gods who attended upon Re, the Sun God.

TEFNUT

Tefnut took her place in the Heliopolitan Ennead as the daughter of the Sun God and the wife of his son, Shu. She personified the element of moisture and was usually depicted in human form wearing a sun's disk encircled by a cobra on her head. Like other goddesses, notably Hathor and Sekhmet, she was often called the Eye of Re.

A very ancient legend, set in the time when Re lived on earth as King of Egypt, tells how Tefnut became estranged from her father and fled into Nubia. The cause of the rift between father and daughter is not known; however, once Tefnut reached Nubia, she transformed herself into a lioness and raged throughout the land emitting flames from her eyes and nostrils, drinking blood and feeding on flesh, both animal and human.

Re missed his Eye, Tefnut, and longed to see her again. He sent for Shu and Thoth, the messenger of the gods, famed for his eloquence, and commanded them to go to Nubia and bring back his daughter. Shu and Thoth, having first disguised themselves as baboons, set off for Nubia. There, Thoth found Tefnut in Bugem, and tried to persuade her to return to Egypt. At first, she refused: she had begun to enjoy herself hunting in the desert. Thoth persevered and painted for her a picture of the gloom that had descended on Egypt because of her absence; and promised her that the game that she now had to hunt for herself would be piled high on the altars that the Egyptians would build for her in gratitude if only she would return to them.

At last, Tefnut agreed to accompany Thoth and Shu back to Egypt; and the two baboons led her home amidst great rejoicing. Attended by a great throng of Nubian musicians, dancers and baboons, Tefnut made a triumphant progress from one city to another until finally she was welcomed home by Re himself and restored to her rightful position as his Eye.

In some versions of this story, Tefnut is replaced by Hathor, who retreats to Nubia in high dudgeon because she has been prevented from destroying Mankind (p. 63); and Shu takes over Thoth's role as chief pacifier of the angry goddess. The original version, however, seems to have belonged to the god, Onuris, whose very name means 'He-who-brought-back-the-Distant-One' and links him with the estranged goddess, the Distant One, Tefnut.

Onuris was the essential warrior-god, a manifestation of the universal theme of the legendary hunter who returns to his people after subduing some monstrous beast. He was usually represented as a man wearing four tall plumes on his head, grasping a long spear in his hands, and poised on the balls of his feet ready to thrust down with the spear at some foe lying prone on the ground.

Onuris had two great sanctuaries, one at This, near Abydos, the town from which the first king of a united Egypt, Menes, originated; the other at Sebennytos (modern name, Samannud) which lies some 90km north of Heliopolis, and which was the capital of the 12th Nome of Lower Egypt, the city from which the kings of Dynasty xxx first originated. The most famous of Sebennytos' sons was Manetho, the historian who was the first man to divide Egyptian history into dynasties of kings. Manetho, who was born at the beginning of the third century BC, was probably a priest in the temple at Sebennytos.

At Sebennytos, Onuris had a mate, a lioness-goddess called Mehit, a name which means 'She-who-has-been-completed'. The word *mehit* was also used by the Egyptians to refer to the Eye of Horus which was gouged out by Seth and healed (or completed) by Hathor (p. 103). Thus, the legend of Onuris and the bringing back of the angry goddess from Nubia is inextricably mixed up with the symbolism of the Eye.

The Eye in the Onuris legend and its derivatives is sometimes said to be the Moon, the Eye of Horus which was taken away from him. More often, however, it is Tefnut as the personification of the Eye of the Sun. For the Egyptians, as for many ancient peoples, the absence of the sun was a time of fear and uncertainty. They were frightened of the dark when the sun was absent from the sky at night; they were uneasy during the winter when the sun lost its warmth, apprehensive lest the crops that lay dormant never spring into life again.

Thus, the return of Tefnut symbolised the return of the sun, bringing light after a period of darkness and life after the season of lifelessness, blessings which Tefnut offered to the Egyptians in addition to the boon that she, Order, had brought to them at the very beginning when her father, Atum, lifted her up in his arms and kissed her, thereby bringing the Mound of Creation into being.

GEB

Geb, the grandson of Atum, was the Earth God; his sister, Nut, was his counterpart as the Sky Goddess. He was often depicted as a recumbent male figure lying beneath a woman, who is Nut. Sometimes he appears as a goose; at other times, as a goose-headed man, or a man carrying a goose on his head. In predynastic times, he was probably worshipped in the form of a sacred goose.

It is perhaps surprising that Geb, the Earth God *par excellence*, should be male in gender. In most cultures, the earth, the bringer-forth of vegetation and living things, is regarded as female: Mother Earth. In at least one place, his shrine at *Bata* in Heliopolis, Geb was worshipped as a bisexual god and credited with having laid the Great Egg from which the sun emerged at the dawn of time in the form of the Benu Bird (p. 47). One of Geb's epithets was 'The Great Cackler', a reference to the cackle he gave as he produced this Egg.

The Phakussa Stele (p. 52) tells of how Geb fell in love with his mother, Tefnut. He yearned for her and wandered about the land in great distress until the day that his father, Shu, departed the earth. On that day, Geb came upon his mother, Tefnut, in the palace of Shu at Memphis. He seized hold of her with great violence and raped her.

Geb does not seem to have been punished for the rape of his mother. Instead, he became King of Egypt in his father's place, and reigned successfully for many years. He was given the title, unique to him, of *Iry-paat-neteru* or 'Heir of the Gods'. Geb named as his heir his eldest son, Osiris, who thus became the first of many Kings, both mythological and human, to sit upon the Egyptian throne, known as 'the Throne of Geb'; and the first to hold the title 'Heir of Geb', which was later borne by the mortal Kings of Egypt.

There was another earth god worshipped by the Egyptians: he was Aker, whom they sometimes depicted as a strip of land with a human head, and at other times as a double-headed lion or sphinx. This fabulous sphinx was supposed to guard the Two Gates, one on the east, the other on the west, which were the only entrances to the Underworld.

Aker was a fearsome deity, greatly feared by all who had to pass by him on their way to the Underworld. Geb, however, was regarded as a god who was at all times benevolently disposed towards the world and mankind.

NUT

Nut was the personification of the vault of heaven. She often appears in the form of a woman carrying on her head what was probably her old fetish—a water pot. She can be depicted as a woman stretched out over the earth with her feet resting on the eastern horizon and her head or her hands touching the western horizon. Her body, or her dress, which is long and blue, is spangled with stars and heavenly bodies. Nut can also be depicted as a cow straddling the earth with her underbelly studded with stars.

The sky itself was represented by ⌐ which shows a flat plate supported by two projections on its lower side. The two projections are the Two Pillars of Heaven, Mount *Bakhau* on the east and Mount *Manu* on the west, with Mount *Manu* providing a pillow for Nut's head and Mount *Bakhau* a footstool for her feet.

In the Heliopolitan creation myth, Nut was the granddaughter of the Sun God, the wife of Geb, the mother of Osiris, Isis, Horus the Elder, Seth and Nephthys, the five children whom she was able to bring into the world only after winning five days in the game of dice that she played with her lover, Thoth (p. 49).

However, Nut was also believed to be the mother of the sun. Each evening, when the sun reached Mount *Manu* on the western horizon, Nut, the sky-goddess, raised her head from her pillow and swallowed it: and each morning, she gave birth to it anew.

Nut was sometimes depicted as a cow because this was the form she assumed when she carried the Sun God, Re, on his journey to heaven after he had decided to abdicate his kingship upon Earth (p. 63). Since Hathor, also, was a cow-goddess, the roles of the two female deities were often interchanged, with Hathor playing Nut's role as sky-goddess, and Nut taking over from Hathor as a goddess of the dead. Thus Nut sometimes takes Hathor's place in the sacred sycamore tree (p. 129) from which she offers succour to the deceased.

Nut's links with the dead were further enhanced thanks to the Egyptian convention of decorating the ceilings of their tombs with stars, thereby turning them into representations of the heaven that the dead man aspired to reach. This theme was taken up on the inner sides of the lids of sarcophagi, which were embellished with stars, and, often, with figures of Nut as a naked woman standing on tip-toe with her arms stretched above her head. Once the lid of the sarcophagus was closed, Nut came face to face with the dead person inside, in which position she was able to protect him throughout eternity.

RE

Re was the self-engendered Eternal Spirit who first appeared on the waters of the Nun as a beautiful child floating on a great blue lotus. To the Egyptians, the water-lily, called *lotus* by the Greeks, was the most perfect type of flower. In contrast to the white lotus (*Nymphaea lotus*) the sacred blue lotus (*Nymphaea cerulea*) had a delightful perfume which suggested to the Egyptians the perfume of Re's sweat, the divine essence.

Re, having created himself by means of magic, turned his attention to the creation of the world. He made the four winds, and the inundation waters. From his sweat, he created gods; from his tears (for which the Egyptian word is *remyt*) he created mankind (in Egyptian, *remeth*, the sort of pun the Egyptians loved to make).

The magic Re used in his creation of the world and everything in it was the Word. Re spoke the Word, and by speaking the Name of things, he created them. To the Egyptians, as indeed to all ancient and primitive peoples, the name of a thing is a magical concept. His name is as vital to a man as his eyes, his hair, his tongue, or any other part of his person.

A North American Indian, for instance, takes care of his name in the belief that he can be injured by misuse of his name just as much as by a wound inflicted on his body. Australian aborigines believe that if an enemy knows your name he can make use of it magically in order to harm you. Thus, Aborigines take care never to tell their real names. They have a name which is used from day to day; and a secret name which is known only to fully initiated members of their tribal group.

The method of creating things by naming them was used by the Great God of the Babylonians; and by the God of the Hebrews—in the New Testament of the Bible, we read: 'In the beginning was the Word, and the Word was with God, and the Word was God' (John I, i). Having created the world by naming all its parts, Re became king of gods and men. He reigned with his daughter, Maat, at his side.

Maat was the personification of Truth and Justice. She was

depicted by Egyptian artists as a woman wearing an ostrich plume on her head. A picture of this feather was often used as the hieroglyphic symbol both for her name and for the noun 'truth'. The feather was used in the Judgement of the Dead, when it was weighed in a balance against the heart of the dead man undergoing the Judgement to see if he were '*maaty*', that is, had lived his life in conformity with truth and justice.

Maat stood for much more than the incarnation of Truth and Justice. It stands for the divinely-appointed order of things, the equilibrium of the universe with the world, the regular movements of the stars, the sun, the moon, the seasons and the sequence of time. Within the world which Re created according to his divine plan, Maat stands for social and religious order, the relationship between man and man, man and the gods, man and the dead.

Kingship, in the person of Re, and Order, in the person of Maat, came to earth at the very beginning. Thus, the creation of the world was simultaneous with the creation of kingship and social order. However, Chaos was an ever-present threat to the existence of this divinely-created order. Only by practising Maat could the Egyptians preserve the harmony of the universe. This belief was the basis of Egyptian religion; and the cult practised in temples was designed to uphold Maat so that Egypt might prosper.

Re ruled the world as king of men and gods only whilst he was in full possession of his powers. At last, however, the time came when the god-king began to grow old: according to Egyptian legend, 'his bones were silver, his flesh was gold and his hair was real lapis-lazuli'—the Egyptian way of describing old age. And his subjects became rebellious.

Chief among these rebellious subjects was the goddess, Isis. She, like Re, was omniscient. She was also, according to legend, 'a woman skilled in words', a great magician. Her ambition was to reign like Re in heaven and earth. But the only way she could achieve her ambition was by learning the Great Name of Re, his secret name. The way in which she did this is recounted in two papyri, one of which is now in the British Museum and the other in the Turin Museum.

Re had many names, but his Great Name was the one which gave him power over gods and men. It had remained hidden in his body since his birth so that no magician might gain power over him. Isis plotted in her heart the means by which she could learn it. Because Re had grown old, he was inclined to slobber at the mouth and shoot his spittle onto the ground. Isis took some of this spittle, kneaded it with soil and made it into a serpent in the form of a dart, which she laid on the path where Re was accustomed to stroll every day.

When Re, accompanied by his retinue of gods, passed by the dart, it took shape as a serpent from which issued a living fire. The serpent stung Re; the god opened his mouth and his cry of pain echoed round the sky. His companions rushed up to him, exclaiming, 'What is the matter?'; gods everywhere asked, 'What can that be?' Re could not find the strength to answer them. His jaws shook, his limbs trembled as the poison seized hold of his flesh even as the Nile in flood seizes hold of the land of Egypt. At last, he managed to still the racing of his heart and summon his followers, calling out, 'Come to me, you who were created from my limbs, who came forth from me!'

When his followers had gathered round him, Re told them what had happened: 'I know in my heart that something deadly has bitten me, but I did not see what it was. I only know that it was not something that I myself have made. I have never experienced suffering like this. I am sure it would not be possible to endure more severe pain.'

Re was profoundly shocked that he should have suffered such an attack. His Great Name ought to have ensured that such a thing could never happen. In desperation, the stricken god summoned his children, especially those gods who were skilled in magic and healing words. Not one of them was able to help their father. At last, Isis came, she who could give the breath of life with her mouth, who could chase away pain with her spells, who could bring the dead back to life with her magic words. She said, 'What is it, divine Father?' And Re told her what had happened to him. He continued: 'I am colder than water, I am hotter than fire. All my limbs sweat yet I am shivering. My eyes are dim, I cannot see the sky. My face is bathed in perspiration just as if it were summertime.'

Then Isis said, 'Tell me your Name, divine Father, for the man who is called by his name is the man who shall live.'

Re cast round in his mind for a name that he could give her that would prove efficacious enough for her magic spells. He did not, of course, intend to give her his Great Name, his secret name. He played for time by listing his achievements, and then declared: 'At dawn, I am called Khepri; at midday, Re; and in the evening, Atum.'

The wily Isis was not impressed. She waited relentlessly while the poison worked its way deeper and deeper into the body of the great god until he could no longer walk. Then she said, 'You have not told me your Name. Tell me your Name so that the poison may go away. For the man who is called by his Name is a man who shall live.'

The poison burned like fire. Re cried out: 'Swear that no one will ever know my Great Name except for yourself and your son, Horus, whom you shall bear to Osiris and who shall reign over the land of

Egypt when Osiris has passed to the West, the Land of the Dead.' And Isis swore an oath: and the secret of Re's Great Name passed from his heart to hers. Immediately, Isis bade the poison leave his body; the poison died and Re lived.

Isis was not the only one to scheme against the ageing Re. It came to his notice one day that mankind was plotting against him. The story of how Re dealt with the plotters is told in the Book of the Divine Cow. The earliest-known version of this Book so far found is on the largest of the four great shrines which protected the sarcophagus of Tutankhamun in the burial chamber of his tomb in the Valley of the Kings at Thebes (Luxor). The text of the story is on the inside of the shrine and is illustrated by a carving of a gigantic cow—the goddess, Nut, whose belly is decorated with stars and who is supported by Shu. Unfortunately, the text is incomplete, although it can be filled in from later versions of the story. The best of these occur in the royal tombs of the late New Kingdom, especially those of the Dynasty XIX rulers, Seti I and his son, Ramesses II, with the best-preserved version surviving in a small antechamber deep inside the tomb of Seti.

Unsure of what to do about those who were plotting against him, Re summoned Hathor, whom he called his 'Eye', Shu, Tefnut, Geb and Nut, as well as the fathers and mothers who had been with him in the Primaeval Waters, and even the god, Nun, himself, the personification of those Waters, so that they might give him advice. Re commanded that they meet him secretly: he did not wish mankind to realise what they were doing.

So the gods were brought before Re, and, having touched the ground at his feet with their foreheads in token of respect, they listened to what he had to say.

Then Nun spoke: 'My son, Re, the god greater than I from whom you came forth and mightier than those whom you have created, sit on your throne with confidence for great would be the fear of you if your Eye were turned against those who are plotting against you.'

Re then told them that many men had fled into the desert because they were afraid of what he would say to them. And the gods recommended that Re should send someone in pursuit of them but not his Eye since mankind had been made from the tears of Re's Eye and the Eye might feel sorry for its 'children'. Instead, Hathor should go in the form of a fierce lioness, who would devour the evil ones in the desert.

Hathor performed her task with such gusto that Re became alarmed. Having tasted blood, she was loath to give up her slaughter. She told Re how pleasant it was to her to have prevailed over mankind and to have earned a new name—*Sekhmet* or 'She-who-prevails'. But Re did not want her to prevail over all of mankind, for he had wished only to teach them a lesson, not to destroy them utterly.

And so he sent his swiftest messengers to Elephantine to bring him quantities of the red ochre that was found in that region. When the red ochre had been brought to him, Re ordered his High Priest in Memphis to grind it up. Meanwhile, barley beer had been prepared by maidservants. The red ochre was added to the beer so that it looked like human blood, and 7,000 jars of the mixture were made ready for inspection by Re and his entourage.

On the morning of the day upon which Hathor intended to complete her destruction of mankind, Re inspected the beer and found it to be excellent. He announced: 'I will save mankind with it!' and ordered that it should be carried to the place where Hathor intended to slay the remainder of mankind. There, the blood-red beer was poured over the land until the fields were flooded to a depth of about 24cms with this soporific.

When Hathor arrived, she found the land covered with what she thought was human blood. Her face glowed in its reflection. She drank deeply; and became so drunk that she forgot all about destroying mankind.

Re met her in the city of Yamit, and welcomed her not as Sekhmet, nor as Hathor, the terrible slayer of mankind, but as the Beautiful One, his Eye. From thenceforward, Yamit became famous for its beautiful women; 'the Beautiful One' became one of Hathor's names; Hathor became the goddess of drunkenness; and a great annual festival was initiated at which servant girls were allowed to brew the intoxicating drink that Re decreed should be made in honour of Hathor.

Unfortunately, Re was still dissatisfied with mankind and with exercising his power on earth. He was weary; he wished for rest. And so Nun commanded the goddess, Nut, to change herself into a cow, so that Re might rest himself upon her back.

When mankind saw the sun's disk riding on the back of a cow, they were astonished. Some of them were angry with their fellows for having plotted against Re so causing him to remove himself from them. They took up their bows and shot arrows at the enemies of Re, who warned them that from henceforward men would always be prepared to slaughter each other. And thus did war come into the world.

Re commanded Nut to ascend high above the earth; and she became the sky. In her womanly form, she wore a blue dress and so the sky became the colour of this dress. From his vantage point on

Nut's back, Re was able to observe the earth from a distance, something which he found very peaceful. He created the Field of Abundance for Nut to stand and browse in, and planted it with green plants. He brought into being the Field of Reeds in which men would be able to pass their Afterlife. He began to create the stars and the planets.

Eventually, Nut became dizzy through standing so far above the earth; she began to shake. Re commanded the god of air, Shu, to stand beneath Nut and support her with his hands. Nut's husband, Geb, was put in charge of the earth.

And so Re had created the earth and all that was in it; the air that men and beasts breathed; the sky and the firmament with its planets and stars; the divine places of the Afterlife. Having abandoned mankind on earth, Re made himself responsible for the Afterlife, where he became the Great Judge of the Dead.

Re also created night and day. During the twelve hours of the night, he sailed through the Netherworld in his Night Barque. At dawn, he emerged on the eastern horizon where a choir of baboons danced and sang with joy at his appearance. Re then boarded his Day Barque and for the twelve hours of the day, he sailed across the sky illuminating the earth with his bright rays.

This daily journey across the sky made the Egyptians very happy. But every night, Re disappeared over the western horizon and mankind was left in the dark, deprived of the light of Re's Eye, the sun. Re decided to provide a substitute. He sent for the god, Thoth, and commanded that he provide light for mankind at night. Re created the moon and gave it into the keeping of Thoth. From thenceforth, the earth was illumined during the day by the Sun God, Re, and during the night by the Moon God, Thoth, acting as Re's representative.

During the New Kingdom, if not before, the Egyptians believed that the powers of darkness, in the guise of fiends led by the monster serpent, Apopis, posed an ever-present threat to the Sun. During the night, they lay in wait for Re; and in the darkest hour before the dawn, they attacked his Barque in an endeavour to prevent the Sun rising.

Every morning, Re beat off the attack, aided by the deities who made up the crew of his Barque. He himself, in the guise of a cat, the Great Cat of Heliopolis, cut off the head of Apopis with a knife. He never vanquished Apopis utterly because at the end of every night, the serpent was found waiting for him again, eager to renew his assault.

During the Old Kingdom, the cult of Re spread from Heliopolis to the rest of Egypt until he achieved nation-wide recognition, enabling his priesthood to exert great political power. From Dynasty III onwards, the building of pyramids shows that Re had become a powerful influence in funerary beliefs and practices.

The origin of the pyramid form of tomb can probably be traced back to predynastic times. Prehistoric Egyptians normally buried their dead in pits dug in the desert—at no time in Egyptian history did the Egyptians waste good agricultural land by burying their dead in it. The grave was marked by a mound of sand piled over the pit.

In Dynasty I, a more elaborate tomb was evolved for the burial of kings and their relatives. This was the *mastaba*, which consisted of a deep burial-shaft surmounted by a superstructure made of mud-brick arranged in a rectangular shape with slightly inclined walls (hence the name, *mastaba*, Arabic for bench).

Excavations of *mastabas* at Sakkara, the necropolis of the ancient capital city of Egypt, Memphis, have revealed the presence of 'mounds' inside the walls of the superstructures of some *mastabas*. The earliest examples are simply cores of sand overlaid with mud-brick; later, a solid brick construction was developed, with its four sides rising in steps. Since the 'mounds' have no architectural function, their purpose must have had a magico-religious significance. They were probably meant to represent the hill which emerged from the Primaeval Waters when the earth was created; and to act as a potent magic symbol to counteract Death.

The stepped mounds inside *mastabas* perhaps influenced the next development in royal tombs. In Dynasty III, King Djoser and his architect, Imhotep, constructed a tomb at Sakkara which consists of six *mastaba* shapes of ever-decreasing base measurements placed one on top of the other until the monument reached a height of over 60 metres, forming a stepped pyramid. The Step Pyramid of Djoser, as this monument is called today, is built entirely of limestone and is the earliest monumental building in dressed stone known to history (p. 164).

The stepped mounds inside *mastabas*, and the step pyramids of Djoser and at least three of his successors, were natural developments from the predynastic pit graves. However, the priests of Re at Heliopolis found a magico-religious explanation for them, an explanation which associated the King with their god, Re.

Re sailed through the sky every day in his Day Barque. What more natural ambition could a dead king have than to join Re on his daily journey and thus spend his Afterlife with him. But how to reach the

Barque? Why, by means of a ladder up to heaven. The stepped mounds inside *mastabas*, and the step pyramids, with the aid of magic spells, provided the ladder.

The earliest geometrically true pyramids were built at Giza in Dynasty IV. The first, and greatest, of these monuments was built by Khufu. His successors, Khafre and Menkaure, each built a pyramid at Giza. Khafre's tomb is comparable in size with that of his father, whose Great Pyramid is over 146 metres high and covers an area of more than 50,000 square metres. Menkaure's pyramid is less than half that size. Together, these three pyramids formed one of the Seven Wonders of the ancient world.

The significance of the true pyramid is not known for certain. It has perhaps something to do with the inspiration derived from the sight of the sun's rays shining down to earth through a gap in the clouds, giving a straight-sided, pyramidal shape; or they may have occurred through natural, architectural progression. They were built during one of the most powerful dynasties in Egyptian history, and have been described as an exercise in nationalism; but doubtless the priesthood of Re found a religious significance for them.

The pyramid form of royal tomb persisted in Egypt for over a thousand years until Re was superceded by Amun as the most powerful god. Many of the pyramids built during this time were equipped with stone pits, some of which are shaped like boats. To date, several of these stone pits have been found to contain actual boats, made of wood. Three of these boats, made of cedar, were found at Dahshur, on the south side of the pyramid of Senwosret III of Dynasty XII. In AD 1954, two pits at the foot of the southern face of the Great Pyramid at Giza were discovered. In one of them, a boat, over 40 metres long, lay dismantled but complete from its keel to the canopied cabin on its deck. The boats may have been used to ferry the dead king and his funerary equipment to his pyramid; their most important function, however, would have been a mythological one: to carry the dead king on his funerary journey to the sky.

The Giza pyramids are the greatest ever built; all later pyramids—and there are over eighty of them—are very much smaller. However, the kings of Dynasties V and VI endeavoured to make up for the smallness of their tombs through the magic of the Pyramid Texts (p. 45) carved within them.

Judged on subject matter and language, these Texts are based on very old rituals and spells. One Spell says: 'A brick is drawn for thee out of the great tomb'—a reference to mud-brick *mastabas*, no longer used by the kings of Dynasty V. Another Spell alludes to predynastic sand burials: 'Throw the sand from off thy face'. The early Pyramid

Texts are obviously Heliopolitan in origin, for there are many references in them to Re.

The death of the king is described in one Spell thus: 'The King departs life in the West . . . he shines forth anew in the East', just as the sun sets (dies) in the West and rises again in the East. His journey to the sky can be accomplished in two ways: by means of a boat, or by ladder. 'The two reed-floats (rafts) of the sky have been set in place for the King so that he might journey in them to the horizon, to Re'; 'a stairway to the sky has been set up for him so that he might ascend to heaven thereby'; and 'the King ascends upon this ladder which his father (Re) made for him'.

Having reached the Afterlife, the King must undergo the Judgement of the Dead before he can take his place as one of the gods, acclaimed and recognised by them. In the early Pyramid Texts, it is Re who is the Great Judge, who sits at the head of the Tribunal of the Gods. After his Judgement, the king is acclaimed and accepted as a member of Re's retinue: 'O pure one! Assume thy throne in the Barque of Re and sail upon the way.'

By Dynasty v, Re had become State God, officially recognised as leader of the pantheon of Egyptian gods. His greatest political success was achieved in Dynasty IV. Until this time, the King of Egypt had been deemed a god. However, in Dynasty IV, Khafre took as one of his royal titles the epithet 'Son of Re', indicating a diminution in the importance of the king since he was now not a god in his own right but merely the son of a god.

This royal link with Re was maintained for the remaining 2,500 years or so of Pharaonic Egypt. Reference to Re is implicit in the way two of the five names borne by a reigning king were written on monuments and official documents. 'Son of Re' and 'King of Upper and Lower Egypt' were the prefixes to the two most important names in the royal titulary. The names themselves were written inside *cartouches*. A *cartouche*— ⊂⊐ —is an elongated version of the hieroglyphic sign ⊙, which represents a loop of rope with a knot at its base and which means *shen* or 'that which the sun encircles'. The King's name written inside the *cartouche* was intended to show that he ruled the world—a world illuminated by Re.

The political success of Re was further enhanced in Dynasty v by several kings of that Dynasty who built their pyramids at Abusir. Every pyramid had attached to it a mortuary temple in which the dead king was supposed to be worshipped forever: at Abusir, for the first time, each pyramid had another sort of temple built near it—a Solar Temple, in which the god, Re, was destined to be worshipped in the very place that was most sacred to the king.

The most outstanding feature of a Solar Temple was the giant obelisk that provided a focal point in the temple. Obelisks were cult symbols of the Sun God, and date back to predynastic times when they were worshipped as models of the miraculous shaft of stone upon which the sun was thought to place itself on first rising. The use of obelisks was especially popular in the New Kingdom. Today, less than half a dozen remain standing in Egypt. Many have been removed by the conquerors of Egypt, from Ashurbanipal, who took two of them to Nineveh, to the Roman Emperors, who took many of them to Rome and Constantinople, the French, who took one to the Place de la Concorde in Paris, and the British, who removed one to London and named it Cleopatra's Needle. There are over fifty obelisks in public squares and parks throughout Europe and Northern America.

By the end of Dynasty VI, the ordinary Egyptian had turned to Osiris for spiritual comfort. The cult of Re had always been a royal cult, concerned with the well-being of the king. It held no direct appeal for the common man. The cult of Osiris, however, was found to be sympathetic by all levels of Egyptian society.

Re was never again to achieve the heights he attained during the Old Kingdom. However, as early as Dynasty II he had been worshipped at Heliopolis in the form of a great black or piebald bull. This animal—the *Mer-wer* or Mnevis Bull—was thought of as the living soul of the Sun God, and was provided with two wives, the cow-goddesses Hathor and Iusas. The lavish endowments provided for him by Ptolemy V Epiphanes (205–180 BC), which are recorded on the Rosetta Stone, demonstrate that Re retained an important place in the Egyptian pantheon to the end of the Pharaonic period.

KHEPRI

At Heliopolis, the god, Khepri, was believed to be a manifestation of the creator god taking shape as the rising sun. His name is derived from the Egyptian word *kheprer*, which means 'to become' or 'to come into existence', an abstract idea which might have been very difficult to illustrate. However, Egyptian makes great use of puns; and in this case, the verb *kheprer* has the same sound as the word for scarabaeus or dung-beetle, hence a picture of such a beetle could be used as the hieroglyphic sign denoting both the beetle itself and the verb 'to come into existence'.

The creator god was believed to have come into existence through his own actions. So, according to Egyptian belief, did the scarabaeus beetle. Thus, the word for beetle, *kheprer*, became the name of the god of spontaneous creation, Khepri. Plutarch explains this:

> 'As for the scarab-beetle, it is held that there are no females of this species; they are all males. They place their seed in a round pellet of material which they roll up into a sphere and roll along, pushing it with their hind legs, imitating by their action the course of the sun from east to west.'

The ball of material, probably dung, is then buried in the sand until the 'seed' is hatched. This idea is reflected in tomb paintings in the Valley of the Kings at Thebes which show the scarab-beetle emerging backwards from the sand dragging the sun with it.

The god, Khepri, normally appears in Egyptian paintings as a human-being with the head of a scarab-beetle. The scarab-beetle itself became one of the most popular motives in Egyptian art. Egyptian scarabs were made in various sizes from many different materials—stone such as limestone or steatite; semi-precious stones such as carnelian, amethyst, green felspar; and faience. They could be almost exact replicas of a dung-beetle or merely stylised versions of it. They could be covered with decorative designs, magical signs, hieroglyphic inscriptions, pictures of gods and kings.

When set in a ring as a bezel or hung on a necklace as a pendant, the scarab was often used as a personal seal. Its flat underside, inscribed with the name and titles of its owner, could be pressed against the clay sealings which were appended to letters and official documents, and even to bolts on the doors of rooms or the lids of chests and containers such as wine jars. Mounted on a plaque in a bracelet or necklace, the scarab was used as a protective amulet. The insect was the symbol of the perpetual renewal of life, and its popularity as a means of protection led to many thousands of scarabs being made of cheap materials with little care taken over their decoration. Hence it is often difficult to distinguish ancient scarabs of inferior quality from the modern, sometimes well-made, versions which are the most popular souvenirs for visitors to Egypt. No such difficulty is encountered with the scarabs used in some of the items of jewellery found, for example, in the tomb of Tutankhamun.

Scarabs were used as funerary talismens. As such, they were usually made of hard stone, faience or gold, and equipped with replicas of a falcon's wings. They were placed inside the mummy bandages over the heart of the dead man; or mounted in a pectoral or ornamental collar and placed on the breast of the mummy. In this position, the wings of the scarab could take the body of the dead man in a protective embrace. Heart scarabs were often inscribed with Chapter 30 of the Book of the Dead, the Spell which instructed the heart on what to do at the Judgement of the Dead—'O my heart, the most intimate part of my being! Do not stand up against me as a witness before the Tribunal'—so that the dead man might emerge triumphant from the Judgement.

Large stone scarabs were made to commemorate historical events, an early exercise in the art of issuing public relations bulletins! The less important historical scarabs bear the name of a king plus an epithet referring to his achievements—the building of a temple, for example. Other scarab bulletins contain more information. The most famous series of such commemorative scarabs was issued in Dynasty XVIII by Amenhotep III: in them he registered in permanent form some of the outstanding events of his reign.

One scarab records the two-day hunt which took place in the second year of his reign in which nearly 100 wild bulls were captured; another registers the fact that in his first ten years as king, Amenhotep III shot '102 fierce lions'.

A third scarab records his marriage to Tiy, daughter of the High Priest of Min, Yuya, and his wife Thuya (p. 188): 'she is the daughter of commoners but now she is the wife of a victorious king'. A fourth scarab gives details of the construction of a pleasure lake for this beloved wife:

'Regnal year 11, 1st day of Inundation, under the Majesty of . . . Amenhotep, Ruler of Thebes, long may he live. The great royal wife, Tiy, long may she live: his Majesty commanded that a lake be constructed for the great royal wife, Tiy, in the city of Djarukha, 3,700 cubits long and 700 cubits wide. His Majesty celebrated the feast of the inauguration of the lake on the 16th day of Inundation when his Majesty was rowed in the royal barge, Splendour of the Aten.'

A fifth scarab, dated to Year 10, records 'a miracle, brought to his Majesty, namely the daughter of the ruler of Naharin, Shuttarna—Kirgipa and persons of her harem, 317 women.' Perhaps the most impressive scarab is the large one made of granite erected by Amenhotep III in the Temple of Amun at Karnak, and which now stands near the north-west corner of the temple's sacred lake.

Khepri, however, is to be found in paintings and reliefs in many a temple or tomb of Ancient Egypt, for he was a pervasive and ever-popular god.

OSIRIS

The myth of Osiris tells how he once ruled Egypt as king until he was betrayed and murdered. He died but was resurrected thanks to his wife, Isis, whose love and loyalty made this resurrection possible. Their son, Horus, avenged his father's wrongs and in his turn became King of Egypt. The story of Osiris, with its emphasis on the ideal family, and the hope that it holds out of immortality through resurrection, had a universal appeal. Osiris thus became one of the most popular Egyptian gods, not only in Egypt itself but throughout the Near East.

His beginnings are obscure. The earliest written references to Osiris are found in the Pyramid Texts. How he was worshipped in prehistoric times and where his original cult-centre was situated is not known. However, by the time he appears in the Pyramid Texts he is a fully developed deity with his own theology and mythology.

Undoubtedly, Osiris was first worshipped as a fertility-god. But as his cult spread throughout Egypt, he displaced indigenous gods in several places, notably in *Djedu*, where he replaced Andjety; and at Abydos, where he superceded Khentyamentiu. At Heliopolis, he became a member of the Great Ennead, and in Memphis he was assimilated to Sokar.

As gods gave way to Osiris, he absorbed their functions and attributes. This process led to the standard depiction of Osiris which shows him as a human male whose body is covered by a tight-fitting white garment that allows only his hands and head to be seen. In his hands, he grasps a crook and a flail. He wears a beard, and on his head he bears either the White Crown of Upper Egypt or the Atef Crown, a form of the White Crown in which the top has been cut off and replaced by a small sun's disk, the whole being flanked by two ostrich plumes.

Osiris' flesh is usually coloured black or green: to the Egyptians, black, being the colour of the rich, alluvial soil from which their crops sprang up year after year, was the colour of resurrection and eternal life. Hence, his black flesh indicates that he has died and risen again. Green, being the colour of plant life, is symbolic of vegetation and youth.

The crown, the crook and the flail infer that Osiris is a king; the white shroud that he is a dead king, for the shroud represents the bandages that were used in mummification. The beard he wears is the ritual false beard as worn by kings that, throughout the dynastic period, was regarded as an emblem of the supernatural thanks to its association with Osiris. In shape, this beard is unlike beards as they were normally depicted by the Egyptians, which are straight: Osiris' beard is long and curved, and is perhaps a stylized version of the beard of a goat, which possibly indicates that Osiris was worshipped at one time in the form of a goat or ram.

Ram-gods were extremely popular with the Egyptians from predynastic times onwards, for rams were considered to be symbols of strength and virility. To name but three: there was Herishef (in Greek, Arsaphes), the ram god of Herakleopolis, whose name means 'He-who-is-on-his-lake' and whose city, which lies some 15km west of Beni Suef, provided the kings of Dynasties IX and X; the Ram of Mendes (see below); and Khnum, the best-known ram-god of all (p. 183).

All of these deities were originally manifest in the ram of the species *palaeoaegypticus*; in dynastic times, this species became more and more rare until it disappeared altogether (*c.*2000 BC). Even before this had happened, the Egyptians had substituted *palaeoaegypticus* rams with rams of other species, and often with the male mountain-goats that abounded in Egypt.

In dynastic times, the soul of Osiris was thought to be lodged in a ram. This sacred ram was worshipped in a town in the Delta named *Djedet*, and was known as Ba-neb-djedet (Ram-lord of *Djedet*), a popular deity down to the Ptolemaic period. The Greeks garbled the last two syllables of Ba-neb-djedet's name into Mendes, and Strabo, Pindar and Diodorus made the Ram of Mendes famous, Pindar, in particular, stressing the fact that this ram was permitted to have intercourse with women. Officially, he was allotted a consort, the dolphin-goddess, Hat-Mehit (The First of the Fish), whose figure was found on the standard of the 16th Nome of Lower Egypt, of which *Djedet* was the capital.

The Egyptian word for 'ram' was *ba*; this same word was used for 'soul'. Hence, although it was as a *ba*-ram that the god of *Djedet* was worshipped in predynastic times, this persona was later refined and the *ba*-soul aspect was emphasised in dynastic times, when the Ram of Mendes was syncretised with Osiris as his soul. In the Late Period, the

Ram of Mendes was given four heads and was then supposed to be the soul not only of Osiris but also of Re, Shu and Geb.

A few miles to the west of *Djedet* lay the similarly named town of *Djedu*, which is the oldest-known centre of the cult of Osiris. This city became known as *per-user*, which the Greeks later translated as Busiris, and which means 'the House of Osiris'. Long before Osiris arrived there, the cult symbol of *Djedu* had been the *Djed*-pillar. This prehistoric fetish gave its name to the city; and since the Egyptian word for *djed*-pillar, *djedu*, was homophonous with the word *djedu* which meant 'stability' or 'endurance', the *Djed*-pillar became a popular motif in jewellery and decoration as the embodiment of these qualities.

The precise significance of the *Djed*-pillar is uncertain. It may have been a representation of the sheaf of corn which played an important part in agricultural rites. In many parts of the world, the last sheaf of corn to be cut at harvest-time is treated in a special way, since it is thought to contain the spirit of the corn; and the *Djed*-pillar is possibly a stylized version of this last sheaf of corn. As such, it is an appropriate cult-symbol for Osiris in one of his aspects, that of corn-god.

When Osiris had become established at *Djedu*, the original symbolism of the *Djed*-pillar became merged with a new belief: the backbone of Osiris was said to be buried at *Djedu*, and the *Djed*-pillar, reminiscent as it is of a backbone, became the embodiment of this sacred relic.

At *Djedu*, Osiris supplanted a more ancient god, Andjety, who was thought to have been a king who once had ruled the city, since representations of him show an old man holding a crook in one hand and a flail in the other, and wearing on his head a double-plumed crown. Osiris took from him these items of royal regalia and incorporated into his own legend the story that he had once been a king who ruled Egypt.

As King of Egypt, Osiris brought the arts of civilization and agriculture to his subjects. He taught them to worship the gods and to obey the laws which he gave them. Before his reign, the Egyptians had been cannibals. However, when Isis, the sister-wife of Osiris, discovered wheat and barley growing wild, Osiris persuaded the Egyptians to give up cannibalism and learn how to cultivate these valuable cereals. He was believed to have been the first to pick fruit from trees and to train vines to grow on poles. He discovered how to tread the grapes picked from the vines in order to make wine. In areas where the vine could not be cultivated, he taught the inhabitants how to brew beer from barley instead.

The Egyptians were not the only ones to whom Osiris brought the blessings of civilization and agriculture. Having installed his wife, Isis, as regent in Egypt, he travelled the world conveying these discoveries to the whole of mankind. Everywhere Osiris went, he earned the gratitude of men for the benefits he bestowed on them and was worshipped as a deity. He was given the epithet, Wennefer, 'the perpetually good being', in recognition of his beneficence.

In one of his aspects, Osiris was worshipped as a god of vegetation, and more especially as a corn-god, who made the earth bring forth its produce in due season. Annually, at the beginning of the fourth month of the Egyptian year, at the time when the Inundation waters were beginning to recede and the fields to reemerge from the flood ready to receive seed, the Egyptians made little clay figures shaped to look like Osiris, and pressed seeds into them. Within a short time, the seeds germinated and a miniature corn-field appeared, shaped like Osiris.

These 'corn-Osiris' figures were symbols of rebirth and regeneration. Just as, every year, the soil of Egypt 'died' under the blistering summer sun, only to be reborn after the Inundation had made it fertile again, so Osiris was regarded as a god of resurrection. 'Corn-Osiris' figures were placed in Egyptian tombs as symbols of the resurrection that the tomb-owner hoped for. Perhaps the most famous 'corn-Osiris' belonged to Tutankhamun. In the store chamber that leads off the burial chamber of his tomb was found a hollow wooden figure, about a metre long, shaped to look like Osiris and lined with linen. It had been filled with Nile silt and planted with corn-seed, which had been kept moist until the grain germinated. The figure was wrapped in linen and housed in a large wooden box.

Other such Osiris figures were found in the tomb of Tutankhamun's grandparents, Yuya and Thuya; and in the tomb of the king who came to the throne four years after Tutankhamun's death, Horemheb. They have been found in non-royal tombs, also, often placed between the legs of mummies, or occasionally, as at Cynopolis, in small pottery or wooden coffins placed in bricked-up recesses in the wall of the tomb.

For king and commoner alike, 'corn-Osirises' were designed to show that just as grain, a seemingly dead substance, can sprout into life, so also could the dead body of a man come to life again. The conception of 'corn-Osiris' figures as symbols of rebirth and regeneration was closely allied to the identification of Osiris with the corn itself as a corn-god, turning him into a deity of joy and sorrow.

Harvest time every year, especially in a year that yields good crops, is a joyful time. It was also, to the Ancient Egyptians, a time of regret, for, with every stroke of his sickle, the Egyptian farmer believed that he was not only reaping the grain but that he was killing it. Symbolically, he was cutting the body of the corn-god before trampling it to pieces on the threshing-floor. It was, accordingly, the custom in Egypt, and elsewhere, for the corn-reapers to lament over the first sheaf to be cut.

The yearly death of the corn, and indeed of other forms of vegetation, was a part of the natural cycle of decay and revival of life. In the ancient Near East, the phenomenon was personified as a god who died annually only to rise again from the dead. This god had many names. In Babylonia and Syria, he was called Tammuz, a form of whom was found outside the Near East, in Greece, where he was known as Adonis. The Phrygians called him Attis and the Egyptians, Osiris.

Tammuz was the lover of the Babylonian mother-goddess, Ishtar, who was carried off to the Underworld by his enemies. Ishtar followed her lover and remained in the Underworld with him, thus removing from men and beasts the urge for sexual intercourse. The great god, Ea, realising that the world was threatened with extinction, persuaded the Queen of the Underworld, Allatu, to sprinkle the lovers with the water of life, thus enabling them to return to the world bringing life and procreation with them.

The Greeks borrowed this myth from the Babylonians, turning the Semitic term *adon*, which means 'lord', the honorific title by which Tammuz's worshippers addressed him, into the appelation, Adonis. Adonis was a beautiful child beloved by the goddess of love, Aphrodite, who gave him into the safe-keeping of Persephone, queen of the dead. When Adonis grew up, he became Persephone's lover. Aphrodite, jealous and wanting Adonis for her own lover, quarrelled with Persephone and appealed to Zeus to settle the issue. Zeus entrusted the case to the muse, Calliope, who decreed that Adonis should spend one third of the year with Aphrodite, one third with Persephone, and have one third to himself in which to recuperate from the amorous attentions of the two goddesses.

Aphrodite cheated, and persuaded Adonis to spend his third of the year with her. Enraged at this, Persephone incited the god, Ares, to change himself into a boar and attack Adonis, which he did whilst the lovers were out hunting on Mount Lebanon. Adonis, gored before Aphrodite's horrified eyes, bled to death; and wherever drops of his blood fell, anemones sprang up. The distraught Aphrodite pleaded with Zeus to allow Adonis to come back to her. Finally, Zeus agreed that Adonis should spend the winter months in the Underworld, but return to earth every spring to spend the summer months with Aphrodite.

Attis was a youth who was loved by the Phrygian mother of the gods, Cybele. One version of his story says that he, like Adonis, was killed by a boar. Another says that he castrated himself and bled to death, whereupon he was turned into a pine tree. In both versions of the story, Attis was said to return from the dead every year.

The essential difference between Osiris and these other gods of resurrection who were supposed to die and rise again is that they returned to earth for at least part of the year. Osiris never returned to earth but remained forever in the Underworld: he lived forever, but not on this earth.

The legend of Osiris as a god of resurrection had its origins in the ancient custom of killing the king, a practice known to many countries other than Egypt. In primitive societies, a king had to be fit and virile, able to demonstrate his own fertility and his prowess as a hunter. When he became old, or unfit through injury or illness, it was feared that his failing capacity to produce human 'seed' would bring a blight on the crops; and that the impairment of his ability to track animals and bring them down by his speed and strength in the chase would affect the well-being of the tribe.

In many ancient societies and, until comparatively recently, in tribes such as the Shilluk of the Sudan, an old or sick king was ritually put to death and a new king chosen to replace him. Other societies did not wait for their king to show signs of infirmity; instead, they appointed him for a fixed term of years, at the end of which either the king or a substitute was killed. The dead king was often buried in the ground as an encouragement for the crops to grow.

In less primitive times, the substitute took the form of a statue which was buried whilst the king was allowed to 'renew' his powers by magical means. The Egyptians of dynastic times adopted this practice as one of the rites that made up the ritual of the so-called *Heb-Sed* ceremony, during which the Egyptian king renewed his power and virility by means of magic (p. 164).

The legendary Osiris was not an old king but a king in the prime of life when he died. The story of his death may have been based on an Egyptian tradition of a real king who once was sacrificed for the good of his people. There is no full account of his story told by the Egyptians themselves, only incomplete references to it in religious and magical texts on papyri and in inscriptions on temple walls which refer to the rites practised in the rituals of Osiris-worship. The most complete version of the Osiris legend is that told by the Greek writer, Plutarch, who wrote his *De Iside et Osiride* in the first century AD. The sources mentioned above indicate that Plutarch's account is substantially correct.

Having brought civilization to Egypt, and then to the rest of the world, Osiris enjoyed an enviable fame and a reputation as a good king. Such was his popularity that his brother Seth became unbearably jealous. The culmination of Seth's envy came when Osiris made his wife, Isis, regent during his absence from Egypt bringing civilization to the rest of the world. If Osiris had made Seth regent, perhaps he would not have plotted against his brother, the king.

By the time Osiris returned to Egypt, Seth had gathered together seventy-two accomplices. He intended to kill Osiris and take for himself their sister, Isis, whom he lusted after. Accordingly, he invited Osiris to a banquet that he was holding in Nedyt to celebrate the twenty-eighth year of Osiris' reign. Meanwhile, Seth had had a beautiful chest made of cedar-wood inlaid with ebony and ivory.

At the end of the banquet, Seth had this chest brought before the assembled guests. Immediately, it became the object of their admiration and envy, so beautiful was it, so fine the workmanship. Seth laughingly promised to give it to the person whom it fitted most exactly when he got into it and lay down. One by one, the seventy-two accomplices tried on the chest for size. But, like the feet that Cinderella's ugly step-sisters tried to squeeze into the glass slipper, to no avail: they were all too tall or too short; too fat or too thin. Finally, the only person left at the banquet who had not tried on the chest was Osiris.

Osiris had hung back from the competition thinking it rather unbecoming for the King of Egypt to participate in such a contest. However, even a king of Egypt was not averse to a free gift, especially one as handsome as this chest. With great dignity, Osiris advanced to the chest, stepped in and lay down. Since Seth had taken the precaution of obtaining the exact measurements of his brother's body and having the chest made to the same size, it was not surprising that the chest fitted Osiris exactly.

Before Osiris could savour the pleasure of ownership of the magnificent chest, the conspirators rushed up to it, slammed down the lid and nailed it up. Not content with trapping Osiris inside the chest, they lapped it round with molten lead. Even before Osiris had had time to suffocate, they had thrown the chest into the Nile where the current carried it down to the Great Green, the name by which the Mediterranean was known to the Egyptians.

Many days later, the chest was washed up on the coast of the Lebanon, near Byblos. At once, a tamarisk tree sprang up on the very spot where the chest lay, enclosing both coffer and the dead Osiris in its trunk. Eventually, the tamarisk grew to such a tremendous size that it attracted the attention of the King of Byblos, who ordered it to be cut down and carried to his palace, where it was trimmed and set up as a pillar in the main hall.

And there Osiris stayed until eventually his wife, Isis, reached Byblos and persuaded the king to give her the pillar. She cut the body of Osiris free from its imprisoning wood and carried it back to Egypt.

As soon as Isis reached Egypt, she hid the body of her husband in a thicket of papyrus and journeyed alone to the island of Chemmis in the Delta. There, according to some versions of the story, she gave birth to Osiris' son whom she had conceived by magical means on the voyage from Byblos. Other versions say that she was pregnant with this son before Osiris was murdered and that she gave birth to him before she set out on the quest to find her husband's body. In these versions, Isis left her son, Horus, in the care of the goddess, Edjo, whilst she journeyed to Byblos; and on her return, she left Osiris' body whilst she went to collect their son.

All versions of the Osiris story agree that, for whatever reason, Isis left his body unattended for a while; and that during this time, Seth, who happened to be out hunting in the marshes of the Delta, came upon the body of the brother he had murdered. This time, Seth determined that Isis should never find the body again. And he cut the body into pieces—some say fourteen, others sixteen—and scattered the pieces up and down the length of Egypt.

Poor Isis had to begin her quest again, her task made so much more difficult by Seth's butchery. Her sister, Nephthys, who was also Seth's wife, offered to help her and together they wandered through Egypt, seeking the parts of Osiris' dismembered body.

They found the body, piece by piece. At each place where a part of Osiris' body was found, Isis fashioned a wax model of that particular member, and left it with the local priests with the injunction that they place it in their temple and worship it. Some say that Isis pretended to the priests that the relics she gave them were not wax models but really were parts of Osiris' body. She also commanded that the priests choose an animal commonly found in their locality and honour it as a representative of Osiris. Thus, the bull called Apis which was already worshipped at Memphis as an animal sacred to the god, Ptah, was thenceforward worshipped also as a representative of Osiris; and the priests of Memphis rejoiced because they thought that they had been entrusted with the head of Osiris.

By distributing parts of Osiris' body to different places in Egypt, Isis ensured that the worship of her husband became widespread throughout the land, from Busiris in the north, which was held to be the last resting-place of his backbone, to Elephantine in the south, where his leg was said to be buried in a cavern on the island of Biga.

The waters of decomposition which issued from this leg were supposed to be the source of the Nile. In later times, the tomb of Osiris' leg on Biga was called 'Abaton' and was regarded as a particularly sacred shrine.

Occasionally, parts of Osiris' body are claimed by several places: his head was buried at Memphis, according to the Memphite priesthood; but the same member was claimed by Abydos! The phenomenon of miraculous multiplication is not unknown today— there are extant enough pieces of 'the True Cross' to make up a small forest.

At last, Isis and Nephthys had collected all the pieces of Osiris' dismembered body, with the exception, according to Plutarch, of his penis, which Seth had thrown into the Nile where it was swallowed by a *Mormyrus*- or *Oxyrhynchus*-fish. The two sisters sat down beside the assembled parts of the body and wept. They wept so loudly that the Great God, Re, took pity on them and sent the jackal-headed god, Anubis, and the ibis-headed god, Thoth, to help them.

Anubis embalmed the members of Osiris' body with costly unguents, and wrapped them in bandages. Then he, and Thoth, with the aid of Isis, Horus and Nephthys, pieced together the parts of the body until it was reassembled in its former shape. The whole body was then swathed in linen bandages and placed on a lion-headed bier inside a pavilion—the first mummy had been made.

Isis changed herself into a kite and used her wings to fan the breath of life into Osiris. He was partially revived, but not enough to be able to take his place upon the throne of Egypt ever again. Instead, he was conveyed to the Underworld, a dark and menacing place. There, he remonstrated with the Great God, Atum, saying:

'O Atum, what is this desolate place into which I have come? It is without water; it is without air; its depth is unfathomable; its darkness is black as night. Must I wander hopelessly here where one cannot live in peace of heart or satisfy the longings of love?'

Atum replied to this cry of despair with the assurance that in the Underworld contentment and peace render unnecessary air and water and love. When Osiris asked if he would ever see the light of day again, Atum told him that he would remain in the Underworld, ruling as King but seeing no other god, whilst his son, Horus, took his place on the throne of Egypt and in the company of gods in the Barque of the Sun God. And when, with foreboding, Osiris asked Atum how many were to be the years of his existence in this dreadful place, he was told that he would live for millions of years until the day came when Atum would destroy what he had created and be united

1. *Re-Horakhty-Atum receiving incense from Tjatui, a priestess of Amen-Re. Vignette from a papyrus containing the Book of the Dead for Tjatui. Dynasty XXI. Thebes.*

2. *Sandstone pyramidion or benben stone from the tomb of Hornefer at Thebes. Dynasty XIX. Height: 45cm. In Dynasty XVIII, the pyramid form of royal tomb was superceded by corridor tombs cut into the cliffs at Western Thebes, and the last vestiges of the pyramid-form in Egypt are found in the shape of the brick or stone pyramidions which were placed above the entrances to the tombs of private individuals.*

3. *Shu holding up the body of the sky goddess, Nut, over the earth god, Geb, in the presence of the god of magic (bottom left corner) and the ram- and human-headed Bas or souls of the Universe. From the Greenfield Papyrus, Dynasty XXI.*

4. *Shu. Faience amulet. Height: 4cm.*

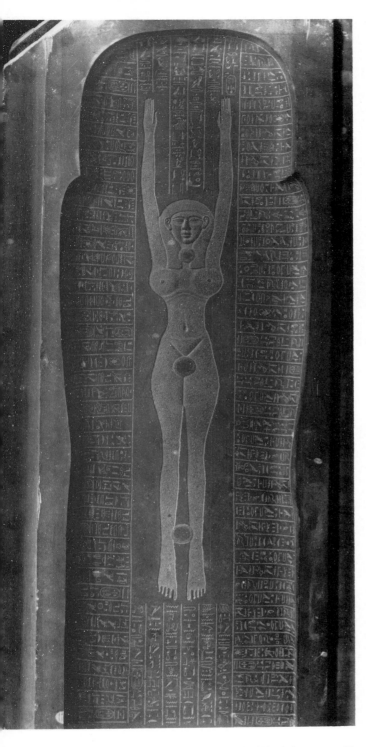

. *Nut carved in low relief, on the inner side of the lid of the great schist*
rcophagus of Princess Ankhnesneferibre, the Divine Wife of Amun (see
age 144) who ruled at Thebes during the reign of Amosis II, Dynasty
XVI. Length: 2.6m, width: 1.16m.

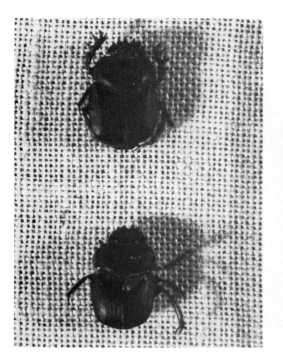

6. *Two preserved scarab beetles*
(Scarabaeus sacer).
Length: 3.5cm.

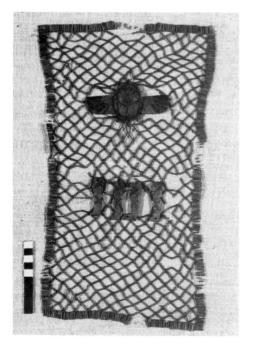

7. *Bead net with winged scarab and the Four Sons of Horus (p. 101), from outer mummy wrappings. Blue-green glaze. Late Period.*
Length: 42.5cm, width: 21cm.

8. *Inscribed gold plaque with separate band of gold bent into an oval shape and affixed to the ba* *of the plaque to provide a mount for a scarab, no* *missing but probably of semi-precious stone. The* *front of the plaque is inscribed with Chapter 30 c* *the Book of the Dead. Plaque 4.3 × 4.7cm.*

The concept of the heart acting as a witness in *the Hall of Judgement appeared for the first time* *in the funerary spells inscribed on Middle Kingd* *coffins; this plaque is one of the earliest examples* *so far found of what became the common practice* *of placing an amulet in the form of a heart scara* *over the breast within the mummy bandages.* *Middle Kingdom or First Intermediate Period.* *Abydos.*

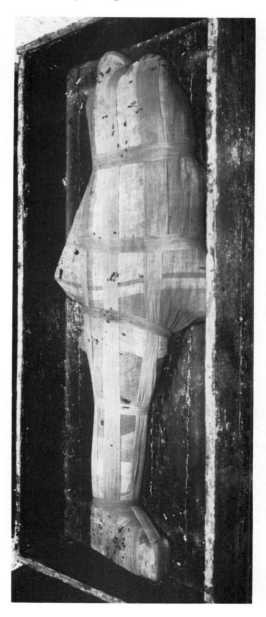

11. *The corn-Osiris of Tutankhamun as it was found by Howard Carter, wrapped in linen winding-sheets and bandaged like a mummy, and laid in a large oblong wooden box.*

9. *Limestone stele showing Osiris and Isis watching the jackal-headed god, Anubis, attending to a mummy that is lying on a lion-headed funerary couch reminiscent of the one found in Tutankhamun's tomb. Graeco-Roman period. Height: 44.5cm, width: 29cm. Abydos.*

10. Djed-*pillar. Faience amulet. Height: 11cm.*

12. *Vignette from the Book of the Dead of Ani, a scribe who lived in Dynasty XIX. Ani, accompanied by his wife, Tutu, stands by the balance in which Anubis is about to weigh his heart. The ibis-headed god, Thoth, stands by with his scribe's palette ready to record the verdict; behind him is Amit. The gods seated at the top of the vignette are, from right to left, Re-Horakhty, Atum, Shu, Tefnut, Geb, Nut, Isis, Horus, Hathor and, seated together on the left, Hu, the embodiment of Divine Utterance and Sia, the embodiment of Wisdom.*

13. *Isis. Faience amulet. Height: 7cm.*

14. *The Temple of Isis at Philae, photographed by Francis Frith in 1857.*

5. *Triad of Osiris, Isis and Horus-the-Child.*
steatite amulet. Ptolemaic Period. Height: 9cm.

16. *Girdle of Isis* (tyt). *Faïence amulet.*
Height: 3.5cm.

7. *The magnificent sarcophagus of Tutankhamun. The corners of the sarcophagus are protected by figures*
of the goddesses Isis, Nephthys, Neit and Selkis carved in high relief. In the picture, Isis appears on the
left, Nephthys on the right, each embracing her corner of the sarcophagus with outstretched arms and spread
wings. Around the base is a dado consisting of djed-*pillar-and* tyt-*symbols of protection.* (in situ in
Tutankhamun's tomb in the Valley of the Kings)

18. *Horus as hawk-headed terminals for the ends of a broad collar or necklace. Faience. 4cm × 4.5cm.*

19. *The Four Sons of Horus: left to right – Duamutef, Qebehsenuf, Imset and Haapy. Canopic stoppers assembled from two incomplete sets: the human-headed stopper (Imset) is of painted terracotta; the rest a of limestone. Middle Kingdom and Late Period (after 800 BC).*

20. *Canopic chest of Tutankhamun in the form of a shrine, the roof of which forms the lid of the chest. When the lid is removed, as in the picture, the stoppers of four Canopic jars are revealed, each fashioned in the likeness of the King's head. The interior of the chest, carved from a single block of alabaster, is hollowed out to the depth of about 13cm, just enough to hold the stoppers which cover four cylindrical holes in the base of the shrine that act as imitation Canopic jars. In each 'Canopic jar' was a miniature gold coffin, wrapped in linen, which contained the viscera of the King. Inscriptions on the miniature coffins place them under the protection of the appropriate guardian goddesses and sons of Horus and, on the corners of the shrine itself, the four goddesses are carved in high relief with arms outstretched in protection. The goddesses that can be seen in the picture are, from left to right, Selkis, Nephthys and Isis. This alabaster Canopic chest was found inside the large shrine of wood overlaid with gold leaf that can be seen standing behind Anubis in the picture in fig. 41*

21. Wadjet-*eye. Faience. Length: 12cm, width: 10cm.*

22. *Limestone funerary stele showing the goddess Kadesh standing on a lion and flanked by the gods Min on her right and Reshpu, god of war and thunder, on her left. Both Kadesh and Reshpu (sometimes called Reshep) were of Syrian origin, and Kadesh was often equated with Astarte. The bottom half of the stele shows its owner, Kaha, foreman of the workers on the royal tombs at Thebes, worshipping Anat. Deir el-Medina. Dynasty XIX. Height: 72cm.*

23. *The Pronaos or Hall of Columns from the Ptolemaic Temple of Hathor at Denderah as photographed, half filled with the sand and rubble accumulated over the centuries since the temple fell into disuse, by Francis Frith in 1857. The columns of the Hall are decorated with typical four-sided Hathor-headed capitals.*

24. *Model sistrum in blue faience, said to have been bought in Luxor in 1908. A notable feature of the sistrum is that instead of being decorated with the usual double Hathor-head, it has a single Hathor-head on the reverse side of which is carved a disk and a crescent, probably to be interpreted as the sun's disk between an (abbreviated) pair of horns – the symbol of Hathor. The handle of the sistrum is inscribed down the front with 'For recitation by Bastet-iru-di-es' (the owner). Late Period c. 800 BC. Length: 14.6cm.*

25. *Mirror with Hathor-headed handle.*

26. *Ta-weret. Faience amulet. Height: 4cm.*

27. *Some of the 'wonderful things' that Carter saw on first entering the Tomb of Tutankhamun. The couch fashioned in the shape of two cows is made of wood coated with gesso and gilded; the bodies of the cows are inlaid with trefoils of blue paste in imitation of cow-hide. Length of bed: 2.21m, Height: 1.79m.*

28. *Tutankhamun's skull-cap, made of fine linen embroidered with minute gold and faience beads in the shape of two cobras (uraei). When found, the fabric of the cap was badly carbonized, although the beads were in good condition and had adhered to the skull of the King. Carter treated the skull-cap with a thin coating of wax and left it as he had found it – on the head of the King, whose body still lies in his tomb in the Valley of the Kings.*

29. *The goddess Isis (right) leading by the hand Nefertari, queen of Ramesses II. Nefertari's headdress consists of a closely-fitting 'cap' shaped like the vulture-goddess Nekhbet surmounted by two tall plumes, symbols of the goddess of Truth, Maat. Painted relief in tomb of Nefertari, Thebes.*

30. *The vulture-goddess, Nekhbet, wearing the Crown of Upper Egypt, and the cobra-goddess, Edjo, wearing the Crown of Lower Egypt and equipped with wings like Nekhbet's. Part of a ceiling decoration in the Ptolemaic temple of Kom Ombo and typical of the way in which ceilings were decorated with representations of the two deities.*

31. *Amun, Mut, his wife, and Khonsu, their son. Relief from exterior of the temple of Ramesses III at Karnak.*

32. *Ptah. Faience amulet depicting him in primitive form. Height: 3.5cm.*

33. Menat *or counterpoise for a necklace, showing Hathor in her fertility aspect, both as a woman and as a cow. Bronze. Length: 16cm.*

34. *The Step Pyramid of Djoser at Sakkara as photographed by Francis Frith in 1857.*

35. *Apis Bull. Faience amulet. Height: 3cm.*

36. *Nefertem. Faience amulet (with centre missing) showing him standing on the back of a Sekhmet-lion (his mother). Original height: 14cm.*

37. *Sekhmet. Faience amulet showing her as a seated woman wearing a sun's disk on her head. Height: 5cm.*

38. *Black granite statue of Sekhmet standing in her shrine in the Temple of Ptah at Karnak. The statue is lit from an opening in the roof but is otherwise in total darkness. Among local people the statue has a reputation for evil. One story recounts how, at some unspecified time in the past, seven boys who were employed on an archaeological excavation as basket boys to remove rubble were buried at the feet of the goddess by a fall of sand and stones. Their bodies were never found – presumably an indication that the goddess had devoured them.*

39. *The two emblems of Anubis, hanging from lotiform poles and set in alabaster pots, that were found standing on reed mats in the north-west and south-west corners of the burial chamber of Tutankhamun. Gilded wood. Height: 1.67m.*

40. *Anubis. Faience amulet. Height: 4cm.*

41. *Anubis guarding the entrance to the innermost Treasury of Tutankhamun's tomb, seated on a chest of painted and gilded wood which contained jewellery and amulets.*

42. *Bronze statue of Thoth as an ibis.*
c. 2nd century BC.

43. *Kohl container, with applicator, in the shape*
of a baboon (Thoth). IInd Intermediate Period.
Height: 5.5cm.

44. *The goddess Seshat and the King performing a temple Foundation Ceremony. Behind Seshat stands*
Horus the Behdetite (see p. 104). Relief in the Ptolemaic Temple of Horus at Edfu.

45. *One of the statues of Min discovered by Petrie at Koptos in 1893–94. Height: 4.22m.*

46. *Alexander the Great, dressed in the conventional costume of an Egyptian king, offering incense and libation to Min in the guise of Amen-Re, Bull-of-his Mother. Relief in Luxor Temple.*

17. *Faience figurine of a cat found in a tomb that was noteworthy for the large number of similar animal representations it contained. Dynasty XVIII. Height: 2cm, length: 7cm.*

18. *Fowling scene from the Dynasty XVIII Theban tomb of Nebamun in which a hunting cat holds a bird in its mouth and deftly grasps two other birds in its hind- and fore-paws. Height of painting: 82cm.*

49. *Bronze statue of the goddess Bastet in cat form. Late Period. Height: 34cm.*

with Osiris in the Primaeval Waters of the Nun. Thus, reluctantly, did Osiris become King of the Underworld.

During his rise from an obscure prehistoric fertility-god to the Egyptian god of the dead *par excellence*, Osiris was incorporated into the mythologies of the two deities who were paramount at the beginning of the historic period in Egypt: Re of Heliopolis and Ptah of Memphis.

At Heliopolis, as we have seen (p. 49), Osiris became part of the Great Ennead as the son of Nut and Geb, born on one of the five epagomenal days, the brother of Isis, Nephthys and Seth, the husband of Isis and the father of Horus, and destined to become King of Egypt after Geb. At Heliopolis, Osiris was regarded as a sky-god. Sometimes, he was said to be the moon; at other times, the constellation, Orion. When, eventually, he supplanted the Sun God as ruler of the Underworld, he was thought of as the dark half of Re, with Re being the sun by day to Osiris' 'dark sun' at night.

At Memphis, Osiris took on his first funerary associations by being identified with Sokar, the ancient Memphite deity of the dead who had been coalesced with Ptah.

Osiris found his true home, his final and best-known resting place, at *Aabdju*, now usually known by the Greek form of the name, Abydos. This most sacred site in Egypt lies between Assiut and Luxor, near the predynastic city of This, which, by late predynastic times, had become the capital of Upper Egypt; and was the Thinite necropolis. When, in 3100 BC, the greatest of the Thinite kings, Menes, united both Upper and Lower Egypt under his rule, he, and his successors, the kings of Dynasties I and II, chose to be buried at Sakkara, the necropolis of the newly-built capital, Memphis. However, they commemorated the fact that their origins were at This by building cenotaphs at Abydos.

At this time, the local god of Abydos was Khenty-amentiu. His name means 'Foremost of the Westerners', a reference to the belief that, just as the sun rose or was 'born' in the east, and set or 'died' in the west, so men when they died followed the sun into the west, where the dead had their abode and where Khenty-amentiu was the 'foremost' or most important god. He himself had supplanted the oldest-known god of Abydos, Wepwawet.

Wepwawet, whose name means 'the Opener of the Ways', was believed to usher the dead on the paths of the Underworld. He was usually represented as a jackal, an appropriate totem animal for a god of the dead since the jackal, then as now, at night frequents the edge of the desert where cemeteries are situated. Unlike Anubis, who is always depicted with a black head, Wepwawet is portrayed with a grey or white head, an indication, perhaps, that he was originally a wolf-god. As well as being the oldest deity of Abydos, Wepwawet was worshipped some 120km to the north in the 13th Nome of Upper Egypt, where he took the form of a wolf, as the Greek name of the Nome capital, Lykopolis (Wolf City) indicates: today, Lykopolis is called Assiut, and is an important provincial capital.

The god who ousted Wepwawet from Abydos, Khenty-amentiu, was represented in human form, his arms folded across his chest, his body entirely swathed in bandages; on his head, the White Crown of Upper Egypt. The bandages indicate that he was a god of the dead, albeit a relatively obscure one. He was local to Abydos where he was worshipped for a very long time, right down to Dynasty XIII, even though Osiris had by that time long since divested him of his attributes and functions and replaced him as the chief god of Abydos.

Osiris arrived at Abydos during Dynasty V. Although the city had enjoyed considerable prestige as the necropolis of This for a long time before the advent of Osiris, his ever-increasing popularity was to ensure that by Dynasty XII Abydos had become one of the most famous religious centres in Egypt. Under the patronage of the kings of Dynasty XII, Osiris enjoyed more power and importance than ever before.

Through his resurrection, Osiris held out the hope of eternal life at first to the King of Egypt alone, but eventually to every Egyptian, for the Egyptians believed that if their friends acted towards them as the gods had acted towards Osiris, they, too, would achieve eternal life. Thus, when an Egyptian died, his body was mummified and wrapped in bandages in imitation of the body of the dead Osiris. The priests attending his burial performed their parts as the gods had performed theirs: the chief female mourners enacted the roles of Isis and Nephthys; the burial rites were conducted by a priest impersonating Anubis. By the end of the Old Kingdom, every dead Egyptian was identified with Osiris and addressed as 'the Osiris such-and-such a name'.

In the Old Kingdom, when Re held sway, the Solar religion as expressed in the Pyramid Texts represents Heaven as an essentially royal domain to which the ordinary man could not aspire. By the end of Dynasty VI, the Pyramid Texts had been largely edited and rewritten to accommodate Osiris. The Old Kingdom belief in a Solar Hereafter was gradually fading as the Osirian beliefs became increasingly popular. By Dynasty XI, the Pyramid Texts had been adapted for use by those who were not entitled to be buried in pyramids, and selections from the Texts were written inside coffins, usually on the walls, sometimes on the base. The Pyramid Texts became the Coffin Texts, a collection of magic spells that enabled the Egyptians to cope with Death and what comes after it.

The Coffin Texts reveal that the Egyptians went in terror of Death and the next world: it was indeed 'the undiscover'd country from whose bourn no traveller returns', and an obsessive fear of the unknown is the hallmark of the Coffin Texts. The Egyptian conception of the Underworld was that it was a nightmarish place—dark, dismal, unsafe, peopled with monsters, genii and all kinds of carnivorous animal. The Coffin Texts provide spells for escaping from such creatures; and spells for the prevention of suffering from evils such as walking upside down or eating excrement.

Everything necessary for life upon earth was thought to be just as necessary for life after death: hence, many spells in the Coffin Texts are for enabling the dead person to breathe pure air; to conserve his sexual powers; to help him find his family again so that they can serve him with funerary offerings of clothing, ointments, drink and, above all, food—a fear of lack of food was uppermost in the minds of the Egyptians.

The obsession with food found in the Coffin Texts is matched only by an obsession concerning the preservation of the body. Hence, many spells refer to the care of the body, especially the head and the heart; other spells confer the ability to move about with ease. The Coffin Texts are concerned with the problem of survival after death; and in the final analysis, this means the preservation of the body. The theory of what happens to the soul and to the dead in the Afterlife, although referred to in the Coffin Texts, is not fully developed until the New Kingdom.

The New Kingdom saw the final triumph of Osiris. In the middle of the sixteenth century BC, the princes of Thebes succeeded in uniting the whole of Egypt under their own rule. During the period of civil war which led up to this event, Osiris' chief shrine, Abydos, was captured by the Theban rulers who were to found the New Kingdom. They used Osiris in their political struggle, and persuaded their subjects that a pilgrimage to Abydos was something that every Egyptian should aspire to make.

In the Middle Kingdom, the Egyptians had often arranged for funerary stelae to be deposited on their behalf at Abydos in place of actually making the journey there. In the New Kingdom, the Journey to Abydos became an essential part of funerary belief: accordingly, Egyptians decorated their tombs with painted pictures of this Journey, which they may or may not have actually undertaken, but which could be accomplished by magical means by the expedient of having it depicted on the walls of their tombs. The most famous of these paintings are at Thebes, where on one wall of many tombs the boats used for the Journey to Abydos are depicted with their sails furled for the voyage downstream; and on the opposite wall with their sails set for the triumphal return journey.

It was the wish of every Egyptian to be buried at Abydos, as near as possible to the place where Osiris was said to be buried. Since this was clearly an impossibility in the majority of cases, those who made a pilgrimage to Abydos were content to leave votive messages to Osiris, written on pieces of broken pot. The vast number of potsherds to be seen today, strewn across the site of Abydos, give the locality its Arabic name, 'Umm el Ga'ab' (Mother of Pots), and bear testimony to how many Egyptians must have visited Abydos over the centuries.

The Theban doctrine of Osiris, which was fully developed by Dynasty XVIII, saw the democratization of the Afterlife. From then on, the Afterlife was available to every follower of Osiris, king or commoner, male or female. It would not be true to say 'rich or poor', since the poor could not afford to make the preparations deemed necessary to make absolutely sure of gaining the Afterlife; but it seems that even the poor had some hope of reaching it. The secret of the enormous popularity enjoyed by Osiris from the New Kingdom to the end of the Pharaonic period lay in the hope of eternal life that he held out to everyone who had made at least some preparations for death.

The Egyptians believed that every man was made up of three parts: the *Ka* ⊔, *the Ba* ⦚ and the *Akh* ⋎. Although it is difficult to find modern concepts which faithfully convey the Egyptian idea of what the *Ba*, the *Ka* and the *Akh* were, the *Ba* is often described as the soul of a man, the *Ka* as his double, the *Akh* as a glorified spirit.

The Egyptians believed that when a man was conceived, the god, Khnum, (or his deputy), made the man's body on a potter's turn-table and at the same time made the man's *Ka*, or double. The *Ka* lived in the man until the moment of his death, when the *Ka* divided into two—into a bird (the *Akh*) which flew to the Afterlife where it once again turned into the *Ka* or double of the dead man; and a human-headed bird, the *Ba*, which stayed behind on earth, living on in the body left behind by the *Akh*.

The Egyptians were not afraid of death as long as they had made the correct preparations for it. These preparations included the building of a tomb—the house of eternity—in which the *Ba* could live on in safety, and at which offerings of food and drink could be made at regular intervals, on which the *Ba* could live. Inside the tomb, the

Ba resided in the body of the dead man. In early times, that body was preserved naturally: it was buried in a pit dug in the sand, which allowed the fluids of decomposition to drain away quickly, thus preventing the body from rotting. The sand also allowed the heat of the sun to penetrate the grave, thus accelerating the rate of dessication.

Once the Egyptians began to build more elaborate tombs, the brick and stone superstructures of these tombs prevented the natural dessication of the body, causing it to rot, thereby destroying the 'home' of the *Ba*. The Egyptians were forced to find a way of preserving the body by artificial means, and the means they found, probably sometime during the late Old Kingdom, was mummification. The whole purpose of tomb building and mummification was to protect the *Ba*. If, however, in spite of everything, the body of a dead man was destroyed after burial, the Egyptians believed that the *Ba* could take up residence in a statue or relief of the dead man. Hence, at an early date, they learned how to carve statues and reliefs—not as decorations but as substitutes for the body.

As long as the *Ba* continued to live on earth, so the dead man could go on living in the Afterlife. It was only if the *Ba* were destroyed that the dead man would suffer the second death, the death that really did come as the end: he was annihilated, made as if he had never come into existence. The dead man could only reach the Afterlife, which was conceived of as being exactly like this life on earth, by undergoing the Judgement of the Dead. From the New Kingdom onwards, it was Osiris who was the supreme judge of the dead.

In order to reach the Hall of Judgement in which Osiris sat, the dead man had to face a perilous journey through the Duat. The Duat is sometimes translated as 'Hell' or 'Hades', but these terms convey ideas that were alien to the Egyptians, and it is perhaps safer to translate 'Duat' as the Underworld.

The Underworld was thought to be a narrow valley with a river running through it—not unlike Egypt! It seems to have been separated from this world—and to the Egyptians, that meant Egypt—by a range of mountains. At the eastern end of this range was a mountain called *Manu*; at the western end, a mountain called *Bakhau*, and it was through openings near these mountains that the sun entered and left the Underworld each night. The dead used the same passes.

Just as Egypt was divided into provinces, so the Underworld was divided into regions. The dead man entered each region via a gate guarded by demons, which he could only get by on giving them the correct password: these passwords, together with a map of the

Underworld, he had taken care to have written on papyrus rolls, such as the Book of the Dead, or the Book of What-is-in-the-Underworld, and buried with him!

At last, the dead man reached the Hall of Judgement, where Osiris sat with forty-two Assessors, each Assessor representing one of the Nomes of Egypt and the Underworld. In front of Osiris, a balance was set up. In one pan of the balance was placed the Feather of Truth; in the other, the heart of the dead man. The god, Thoth, stood by to register the verdict and the god, Anubis, waited to release the balance.

The dead man, accompanied by his *Ba*, stood in front of Osiris and made his confession. This confession was written down in Chapter 125 of the Book of the Dead. And it is not a confession of sins as we would understand it. The dead man lists the things that he has *not* done: he denies that he has stolen, killed, cheated, blasphemed, lied, spoken slanderously, gossiped, committed sodomy, masturbated, committed adultery and so on. The words 'I have not' preface every 'sin'; a fact that has led Egyptologists to call this list the 'Negative Confession'.

Having made his 'Confession', the dead man waited whilst his heart was weighed in the balance against the Feather of Truth. If the Feather weighed down the heart, or if the balance did not move, the man had made a true 'confession'. If the heart, heavy with guilt, weighed down the Feather, then the man was found 'guilty'.

Close to the balance sat the monster, Amit: a composite animal with the head of a crocodile, the body of a lion and the hind-quarters of a hippopotamus. He waited to eat the heart of a man found guilty. There is no record that Amit ever had to perform this task. Having taken the precaution of placing a papyrus in his tomb with the Negative Confession written on it, the Egyptian believed that what was set down on the papyrus became fact; no matter what sins he had committed, the Negative Confession wiped them out. Although the Egyptians seem to have had a strong ethical sense, they nullified it by the use of magic.

Throughout the centuries, Abydos maintained its position as the most important religious centre in Egypt. Many shrines and temples were erected there, the earliest of which must have been one built of mud-brick and dedicated to Khenty-amentiu, later to be displaced by Osiris. In Dynasty XII, Senwosret III built for himself a mortuary temple at Abydos in addition to the mortuary temple connected to his pyramid at Dahshur. The first king of Dynasty XVIII, Ahmose, built a cenotaph at Abydos for his grandmother, Tetisheri, and several other temples are known to have been built there by kings of Dynasties XVII and XVIII, although their sites have not yet been located; and in Dynasty XIX, Ramesses II added to their number.

The most famous temple at Abydos, indeed, one of the most renowned temples in Egypt, largely because of the beauty of the reliefs within the building, is the one begun by Seti I in Dynasty XIX and completed by his son, Ramesses II.

Seti's temple has an unusual L-shaped plan; and seven sanctuaries: one dedicated to Seti himself, the others to Ptah, Re-Horakhty, Amun, Isis, Horus and Osiris. Behind the temple is the building known as the Osireion, which was designed to be a re-creation of the Island of Creation set in the waters of the Nun. It was a cenotaph for Seti, who was actually buried in the Valley of the Kings at Thebes, and it is possible that the King lay in state in it before being taken on his last journey to Thebes. The Osireion is constructed from massive granite blocks in a style reminiscent of that of the Old Kingdom. Its central part is open to the sky, and it was here, probably, that barley was germinated as a symbol of the resurrection of Osiris.

At Abydos, the Osiris Mysteries were enacted every year during the last month of Inundation (October) when the flood waters were receding. In the New Kingdom, the Mysteries lasted for eight days, and began when a statue of Osiris was carried on the shoulders of his priests towards his tomb. The procession was led by a priest wearing a jackal-mask who represented Wepwawet, the Opener of the Ways; and in it were other priests and priestesses impersonating the chief actors in the Osiris legend.

The following three days and nights were filled with lamentations: having buried the statue of Osiris, the mourners, led by 'Isis' and 'Nephthys', grieved for the god. Next came the reenactment of the trial of Seth before the Tribunal of the Gods; and a mock battle between the followers of Seth and those of Osiris. Eventually, Osiris made a triumphant reappearance in his sacred Barque, called *Neshmet*, and, finally, the most sacred act in the Mysteries was carried out—the erection of the *Djed*-pillar, the ancient representation of the backbone of Osiris, an act which symbolised the resurrection of the god.

The cult of Osiris lasted for over 2,000 years. His final transmogrification came under Ptolemy I Soter (304–282 BC) who introduced a new god into Egypt, a god called Serapis, in an attempt to provide all his subjects, both Greek and Egyptian, with a divinity whom both cultures would find sympathetic.

Serapis was a combination of Osiris and the sacred bull Apis of Memphis (p. 165), but with many Hellenistic elements also. He borrowed some of his attributes from Zeus, Asklepios and Dionysus:

hence, he was a god of fertility and of the Underworld who was also a physician.

His cult was centred on Alexandria, where his temple, the Serapeum, was regarded as a place of pilgrimage throughout the Greek and Roman world until its destruction on the orders of the Emperor Theodosius in AD 389. The old burial place of the Apis Bulls at Sakkara (also called the Serapeum) was granted a new lease of life because of the introduction of Serapis. However, the Egyptians themselves never fully accepted this hybrid deity with his Hellenistic overtones.

Osiris is probably the best-known of all Egyptian gods. His appeal lay in the belief that he had lived on earth as a man who brought nothing but good to mankind but who was betrayed and murdered. His resurrection and the hope of eternal life that he held out to everyone further enhanced his popularity, which was unrivalled until Roman times when the popularity of his wife, Isis, gained ground. Only the advent of Jesus Christ, who brought the same message to mankind, eclipsed the fame of this the most sympathetic of all the deities in the Egyptian pantheon.

ISIS

Isis was more popular than any other goddess in the Egyptian pantheon. Nothing is known of her origins, although it is more than probable that at the outset she was a fetish-goddess who was worshipped in a locality in the Delta situated close to Busiris, the oldest-known centre of the cult of Osiris.

The standard depiction of Isis shows her as a woman wearing on her head the hieroglyphic sign, ◿, which represents a seat or a throne. It is possible that originally Isis wore on her head her fetish-object, which later became confused with the hieroglyph ◿, thus connecting Isis with the royal throne, perhaps as a personification of it. She was known as the 'goddess of many names' and indeed she is found as a form of every great goddess from Nut and Hathor (from whom she borrowed the cow's horns she is sometimes depicted wearing) to Astarte; the Greeks equated her with their own goddess of the Earth, Demeter.

Isis was a universal goddess; she took her place in the sky as Sirius (the Dog Star) but there was no town or city in Egypt that claimed recognition as the burial place of Isis. For many years, therefore, she was not exclusively connected with any one town or temple. Instead, a part of every temple in the land was reserved for her worship. At Denderah, for example, Isis was given a small temple to the south of the main temple which was dedicated to Hathor; and in it her birth was recorded and celebrated.

The first great temple built specifically in honour of Isis was begun in Dynasty xxx by Nectanebo II (360–343 BC) who built the Temple of Isis at Behbeit el-Hagar, which lies between Tanta and Damietta in the Eastern Delta. The temple, which was known to the Greeks as the Iseum, was completed by Ptolemy Euergetes I and Isis, together with Osiris and Horus, was worshipped there until the sixth century AD.

Perhaps the most famous temple dedicated to Isis is that at Philae, the island which lies just to the south of Elephantine (Aswan) on the southern border of Egypt. The earliest parts of the temple were erected by Nectanebo I (380–362 BC) but Ptolemaic kings and Roman emperors built there also. The great hall of the temple was turned into a church under the Byzantine Emperor, Justinian (AD 527–565). Philae has come into prominence once again in the last few years due to the building of the High Dam at Aswan. In order to save the temples and shrines on Philae Island from drowning under the water of Lake Nasser, they have been dismantled and reerected on the nearby island of Agilkia.

Originally, Isis was significant because of her relationship to other divinities: she took her place in the Heliopolitan Ennead as the daughter of Geb and Nut, the wife of Osiris and the sister of Seth and Nephthys. She was allotted a role as protector-goddess: Isis, together with Nephthys, Neit and Selkis, guarded the four corners of royal sarcophagi; the mummified liver of a dead man was set under her protection; she and Nephthys were regarded as the chief divine mourners. Isis' role as mourner and protector of the dead arises from her association with Osiris and the story of her quest to find his body after his murder by Seth (p. 78).

Isis was often depicted as a female figure with arms outstretched and placed around the figure of Osiris; or as a mother suckling her son, Horus, making her the prototype of the faithful wife and devoted mother. Her reputation as a great magician, as exemplified by the story of Re and his Great Name (p. 60), would have done her no harm in the esteem of the Egyptians, who were great respecters of magic. But it is as the faithful wife and, more especially, as the devoted mother, that she was most revered.

The fullest account of how Isis kept faith with Osiris is found in Plutarch's *De Iside et Osiride*, which is, obviously, a very late version of the story. After the murder of Osiris, the grief-stricken Isis set out to find his body, which Seth had thrown into the Nile. She journeyed up and down the land of Egypt and beyond, enquiring of everyone she met whether they had seen her beloved husband.

At last, the goddess came across some children playing on the shore of the Great Green. They told her of the beautiful chest that they had seen floating in the sea and being carried eastwards on the waves. And so Isis followed the shoreline of the Great Green until she came to Byblos in the Lebanon. There, she used her magic arts to learn the whereabouts of her husband's body and discovered that it had been enclosed in the trunk of the great tamarisk tree that was now a pillar in the main hall of the King's palace.

Isis disguised herself as an old woman and sat down by a well. She spoke to no one until, one day, the handmaidens of the Queen of Byblos passed by. To them, she spoke beguilingly and showed them how to braid their hair in new ways; and as she bent over them dressing their locks, she impregnated the tresses with the divine perfume of her own body.

When the Queen saw her maidservants' hair and smelled the sweet smell that emanated from it, she asked her women who had taught them to dress their hair in this new way, and they told her of the old woman who sat by the well. The Queen sent for the old woman; and, realising that she was an Egyptian, thought that she might be one who knew the magical arts for which Egypt was famous: and so she asked her to be the nurse of her baby son. And Isis agreed.

The little prince of Byblos was ailing and had not been expected to live long. The Queen hoped that the old Egyptian woman would use her magic to save him. Her hope proved well-founded, for, under Isis' care, the prince grew better every day. Indeed, he improved so quickly that the Queen was curious to know what magic the old woman was using.

One night, she hid herself in the baby's room. For a long time, she waited in vain for something to happen. Then she saw the old woman leave the room, and followed her until she reached the main hall of the palace. There, the old woman changed into a swallow and flew round and round the great pillar that had been made from the tamarisk tree, twittering mournfully. The Queen watched for a while, and then, realising that her son had been left alone, ran back to his room.

To her horror, the baby was standing in the middle of the floor engulfed in flames. The Queen uttered a loud shriek and rushed forward to snatch her son from the fire. Before she had had time to realise that the baby was quite unharmed, she was confronted by Isis, not in the guise of an old woman or a swallow, but in her full splendour as a goddess. The Queen fell to her knees before her as she said:

'I was burning away the mortal parts of your child so that he might live forever. Now, however, you have broken the spell, and he will die as all men must die.'

When the King of Byblos learned of what had happened, he begged Isis to forgive his wife. Isis agreed, providing that the King would give her the magnificent tamarisk pillar in his hall. Only too glad to appease the goddess so easily, the King had the pillar cut down.

Isis cut open the pillar and drew forth the chest which contained the body of Osiris. She threw herself onto the chest and lamented so loudly that one of the King's children died of fright. Then she wrapped the tree-trunk in fine linen and poured costly ointments over it. She gave it to the King of Byblos, who built a temple for it in which the people of Byblos could worship the tree-trunk: the temple stands to this day.

Isis took the chest with its precious contents and placed it in a boat. Maneros, the King's eldest son, went with her to sail the vessel. As soon as they had put to sea, Isis opened the chest and gazed sorrowfully upon the face of her dead husband. As she leaned forward to kiss him, Maneros approached the divine couple, and Isis turned to look at him, her face filled with such grief that the prince backed away in horror and fell over the side of the boat. Maneros was drowned, and for many years the Egyptians commemorated him by calling upon him in their harvest songs as they lamented over the cutting of the first sheaf of corn.

And so Isis brought the body of her husband home to Egypt. She grieved that she had no son to inherit the throne of his father which would now fall to the murderer, Seth. She determined that her husband, Osiris, should have a son to avenge him and claim his rightful inheritance. One version of her story says that she changed herself into a kite and produced light from her feathers and air from her wings. By this means she made Osiris' penis rise up from his inert body. She drew from him his essence and with this she made for him a son and heir whom she carried within her body.

Osiris became King of the Underworld and Isis was left alone to protect his seed with which she was pregnant and bring it to fruition; to guard her unborn child from Seth. She tried to hide herself from Seth but he caught her and imprisoned her in a spinning-mill.

What happened next is told on a stele made for King Nectanebo II, a late version of what is clearly a very old legend. The stele was found in AD 1828 at Alexandria and is now called the 'Metternich Stele'.[4]

The god, Thoth, realised that Isis was in grave danger from Seth; he was fearful of what would happen to her when Seth discovered that she was pregnant. And so he rescued her from the spinning-mill. Thoth advised Isis to go into hiding until her little boy grew to the age at which he could claim his inheritance. After her escape, Isis waited until evening before setting out for the Delta where she intended to hide herself in the papyrus thickets and marshes which covered the area. She was accompanied on her perilous journey by seven scorpions, the leader of which was called Tefen.

On her journey to the Delta, the weary Isis and her companions came to the town of *Per-sui* and decided to ask for refuge for the night at the house of a certain rich lady named Usert. Usert shut her door in Isis' face, an act that so vexed the scorpions that they put their venom into the sting of Tefen, who crept under the double doors of Usert's house and stung her son. Meanwhile, a little fisher-girl had offered shelter to Isis and her companions in her own humble home.

The venom of Tefen, enriched as it was by his fellow scorpions, caused Usert's little boy untold agony. His frantic mother rushed into the town calling for help: but everyone ignored her. Isis found that she was sorry for the child, who was, after all, innocent. She decided to cure him and called to his mother, telling her to bring the little boy to her, for she was one who knew how to expel poison with her magic spell. And so Isis laid her hand on the child, who lay panting for breath, and recited:

'O poison of Tefen, come forth and drip onto the ground.
May the child live and the poison die.'

Usert was overcome with remorse for her callous treatment of Isis. Filled with gratitude, she sought to make amends by filling the hut of the little fisher-girl who had sheltered the goddess with valuable possessions from her own house.

Isis went on with her journey and eventually came to Chemmis in the Delta. There she gave birth to her son, Horus, whom she named Horus-Avenger-of-his-Father. She took off her girdle and tied it round the baby for his protection. It is the knot of this magic girdle that was used to form the amulet, *Tyt*, which became a symbol of protection to the Egyptians.

Although Isis was a goddess, her divine status availed her not at all in Chemmis. She was a fugitive, terrified lest Seth find her and her baby son; and she was hungry—there was no one to feed her and care for her. Eventually, she was forced to leave Horus alone and, disguised as a beggar-woman, go in search of food.

All day she wandered, seeking things to eat, longing all the while to see her little boy. For some reason she must have removed her protective girdle from him before she left because when, at the end of the day, she returned to the place where she had left him, she found the child lying on the ground, water streaming from his eyes and saliva dribbling from his mouth.

Isis rushed to her son, her innocent, fatherless child. She picked him up and cradled him in her arms. Sobbing, she cried out, 'Here I am, here I am'. But the child lay still as a stone. Thinking that her son was in distress because he had been left all day without food, Isis tried to suckle him. But even the smell of his mother's milk and the sensation of her nipple pressed against his mouth failed to rouse the baby.

Isis did not know where to turn for help. She dared not call out to the gods, for fear of Seth. Instead, she appealed to the marsh-dwellers, who left their huts and came hurrying to exclaim over Isis in her sorrow. None of them knew how to cure her son, who lay rigid on the ground showing no signs of life. Isis began to fear that Seth had attacked her child. Eventually, a woman came to Isis, a great lady in her town with a reputation for learning. She assured Isis that Horus' malady was no trick of Seth's devising because Atum had decreed that Seth should not enter Chemmis. She advised Isis to seek another reason for the sickness and suggested that Horus had been bitten by a snake or a scorpion.

Isis laid her nose to her child's mouth and sniffed 'to find out whether there was any smell in his skull'. She discovered that Horus had been poisoned by a scorpion. Ironically, it seems that she was unable to cure her own son as she had the child stung by Tefen. The cries of anguish that she uttered when she found that Horus had been bitten brought Nephthys and Selkis to her: their combined voices reached Re in his Barque of Millions of Years, so that the boat came to a standstill and darkness descended on the earth.

Thoth alighted from the boat and recited the spell by which Horus would be restored to health:

> 'Come back, O Poison. You are exorcised by the spell of Re himself . . . the Barque of the Sun God will stand still . . . until Horus recovers—to his mother's delight. Fall onto the earth, O Poison . . . darkness will cover everything . . . wells will be dry, crops will wither . . . until Horus recovers—to his mother's delight.'

At last, the poison was overcome. Thoth, with a final injunction to those who dwelt in Chemmis that they should guard the child, Horus, until he grew up, returned to the Barque of Re to report to the Sun God that Horus was alive and well—to his mother's delight.

And so, Isis waited patiently during the years when Horus was growing up in Chemmis, guarded according to Thoth's decree. Eventually, the day came when he was old enough for her to take him before the Tribunal of the Gods to claim his inheritance. There, Horus found that the sympathies of Re were with Seth: Re preferred that the kingship should be in the hands of an experienced man rather than in those of a youth scarcely out of childhood.

The story of what happened next is told in a papyrus written in the Late Period and now kept in the Chester Beatty Library in Dublin (p. 102). After much arguing amongst the gods in the Tribunal, Re decreed that the company of gods should be ferried across to the Island in the Midst, there to decide the fate of Horus and Seth. Re gave instructions to Anty, the ferryman, not to let any woman who resembled Isis cross over to the Island; for he intended that the gods should settle the issue without interference from the wily Isis.

But Isis was determined to avenge her husband's murder and uphold her son's rights by ensuring that Seth should never sit upon the Throne of Egypt. She disguised herself as an old woman and, approaching Anty the ferryman as he was sitting near his boat, she succeeded in bribing him with the gold ring that she wore on her finger to ferry her across to the Island in the Midst.

The Ennead was sitting down eating bread when Isis arrived on the Island. Seth looked up and saw her whilst she was still some way off. Before he could see her more clearly, Isis recited one of her magic spells and changed herself into a shapely young woman. Thereupon Seth loved her to distraction. He sprang up from where he was sitting eating bread and went to meet the beautiful girl before any of the other gods had had a glimpse of her. He stood behind a tree and called out, 'Yoo-hoo, pretty maid! Here I am!'

But the 'pretty maid' repulsed Seth's advances whilst she wrung his heart with the following tale:

'I was married to a cattle herdsman. I bore him a male child and the lad grew up, tending his father's cattle. But then a foreigner came. He sat down in my byre and said this, speaking to my little boy: "I will beat you and take away the cattle which belonged to your father and throw you out".'

'And now,' said the wily Isis, 'I should like you to act as my little boy's champion.'

The besotted Seth, realising that the only way to gain the affections of this shapely young woman with whom he had fallen in love at first sight, immediately offered his services, stating indignantly that it was outrageous that the cattle belonging to her husband should be given to a stranger whilst her son was still alive.

Poor Seth. He had not noticed that when his 'pretty maid' spoke of 'cattle' she was using a word that meant not only cattle but was also used as a synonym for 'Egyptians'. His answer, therefore, meant that the Egyptians belonging to Isis' husband, Osiris, should be given to her son, Horus.

With a loud shriek, Isis changed herself into a kite and flew up to perch on top of an acacia tree, calling out to the discomforted Seth: 'Now it's your turn to weep! You have condemned yourself out of your own mouth. So what are you complaining about?' Realising how he had been tricked, Seth began to cry. Still crying, he ran to Re-Horakhty, who enquired in a resigned tone of voice what was the matter with him.

Seth told Re how Isis had beguiled him by changing herself into a shapely young girl and telling him the sad story of how her husband had died and how a stranger had stolen the cattle that had been left to her little boy. And Re asked Seth what his reply had been. He was told:

'I said to her, "Is it to the foreigner that the cattle should be given while the child of your good man is still alive?" So said I to her. "The face of the stranger should be beaten with a stick. He should be thrown out and your little boy·be put in his father's place." So said I to her.'

And Re said to him: 'Well, you have passed judgement on yourself. So what are you complaining of?'

Seth was furious. He had the ferryman, Anty, bastinadoed until the soles of his feet were entirely removed for disobeying orders for the sake of a little gold ring. But he could not prevent the Crown of Egypt being placed upon Horus' head.

In this account of how Isis tricked Seth, she changed herself into a kite. We have seen how she changed herself into a kite on more than one occasion in order to breathe life into Osiris. It is Isis' propensity for changing herself into a kite in order to achieve her purposes that gave rise to the depictions of her as a human female with wings, as when, for instance, she is protecting the royal sarcophagus.

Isis is sometimes represented as a headless goddess. The reason for this is also to be found in the story of Horus' struggles against Seth as related in the Chester Beatty Papyrus. Seth was determined that the incidents that took place on the Island in the Midst should not be the end of the matter. He challenged Horus to a race, a race which ended with the contestants fighting each other with harpoons. When Seth's harpoon struck Horus, he cried out to his mother to use her magic spells to make the harpoon drop from him. This she did. But when Seth was in his turn struck with Horus' harpoon, Isis felt sorry for her brother. Once again she used her magic, this time to make the harpoon drop from the body of Seth. At this, Horus became very angry. With his face as savage as a panther's, he took hold of his axe and chopped off his mother's head, and, clasping the head to his bosom, stalked off to the mountains. Meanwhile, Isis had changed herself into a headless statue made of flint until a new head could be made for her.

Re was angry at what Horus had done; but Isis forgave her son. She continued with her struggle to ensure that he inherited the Throne of Egypt; and eventually, she triumphed.

During the Late Period especially, Isis became a universal goddess by virtue of her assimilation with deities such as Astarte, Hathor, Bastet, Nut, Sothis (with whom she merged and was worshipped under the name of Isisothis); and Renenutet. Renenutet (sometimes called Ernutet or Thermuthis), whose name means 'the provider of nourishment', was the goddess of fertility and the harvest. She was personified as a cobra and was much respected during harvest-time when the Egyptian peasant was apt to encounter manifestations of her as he cut his wheat or barley. Renenutet was the mother of Nepri, the personification of corn, who was equated with Osiris, the corn-god. The obvious parallel between Renenutet and her son, and Isis and the Horus-child, led to a merging of the two goddesses during the Late Period when they were worshipped as Isermuthis.

The cult of Isis was widespread in the Egypt of the dynastic period. From Egypt it spread northwards to Phoenicia, Syria and Palestine; to Asia Minor; to Cyprus, Rhodes, Crete, Samos and other islands in the Aegean; to many parts of mainland Greece—Corinth, Argos and Thessaly amongst them; to Malta and Sicily; and, finally, to Rome. In the first century BC, Isis was perhaps the most popular goddess in the Eternal City, from which her cult spread to the furthest limits of the Roman Empire, including Britain: her only rival was Mithras.

Just as Isis was identified in Egypt with many other Egyptian goddesses, so in foreign lands was she worshipped as a form of many native goddesses. In *The Golden Ass*, Apuleius lists some of her names: in Phrygia, she was the 'Mother of the Gods'; to the Athenians, she was Minerva; in Cyprus, she was Venus of Paphos; the Cretans called her Diana; the Sicilians, Proserpine. Only the Egyptians called her by her true name: 'Isis the Queen'.

The cult of Isis in Egypt and elsewhere was superseded only by that of the Virgin Mary and the Infant Jesus; and even then, she was not forgotten. The iconography of Mary and the Christ Child owes much to that of Isis and her child, Horus, who was often depicted sitting on his mother's knee. Perhaps the most graceful compliment paid to Isis, Queen of the Gods, is found in the aria 'O Isis und Osiris' which Mozart wrote for *Die Zauberflöte*, thereby ensuring that the goddess' name is remembered even today.

HORUS

Falcons were more numerous in Ancient Egypt than they are in that country today. These impressive birds, with their fine plumage and their ability to hover motionless above the earth before swooping on the prey that they have seen from afar, or to swerve upwards into the sky, higher and higher until they disappear from sight, appealed to the Ancient Egyptians' sense of awe at the mysteries of Nature. Thus, falcons were worshipped at many places, under many different names. Several gods took on the form of a falcon from time to time—Re, Montu and Sokar amongst them; but the most famous of the falcon-gods were those called Horus. There were several deities bearing this name, each with his own cult-centre and legends; over the years, however, their cults and legends became inextricably mixed until finally all falcon-gods were eclipsed by the most popular falcon of all, Horus of Edfu, who manifested himself in the shape of a peregrine.

Who was Horus and what was his place of origin, his attributes and legends, that he could displace so many indigenous gods?

In the beginning, Horus was a sky-god. His Egyptian name, *Hor*, can mean either 'face' or 'distant'; slightly modified to *horet* it means 'sky'. The Distant One is an appropriate name for a falcon since this is a bird that seems to fly further and higher than any other as it ranges widely over the heavens: thus Horus was visualised as the face of the sky. In this face, the left eye was the moon and the right eye was the sun; and the deity to whom the face belonged was worshipped as 'the Great Horus' or 'Horus the Elder', whom the Greeks called Haroeris, the sky-god who had come into existence before mankind and who manifested himself on earth in the form of a falcon. This falcon could also represent a moonless night: as *Hor-Khenty-en-irty* (Horus-Foremost-one-without-Eyes) he was worshipped as the face of the sky at the time when neither sun nor moon could be seen.

There is some argument as to whether Horus was originally a god of Lower Egypt or of Upper Egypt: two places, *Behdet* and *Nekhen* are

98

rival claimants for the distinction of having been the first to establish his cult. The exact location of *Behdet* is uncertain: it undoubtedly lay in the Western Delta, close to the ancient town of *Imarut* (The Town of the Trees), the predynastic centre of the cult of a tree-goddess, Sekhet-Hor, who, according to legend, changed herself into a cow, a form of the goddess Hathor, in order to protect Horus when he was a child.

Imarut lay in what eventually became the 3rd Nome of Lower Egypt, and in the New Kingdom, it became Nome capital. In later years it was called *Demit-en-Hor* (Town of Horus), which is preserved today in the Arabic name of the modern town that stands near the site, Damanhûr. At *Behdet*, Horus came to be worshipped not in purely falcon-form but as a hawk-headed man equipped with bow and arrows, and a spear whose point was triangular and backed by the head of a hawk: Horus of *Behdet* was a warlike god.

One of the earliest Upper Egyptian centres of a falcon-cult was at *Nekhen* (modern name, Kom el-Ahmar), on the west bank of the Nile some 80km south of Luxor (Thebes), a very important predynastic settlement that became the capital city of the 3rd Upper Egyptian Nome in the dynastic period, a position that it held until the New Kingdom. The jackal-headed figures depicted in reliefs and known as 'the Souls of *Nekhen*' probably represent the early rulers of the city, analagous to 'The Souls of *Pe*' (p. 134); and just as *Pe* was linked with *Dep*, so *Nekhen* became the twin town of *Nekheb* (p. 136).

The chief god of predynastic *Nekhen* was not Horus but *Nekheny* or 'the Nekhenite', a falcon who wore two tall plumes on his head. The finest portrait of the falcon of *Nekhen* is the gold head found there in AD 1898 by Quibell and now in Cairo Museum. By the time this head had been made—Dynasty VI—*Nekheny* had long been assimilated with Horus who thus became Horus the Nekhenite. The Greeks acknowledged that *Nekhen* was truly 'The City of the Hawk' and called it Hierakonpolis.

Some of the authorities who maintain that the cult of Horus originated in the Delta suggest that it made its way into Upper Egypt when the inhabitants of the North sailed as far south as *Nebet* (modern name, Tukh) and conquered the followers of the local god, Seth. Certainly, this was a tradition enshrined in inscriptions in the temple that was built at Edfu (p. 104) in Ptolemaic times. Some even go so far as to say that all the legends concerning Horus' struggles with his great enemy, Seth, are based on fact and symbolise the conquest of the South by Horus' followers from the North.

On the other hand, others suggest that Horus originated in Upper Egypt, and that his cult spread northwards as the Upper Egyptian kings Scorpion and Narmer/Menes subjugated that part of the land. This theory might account for the monogram on the famous Narmer Palette (p. 125) which shows a falcon perched on a papyrus plant from which a human head protrudes. A rope tied through the nose on the head is held by a hand projecting from the falcon's breast. The monogram is thought to depict Horus bringing the people of the North, symbolised by the papyrus of Lower Egypt, as captives to the King of Upper Egypt—an act, perhaps, that he would be more likely to perform as an Upper Egyptian god.

Long before the Unification of Egypt, Horus had achieved the status of royal god *par excellence*. This was due to the fact that he had important sanctuaries in both halves of the country in cities that were seats of power for the native rulers—*Pe* in Lower Egypt and *Nekhen* in Upper Egypt—by virtue of which he became patron deity of both lines of kings.

Horus was the earliest state god of Egypt. In both halves of the country, the reigning king was considered to be the earthly embodiment of Horus and was called 'the Living Horus'. After the Unification, the King of Upper and Lower Egypt adopted as part of his official titulary the Horus Name, symbolic of his role as Horus incarnate. This name was inscribed in the top half of the *serekh*, a rectangular frame at the bottom of which is a design that imitates the recessed or panelled facade of the royal palace, and on top of which Horus, often wearing the Double Crown of Egypt, is perched.

Another of the names in the king's titulary was the Golden Horus Name, which was written as a monogram showing a falcon sitting on the hieroglyphic sign for gold, 🜚. Some authorities say that the sign for gold, read *nebu*, symbolises Seth, whose cult-centre was in the city called *Nebet* (Gold Town; see above) and commemorates the victory of Horus over Seth. Others say that the Golden Horus Name simply indicates a concept of the king being a falcon made of gold, although whether this falcon is Horus or some other god remains a mystery.

Although Horus was the earliest state god of Egypt, it was not long before Re of Heliopolis made a bid for that position. However, the priests of both deities seem to have come to an amicable arrangement: at an early date, the character of Horus had changed from that of a sky-god to being, more specifically, a sun-god; and it was in this guise that he was received at Heliopolis, the oldest centre of the cult of the sun. There he was coalesced with Re and became Re-Hor-akhty or Re-and-Horus-of-the-Two-Horizons, that is, the two horizons of sunrise and sunset; and represented as a man with the head of a hawk surmounted by a sun's disk.

Horus was fitted into Heliopolitan theology not in his own form of sun-god but as the son of Osiris and Isis, born posthumously in the Delta where Isis protected him from his father's murderer, Seth, until he was old enough to claim his inheritance, the Throne of Egypt. This Horus was called variously *Hor-sa-Isis* (Horus-son-of-Isis; in Greek, Harsiesis); *Hor-nedj-her-itef* (Horus-avenger-of-his-father; in Greek, Harendotes); and *Hor-pa-khred* (Horus-the-child (of Isis); in Greek, Harpocrates). Harpocrates, who was represented as a young boy wearing the long, curled side-lock of hair that denoted youth and sucking the finger of his right hand, was especially popular during the Late Period.

Horus-son-of-Isis (Harsiesis) was thought to be a friend of the dead, concerned to protect them. He was helped in his task by the four genii known as 'the Four Sons of Horus', whose mother was said to be Isis, Horus' own mother. They were: Imset, who was man-headed; Haapy, baboon-headed; Duamutef, jackal-headed; and Qebehsenuf, hawk-headed. They in turn were helped in their task by four goddesses: Isis and her sister, Nephthys; Neit, the great creator-goddess of Sais; and Selkis (sometimes known as Selket or Serquet), the scorpion-goddess who was a manifestation of the scorching heat of the sun. Their role was to guard the viscera that had been removed from the body during mummification and placed in the vessels that we call 'Canopic jars'.

The Greeks gave the name Kanopus to the port in the Western Delta, near Alexandria and now called Abukir, where tradition had it that Kanopus, the pilot who guided Menelaus and Helen to Egypt after the fall of Troy, was buried. Osiris had been worshipped in this place since predynastic times in the form of a jar with the head of a god, and so when modern Egyptologists found jars in tombs which contained the viscera of the tomb-owner and had stoppers shaped, in some cases, like human heads (actually the head of Imset), they called such vessels 'Canopic jars'.

From Ramesside times, the stoppers of Canopic jars were fashioned in the form of the head of the particular Son of Horus whose task it was to guard that jar's contents. The jar containing the liver was set under the protection of Isis and Imset: its stopper, therefore, was carved in the shape of a man's head. That containing the lungs was protected by Nephthys and Haapy: its stopper was shaped like the head of a baboon; that containing the stomach was guarded by Neit and Duamutef: its stopper was jackal-headed; and that containing the intestines was protected by Selkis and Qebehsenuf and topped by a hawk-headed stopper.

At first, the priests of Heliopolis made a distinction between Horus the Sun God and Horus, son of Isis; but eventually the two gods merged and Horus the Sun God was absorbed to a great extent by Horus, son of Isis, who achieved great popularity throughout Egypt, not merely because of his friendship towards the dead when he interceded for them with his father, Osiris, at their Judgement before the Assessors (p. 85), but also because of the heroic role he played in the stories told of his fight against Seth, a contest which lasted for eighty years.

The story of this contest is told in a papyrus that is thought to have been written, in hieratic, during the reign of Ramesses V. It was found in the nineteenth century AD at Thebes (Luxor) and is now in the Chester Beatty Library in Dublin.[5] The story of the Contendings of Horus and Seth as told in the Chester Beatty Papyrus is related by the story-teller in a series of episodes in which the gods, from Re downwards, do not appear in an awe-inspiring light, but rather as indecisive, fickle and easily persuaded to back each of the contestants in turn.

The Papyrus relates how Horus and Seth came before the Tribunal of the Gods whose task it was to decide which one should have the Throne of Egypt. After much discussion, the gods awarded the throne to Horus, whereupon Seth sprang up and threatened to kill one god every day with his sceptre, which he claimed weighed 4,500lb—more than two tons!

Immediately, Re decreed that they should cross over to an island in the middle of the Nile to debate the matter further (p. 94). Again, the Crown was awarded to Horus, but Seth insisted on a trial of strength. He suggested that he and Horus should change themselves into hippopotami and jump into the waters of the Great Green (Mediterranean), and whoever emerged first within the space of three whole months should lose the Crown of Egypt. The two gods duly turned into hippopotami and plunged into the water. Whereupon, Isis decided to take a hand: she made a rope and a copper harpoon and threw them into the water at the place where Horus and Seth had jumped in.

Unfortunately, the harpoon hit her son, Horus, who yelled to his mother for help. Isis commanded the harpoon to leave the body of her son, retrieved it and threw it into the water again. This time it hit her intended target, Seth, who yelled in his turn: 'What have I done to you, Isis? Call to your blade to let go of me, for I am your maternal brother, Isis!' Then Isis was sorry for him and made her blade loose him.

This not unnaturally angered Horus, who jumped out of the water holding his great axe in his hand. He chopped off his mother's head, tucked it into his bosom, and stalked off into the mountains in high dudgeon.

Re was angry with Horus for what he had done to Isis, and, after restoring her head by magic, he commanded the gods to go in search of her errant son and bring him before him to account for his actions. Seth was the first to find Horus, who lay asleep on a mountainside. He threw him over on his back, straddled him and gouged out his eyes. And then he buried the eyeballs in the mountain, where they turned into bulbs which grew into two lotuses.

Seth, meanwhile, had returned to Re to report that he could not find Horus. But Hathor did not believe him and went in search of Horus herself. She discovered him lying weeping in the desert, terribly injured by the loss of his eyes. Immediately, she caught a female gazelle and milked her; and said to Horus, 'Open your eyes so that I may put this milk into their sockets.' She did so, and Horus' eyes were restored to him. From then on they were called his *Wadjet*-eyes, or healed eyes; and the *Wadjet* symbol became one of the most potent and popular of Egyptian signs, used as an emblem or as an amulet worn as a protective piece of jewellery, or in the wrappings of mummies.

Isis forgave her son for beheading her! And eventually the gods settled the dispute over the Throne of Egypt by despatching a letter to Osiris in the Underworld asking for his opinion on the matter; to which he replied:

'Why should my son, Horus, be cheated since it was I who made you strong. It was I who made the barley and the emmer (wheat) to feed gods and men—no other god found himself able to do so!'

Osiris' letter elicited a rash response from Re:

'Even if you had never come into existence, even if you had never been born, the barley and the emmer would still have come into being.'—

a claim that brought forth such an angry letter from Osiris that Re was persuaded that it would be wise to give the Crown of Egypt to Osiris' son, Horus. He did so, and before all the gods, Horus was placed upon the throne as King of Upper and Lower Egypt.

In due course, Horus handed on the Throne of Egypt, from thenceforward called the Horus Throne, to a human successor. From that time on, every reigning King of Egypt was 'the Horus'; and every dead King, 'the Osiris'. One of the ways in which a king legitimised his claim to the throne was by acting as a Horus to his predecessor's Osiris. The dead king need not necessarily have been the new king's father: by the act of burying his predecessor, the new king became in effect his 'son' and heir.

Thus, it was possible for a Crown Prince to lose his throne if he were abroad at the time of his father's death and unable to get back to Egypt within the seventy days allotted for the ritual preparations for the dead king's burial. Sometimes, a king died before producing a male child to succeed him. Tutankhamun was one such king, and in this case, the dead king was succeeded by Ay, his uncle who was not of the blood royal. However, Ay could legitimately claim the throne and become king because he acted as Horus to Tutankhamun's Osiris by burying him.

The myths concerning Horus' struggles against Seth are made much of in the temple that was the Upper Egyptian centre of the cult of Horus—Edfu—where he was worshipped both as Horus the Behdetite, the great sky-god and as Horus, son of Isis: thus Horus of Edfu, as a combination of these two powerful deities, could take shape as a hawk-headed man or as a falcon; and his temple at Edfu contained statues and reliefs of Horus in both forms.

Edfu, or to give it the name by which it was known to the Ancient Egyptians, *Wetjeset-Hor* (which means 'the Place where Horus is Extolled'), lies on the west bank of the Nile some 100km south of Luxor. It was the capital of the 2nd Nome of Upper Egypt and the site of a temple dedicated to Horus from an early date. Although the earliest shrines erected on the site can not now be traced because they are, presumably, beneath the foundations of the great stone temple that stands there today in a remarkable state of preservation, there is a record that Imhotep built a temple at Edfu in Dynasty III using a plan that 'fell from heaven'.

The Temple of Horus at Edfu had two names, one sacred, the other secular. The sacred name was *Behdet*, which means 'throne' or 'seat', and seems to have been used since Dynasty III, probably adopted because by that time the true origins of Horus had become obscured and he was thought to have transferred his home from *Behdet* in the Delta to *Wetjeset-Hor* in Upper Egypt, from then onwards also called *Behdet*.

The official secular name of the temple was *Djeba*, which means 'Retribution Town', a reference to the fact that the enemies of Horus, notably Seth and his confederates, were brought to justice there. The word *Djeba* became Etbo in Coptic, and hence was the origin of the modern, Arabic name of the town, Edfu. The Greeks, who identified Horus with their own sun-god, Apollo, called the place Apollinopolis Magna.

The Temple of Horus as seen today was built during the Ptolemaic period. It was begun in 237 BC by Ptolemy III (also known as Euergetes I) and finished in 57 BC, and was the only Ptolemaic temple to be completed and that within a comparatively short space of time. Today, it is the best preserved of all Egyptian temples.

Because Ptolemaic temples were built during a period when Egypt was ruled by foreigners, namely Macedonian Greeks, and many of its old customs and beliefs were under threat, the priests of those temples inscribed on their walls as much information as they could concerning temple ritual and festivals, information which in former times they had either carried in their heads, to be passed on from generation to generation by word of mouth, or on scrolls of papyrus which they had found to their cost could be removed from their safekeeping, destroyed and their precious contents lost. They took care to write the inscriptions on the walls of the temples in a complicated script deliberately designed to ensure that even those few who could read would have great difficulty in understanding it: temple secrets were to be maintained!

In the huge Temple of Edfu, seemingly every wall and pillar is covered by hieroglyphs. The enormous amount of inscription, not all of which is as yet fully translated, gives us, amongst other things, some idea of the history of the construction of the temple; descriptions of the building, with each part, large or small, being named and its dimensions and purpose given, its decorations described. The daily rituals are listed, as are the great festivals; even the route taken by the processions of priests taking part in these festivals, and the doors through which they passed in and out of the temple, can often be traced.

Apart from the ceremonies that celebrated the Foundation of the Temple, and its Consecration, and the annual New Year Festival, most of the important ceremonies particular to Edfu were based on the myths concerning Horus, his birth and his struggles against Seth.

Several major deities had their own legends in which the deity was credited with the creation of the world, and Horus was no exception. At Edfu, the story is told of how, in the beginning, Chaos reigned, all was in darkness and the waters of the Nun covered the earth—silent, inert, deep. And then, two amorphous deities, the Great One and the Distant One, appeared above a small island that had emerged out of the Primaeval Waters. From the flotsam that clung to the edges of this island, one of the deities picked up a stick, split it into two pieces and stuck one of them into the ground, near the water's edge.

No sooner had he done so than a falcon emerged from the surrounding darkness and alighted on the stick. Immediately, light broke over Chaos, and the falcon sitting on his perch transformed the island into a holy place. The antiquity of this tradition is attested by the fact that, in the Archaic Period, the hieroglyphic sign for 'god' consisted of a falcon sitting on a perch.

Eventually, the waters of Chaos receded; the island became bigger and bigger until it became the earth, which, to the Egyptians, was Egypt. Men appeared, and built a shelter round the falcon to protect him, thereby creating the first temple. Thus did Horus the Falcon become the creator of the world, and incidentally the owner of the first temple. We have seen already that Horus, son of Isis, was at one time King of Egypt until he handed on the throne to mortal kings. It was natural, therefore, that one of the great ceremonies held in his temple of Edfu should be the annual celebration of the Coronation of the Sacred Falcon.

This took place during the first five days of the first month of Winter (the fifth month of the Egyptian year—November). The statue of the falcon Horus was taken in procession out of the main body of the temple into a small building outside—the Temple of the Sacred Falcon. The statue was carried by four priests—the two in front wearing falcon masks and the two behind, jackal masks, representing the ancient kings of *Nekhen* and *Pe* respectively. The whole procession proceeded in silence, 'no man speaking to his fellow'.

In the Temple of the Sacred Falcon, the 'new king' was chosen—not from amongst men, but from amongst several falcons that had been brought in from the special grove near the temple where they had been bred for the purpose. Once the Sacred Falcon had been chosen, he was taken to the bridge that linked the two wings (pylons) of the main gate of the temple. There, the statue of Horus displayed his newly-chosen heir, the living falcon, to the people, after which the procession made its way back to the interior of the temple where the sacred falcon was crowned and invested with the royal regalia. At the end of the day, the living falcon, having played its role in the great ceremony of the day, was returned to the grove of the sacred falcons, there to live out its life until, when it died, it was mummified and buried in the necropolis that had been set aside to receive the sacred birds.

The Coronation of the Sacred Falcon was much more than the yearly selection of a new sacred falcon: it commemorated the coronation of the King of Egypt. Thus the date of the Festival was significant—the first day of the fifth month: in other words, the day after the month in which the resurrection of Osiris took place (p. 87), the day on which his son Horus ascended the throne.

Another major annual festival at Edfu was the Festival of Victory, celebrated for five days, starting on the 21st day of the second month of Winter (December). It is, in effect, a sacred drama, concerned with the victory of Horus over his enemy, Seth. The 'script' of this drama is found on the inner surface of the great wall that runs round the main body of the temple, on the western side of the wall; and it is said to be the first play ever written. In AD 1971, it was revived by students of Padgate College, Lancashire, in a performance entitled *The Triumph of Horus*.[6]

It is probable that, in Ancient Egypt, although not at Padgate, *The Triumph of Horus* was concluded with the recitation of *The Legend of the Winged Disk*, which is carved on the same wall as *The Triumph of Horus*. This legend, 'dated' to the 363rd year of the reign of Re-Hor-akhty, tells of how Re and his soldiers were in Nubia when the inhabitants of that land began to talk seditiously against him, for which reason Nubia was thereafter called *Wawat* (a pun on the Egyptian verb 'to conspire').

Re commanded Horus the Behdetite to deal with the rebellious Nubians. And Horus flew up into the sky in the form of a great winged sun-disk and shone so ferociously upon the rebels that they were blinded and in panic killed one another.

Re was pleased and decreed that Horus should thenceforward be his champion; and gave him a new name, 'He-of-the-Dappled-Plumage'. In the form of the Winged Disk, Horus pursued the enemies of Re. Whether these enemies took the form of crocodiles or hippopotami, whether they fled from him on land or on sea, Horus defeated them with his axe and his spear. And at each place where he did this, his achievement was commemorated by Re who gave the place a new name; and often, Horus a new epithet.

Eventually, Re's enemy was seen in his true guise: Seth, who raged and cursed and earned the name 'Stinking Face'. Horus of *Behdet* waged war against Seth for a long time, until, finally, he overthrew his ancient enemy and brought him in chains before Re. Then Horus-son-of-Isis cut off the head of the Enemy (Seth) and dragged him by his feet through the land, with his spears stuck into his back.

Horus of *Behdet* had the form of a man with the head of a hawk, crowned with the Double Crown of Egypt and wearing two plumes and two cobras on his head; in his hands he held a metal axe, a harpoon and a chain. Horus-son-of-Isis transformed himself and assumed the shape of Horus of *Behdet*. And together they killed the enemies of Re. Their followers were called *mesentiu*, 'the Harpooners'; and Horus was named Lord of Mesen (the Place of the Harpoon—another name for Edfu), Prince of the Two Halves of Egypt.

And an image of the Winged Disk was set up in every temple in every town; Seth was despatched to thunder in the sky; and Horus became Lord of Egypt.

The cultus statues of Horus at Edfu show him in purely falcon form; and in reliefs, he is usually depicted as the falcon-headed man. Horus-son-of-Isis was never a falcon-god. It is clear, however, that long before the Ptolemaic Temple of Edfu was built, the images of the two gods had become inextricably mixed in the minds of the Egyptians. Thus Horus is often a confusing god for modern man to sort out, and it is perhaps wise to adopt the attitude of the Ancient Egyptians and accept that this confusion between the attributes and myths of the two deities is nothing to worry about.

Although the worship of Horus, whether distinguished as Horus the Falcon or Horus-son-of-Isis, was pervasive throughout Egyptian history, it is interesting to remember that in predynastic times falcon-gods were worshipped under names other than Horus at places such as *Djew-Qa* in Upper Egypt and *Khem* and *Per-Soped* in Lower Egypt; and that only gradually, as the fame of Horus spread, were the cults of these other falcon-deities superseded by his.

Djew-Qa (later *Tjebu*; modern name, Qaw el-Kebir) was the capital of the 10th Upper Egyptian Nome, and had worshipped an indigenous falcon-god named Anty (He-with-the-Talons) since predynastic times until, sometime in the Dynastic period, Anty, like so many other falcon-gods, was assimilated with Horus.

For some reason, probably because the names had a similar sound, Anty was identified by the Greeks with their mythical giant, Antaeus. Antaeus was the son of Poseidon and Mother Earth, and King of Libya. He used to challenge strangers to wrestle with him until they were exhausted, whereupon he killed them. His final bout was with Herakles, and he lost the contest. However, he is commemorated in the Greek name of the city of *Djew-Qa*, which is not named after either of its falcon-gods but after Antaeus, being called Antaeopolis.

At *Khem* (Greek Letopolis; modern name, Ausim), the capital of the 2nd Nome of Lower Egypt, which lies some 13km northwest of Cairo, a falcon was worshipped originally under the name of *Khenty-khem* (The Foremost One of Khem); and then as *Khenty-irty* (which means, perhaps, 'the Sharpeyed One'). At least as far back as Dynasty IV, Horus replaced the ancient falcon-god of *Khem* and, incidentally, took on a warlike aspect: his enemies were beheaded there. In the Pyramid Texts, these enemies were called *sabet*-snakes (multi-coloured snakes, possibly cobras) and there was evidently an ancient ritual at *Khem* in which their heads were cut off.

A falcon-god of yet another Lower Egyptian Nome, the 20th, also became identified with Horus. This god, Soped, gave his name to the Nome capital, *Per-Soped* or the House of Soped (today called Saft el-

Hina), the city which lay at the entrance to the Wadi Tumulat, an important route to the Sinai peninsula. Hence, Soped was the guardian of Egypt's eastern border and considered to be lord of foreign lands. Coalesced with Soped, Horus became Lord of the East.

As the cult of Horus grew, he was welcomed at places that did not have falcon-gods of their own but worshipped other forms of animal, which, once Horus had arrived on the scene, were absorbed by him. One such case was *Kem-wer*, which·lies on the east bank of the Damietta branch of the Nile, and was the capital of the 10th Lower Egyptian Nome. Its modern name, Tell Atrib, is derived from the Greek Athribis, and owes nothing to the original name of the town, *Kem-wer*, which means 'The Great Black Bull'.

The oldest name of the town refers to the bull that once was worshipped there until, in dynastic times, it was replaced by a crocodile-god named Khentekhai. Perhaps as early as Dynasty IV, Horus had become the most important deity at *Kem-wer*, not only syncretising with the crocodile-god but also taking over the name of Khentekhai.

At *Kem-wer*, Horus-Khentykhai was also worshipped in the form of a falcon-headed man holding two eyes (*Wadjet*) representing the sun and the moon in his hands. He is called *Hor-merty*. The second syllable of the name, *merty*, is written in hieroglyphs using the sign that usually means 'to love'; hence it is possible that the translation of the name *Hor-merty* should be 'Horus-with-the-two-beloved-eyes'. It is only one of several names of Horus which connect him with eyes.

To the Egyptians, as to many peoples, the eye was extremely important. We still say that 'the eye is the mirror of the soul'; and many people today, in Egypt and elsewhere, fear the Evil Eye. Hence, the Divine Eye was, to the Egyptians, a symbol of great significance. It could take many forms—Edjo, Tefnut and Hathor, for instance, were each known as the Eye of Re; the *Wadjet*-eye of Horus (p. 103) had religious and protective connotations.

Whenever the Egyptians depicted the Divine Eye, it was not a human eye that formed the inspiration for their model, but the eye of a peregrine falcon, stylised to show a bright pupil set in the socket of a human eye drawn full-face, under which is the characteristic mark that is found under a peregrine's eyes, the so-called 'moustachial streak', which on the actual bird is black and stands out conspicuously against its white chin and cheeks.

Hebenu (modern name Zawyet el-Amwat, sometimes known as Zawyet el-Maiyitin) was the capital of the 16th Upper Egyptian Nome, the Oryx Nome. It lies on the east bank of the Nile, a few kilometres south of Minia. The sacred animal of this Nome was the desert oryx, the graceful antelope that had become associated with

109

Seth. When Horus moved into *Hebenu*, he was regarded as the vanquisher of the oryx, symbolically representing his great enemy, Seth; and in the Late Period this aspect was reflected in the drawing of the Nome sign, which depicted Horus as a falcon, standing with his talons sunk into the back of an oryx.

Another place where Horus displaced an original god who was not a falcon was *Tjel* (or Sile), the modern Tell Abu Sefah, a town which lay within the 14th Nome of Lower Egypt some 3km east of Kantara on what is now the Suez Canal. The name of the Nome capital, *Khent-iabet*, which means 'Front of the East', illustrates the strategic importance of the area: *Tjel* itself was the site of a great fortress, possibly called *Mesen*, that the Egyptians built to guard their north-eastern frontier. The indigenous god of *Tjel* was a lion whose special function was to protect Egypt against foreigners and invaders from the east. Horus took over from the Lion of *Tjel* as guardian of Egypt's north-eastern border and by so doing became the 'Lord of *Mesen*'.

Horus was worshipped at another *Mesen* in the Delta. It is not certain where this *Mesen* was, but it is known to have been in the Western Delta, and was, perhaps, near the city of *Pe*. According to legend, Isis bore her son, Horus, on the island of Chemmis, near *Pe*, where he was protected by the goddess of the neighbouring city of *Dep*, Edjo. *Pe* was a city whose god was originally a heron, or perhaps some kind of hawk, which was ousted by Horus. In Chapter 112 of the Book of the Dead, the inhabitants of *Pe* are asked whether they know how it came about that *Pe* was given to Horus and are told: 'Re gave it to him as a compensation for the injury to his eye.'

Apparently, Horus woke up one day with a sore eye, and took himself off to Re to ask him to inspect it to see if he could find the cause of the soreness. Re examined the eye, and said, 'Look, can you see that black pig?' Horus looked, and was immediately smitten with a blow on his eye, rendering it even more painful than it had been before.

Horus was very angry at this; it seemed obvious to him that it was the second time that Seth (who was, of course, the black pig) had inflicted a blow upon his eye. Re healed the injured member and decreed that henceforward all pigs should be an abomination to Horus. And *Pe* was given to him as compensation for his injury.

Although Horus was usually depicted as a falcon, or as a falcon-headed man, there is one famous instance of him appearing in another guise: the Sphinx of Giza, that most illustrious symbol of Ancient Egypt. In Dynasty IV, when Khephren built a pyramid at Giza, he ordered that a knoll of limestone some 400 metres to the east of his pyramid be carved to look like a crouched lion; and that the head of the animal be not that of a lion but of himself, Khephren, who thus became identified with the Heliopolitan tradition of the horizon being guarded by lions (p. 51), not, this time however, by Shu and Tefnut, but by Horakhty (Horus of the Two Horizons, p. 100) in the guise of a lion.

Statues of lions with heads representing kings, gods or the animals associated with those gods—the ram of Amun, for instance—became very popular in Egypt, especially when arranged in double rows along the path that led to the entrance of a temple, as guardians of the sanctuary; for they were thought to have the power to protect both kings and gods. The Egyptians called such statues *shesep-ankh* or 'living statues': today, they are known by the Greek word, sphinx.

The Greeks themselves had a sphinx, but this sphinx was the cruel winged lioness with a woman's head who appeared in the story of Oedipus challenging travellers on the road to Thebes (the one in Greece) with the riddle:

What goes on four legs, on two and then three,
But the more legs it goes on the weaker it be?

Those who could not answer correctly were killed. Oedipus destroyed the Theban Sphinx with the answer to her riddle: Man. As a baby he crawls on all fours; in the prime of life he walks on two legs; but in old age he has to use a third 'leg'—a stick.

The Great Sphinx of Giza, at some 70 metres in length, is the largest and most renowned of Egyptian sphinxes. Some thousand years after it was constructed, a young prince of Dynasty XVIII was hunting in the desert near the Giza plateau. He decided to rest near the Sphinx, whom he called Horakhty-Re-Atum-Khepri, and fell asleep in its shadow. The Sphinx sent him a dream in which it promised him the Throne of Egypt if he would clear the sand that the wind had blown over its body.

The prince had the encroaching sand cleared away, and when in due course he became King, he, Thothmes IV, left a record of his actions between the paws of the Sphinx—the Dream Stele, still to be seen there today; and from thenceforward, the Great Sphinx of Giza was identified, not with the long-dead Khephren, but with Horus alone, under the name of Horenakhet—Horus-on-the-Horizon—whom the Greeks called Harmakhis.

A visitor to Giza today, looking at the impressive Sphinx, Harmakhis, might consider that the old Arabic saying, 'The world fears time, but time fears the pyramids', could equally well be applied to the Sphinx. But perhaps the most impressive image of Horus is to be seen in the courtyard of his temple at Edfu, where a giant statue of the falcon-god, magnificently carved to show all his strength and ferocity, gazes imperiously from his piercing eyes at those who enter his domain.

SETH

Seth was one of the oldest Egyptian deities. In predynastic times he was worshipped as an idol that seems to have been assembled from the features of several animals into an elegant imaginary beast—the so-called 'Seth-animal'—a creature that has the body of a greyhound; a long, fork-ended tail standing upright from its body; an elongated, curved muzzle or snout; long, pricked-up ears with flattened tips; and almond-shaped eyes. It has been suggested that the Seth-animal was a species of dog, now extinct but resembling a saluki; or a pig, a jerboa, a giraffe, an ant-eater, a wart-hog or an okapi! However, there is no known zoological equivalent for the fabulous Seth-animal.

The earliest centre of the cult of Seth was at *Nebet*, which lay on the west bank of the Nile some 30km north of Luxor near the modern town of Tukh. *Nebet* was close to the entrance of the Wadi Hammamat through which the eastern desert with its gold deposits could be reached. It was probably due to gold that the town achieved its importance, a fact that is reflected in the name of the place—*Nebet* means 'Gold Town'. Seth himself was called *Nebty*, 'He-of-Gold-Town'.

The importance of *Nebet* dates back to the predynastic era; some of the oldest settlements of Upper Egypt have been found in the area, notably at the nearby site of Naqada, which Petrie excavated in AD 1895, afterwards using the name to describe the last two predynastic cultures of the whole of Upper Egypt, Naqada I and II.

Other predynastic centres of the cult of Seth were found in northern Upper Egypt, two major sites being in the 11th and 19th Nomes. The original Nome standard of the 11th Nome consisted of a Seth-animal on a pole. In Dynastic times, this animal was depicted with a dagger sticking into its head, a sign that by this time Seth was regarded as a force for evil, and his animal as potentially harmful. This aspect is reflected in the Egyptian name for the capital of the 11th Nome, *Sha-sehetep*, which means 'the Pig [i.e. Seth]-is-Pacified'. The Greek name for the town was Hypselis; today it is called Shutb. It lies some 8km south of Assiut.

1 Pectoral (3.8cm high by 5.7cm long) from a Dynasty XII necklace reputed to have come from Dahshur and now in Eton College, Windsor. In the centre is a representation of the goddess, Bat (the personification of the sistrum of Hathor), supporting on her head a sun's disk flanked by two cobras (Edjo and Nekhbet as uraei). To the left and right of the disk are Wadjet-eyes (symbols of Horus). To the left of Bat is Horus as a sphinx, to her right the Seth-animal: they are confronting each other not as enemies but as allies in the protection of the royal wearer of the pectoral

The capital of the 19th Nome of Upper Egypt, *Per-medjed*, which today is called el-Bahnasa, lies some 160km north of Assiut. In ancient times it worshipped a fish, *Mormyrus kannume*, which appropriately enough, since Seth was also worshipped there, was supposed to have swallowed the penis of his great enemy, Osiris (p. 80). Little is known of the town from pharaonic times; it became prominent in the Graeco-Roman period when it was called Oxyrhynchus. Today, it is famous chiefly because of the thousands of Greek papyri that Grenfell and Hunt found in its rubbish heaps during their excavations of AD 1896–1907.

From earliest times, Seth was regarded as the Upper Egyptian god *par excellence*. Legend had it that Geb, the Earth God, divided Egypt into two halves, giving the northern part to Horus and the southern to Seth. The famous limestone mace-head found at Hierakonpolis, known as the Scorpion Mace-head because it is carved with reliefs showing episodes from the life of the pre-dynastic king of Upper Egypt named Scorpion, shows two standards bearing Seth-animals. This would seem to indicate that the followers of Seth were allies of Scorpion, himself an adherent of Horus, when he initiated the conquest of Lower Egypt by the South.

After the Unification, the kings of Egypt adopted Horus names (p. 100); but they allotted to Seth a role as representative of Upper Egypt. The queens of the period were given the titles 'She-who-unites-the Two-Lords [i.e. Horus and Seth]' and 'She-who-sees-Horus-and-Seth'.

In the reign of the fourth king of Dynasty II, Sekhemib, a religious revolution of some sort seems to have taken place. Horus was displaced as royal god, and Seth received the allegiance of Sekhemib, who changed his name to Peribsen, and, whereas the *serekh* (p. 100) bearing the former name was surmounted by the Hawk-god, that bearing the latter name was instead graced by the figure of the Seth-animal.

Although Sekhemib/Peribsen's successor, Sendji, reinstated Horus, the last king of the Dynasty did not entirely forsake Seth in favour of Horus, since the *serekh* carved with his name, Khasek-hemwy, bears both Hawk and Seth-animal, a sign, perhaps, that a reconciliation had been achieved.

For a long time, Seth was regarded as a beneficent god by a large part of the population of Egypt. However, he was also at all times identified with the desert that lay to the east of the centre of his cult, *Nebet*: an association which extended eventually to all deserts. To the Egyptians, the desert which surrounded their land was inhospitable, arid and dangerous, a place where gods, wild animals and the dead held sway. The fertile land of Egypt on which they grew their crops was called the Black Land; the desert was the Red Land.

As god of the deserts, Seth was called the Red God, and associated with every frightening element which the Egyptians thought eman-ated from them: wind and rain, storm and thunder. Since the roads which led out of Egypt passed through her deserts; and, indeed, one of the words commonly used by the Egyptians for 'desert' was the same as that for 'foreign land'; Seth became known as Lord of Foreign Lands.

Around 1670 BC, invaders from the foreign lands which lay to the east of Egypt began to infiltrate the eastern part of the Delta, gradually establishing a hold over the Delta and Lower Egypt. These invaders, known as the Hyksos, provided the kings of Dynasties XV and XVI. They flourished for over a hundred years until they were driven out of Egypt by Ahmose, the founder of Dynasty XVIII. The Hyksos built a capital in the north east Delta, probably at the site of the modern village of Qantir, and called it Avaris. Seth had long been worshipped in the area: the Hyksos identified him with their own god of war, Baal, and worshipped him under the name of Sutekh.

2 *Stele showing the god Seth being worshipped by Aapahte, deputy of the gang of workmen on the royal tombs at Thebes, Deir el-Medina, Dynasty* XIX

Although Seth had a wife—his sister, Nephthys—at Avaris, he was given two other consorts: the western Semitic goddesses, Anath and Astarte. Anath was a war-goddess who was represented in human form equipped with shield and battle-axe and wearing on her head what appears to be the Upper Egyptian crown surrounded by plumes. She was regarded as the daughter of Re. Astarte was a goddess of war who was identified with Sekhmet; and, more particularly, a goddess of love and therefore equated with Hathor. She could be depicted with the head of a lioness, but she appeared more often as a naked woman standing in a chariot and driving a team of horses. Even after the departure of the Hyksos, these two consorts of Seth were worshipped by the Egyptians themselves, with Anath achieving the height of her popularity during the Ramesside period, whilst Astarte was venerated from Dynasty XVIII to the Ptolemaic era.

After the expulsion of the Hyksos shortly before 1550 BC, the city of Avaris sank into obscurity. Then, in 1315 BC, Horemheb, last king of Dynasty XVIII, died childless and was succeeded by Pramesse, one of his generals, who ascended the throne as Ramesses, first king of Dynasty XIX. Ramesses I came from a Delta family which seems to have been particularly devoted to Seth of Avaris. His son and heir, Seti I, was named after the god; and on a stele found at Tanis, Seti's son, Ramesses II, records that when his father was still Crown Prince and a commander in the army, he came to Avaris to celebrate the four-hundredth anniversary of the foundation of the city and its dedication to Seth. Ramesses II himself used the site of Avaris as the foundation for his new city of *Pi-Ramessu* (The House of Ramesses).

Although the state god of Egypt at that time was Amun of Thebes, in the Delta Seth was of greater importance. Ramesses emphasised his allegiance to him by naming his favourite daughter Bint-Anath (Daughter of Anath, Seth's consort) and by building a temple for Anath at *Pi-Ramessu*; and, as we learn from a description of Ramesses' famous battle against the Hittites at Kadesh, one of the divisions of the Egyptian army was named after Seth's warlike form, Sutekh. In the Ramesside period, Seth was not regarded as merely the deity of the harmful elements in the desert but as the patron of the life-sustaining oases.

Seth had always had two aspects to his character: one good, the other malevolent. Throughout their history, the Egyptians held an ambivalent attitude towards him: they feared his capacity for evil yet they had a sneaking admiration for his power and ferocity. From time to time, political expediency or the personal preference of the ruler dictated that he should be a favoured god; but his role at other times was that of the personification of evil: the Greeks called him Typhon.

In Greek mythology, Typhon, the child of Mother Earth and Tartarus (the place of torture in Hades), was the largest monster ever born. He had an ass' head and immensely long arms which ended in countless serpents' heads instead of hands. In place of legs, the lower part of his body was yet more serpents. He had vast wings which blotted out the sun; from his eyes he flashed fire; from his mouth, he belched forth flaming rocks.

After his birth, Typhon rushed towards Olympus, from which the gods fled in terror at his coming, only pausing in their flight when they reached Egypt, where they disguised themselves as animals so that they would not be noticed among the Egyptian gods! Only Athene stood against Typhon, until eventually Zeus overcame him with his thunderbolts. The severely wounded monster fled to Sicily where Zeus threw Mount Etna on top of him. To this day, Typhon sometimes hurls molten rock and fire from its cone.

Some authorities believe that the myth of Typhon was based on an actual event—the flight of priests and priestesses in the fifteenth century BC from the volcanic eruption on the Aegean island of Thera (Santorini) which destroyed the Minoan civilization on Crete.

Typhon, like Seth, was thus a god of violence and turmoil. The colour red became associated with them both: with Typhon because he became a volcano and with Seth because of his links with the desert. Hence, red-haired animals, and even red-haired men, were held in abhorrence by Greeks and Egyptians.

Seth's turbulent nature was apparent from his very beginning. Plutarch says that Seth entered the world by bursting through the side of his mother, Nut. All kinds of dangerous and unpleasant animals were associated with him: the scorpion, the serpent, the hippopotamus, the crocodile, the wild ass, the wild boar; and the pig.

In ancient Egypt, as in Syria-Palestine, the pig was held in abomination. Although the Egyptians kept pigs and are said to have used them during the sowing season to trample the seed into the soft, muddy ground, they did not eat them. This reluctance to eat pork was probably for practical reasons: pig meat rapidly becomes unfit to eat in a hot climate. However, just as Jews and Muslims were later to be forbidden to eat pig by religious law, so the Egyptians invented a mythological reason for not doing so. The pig was a representation of Seth, probably because in predynastic times it had been an object of worship in one district or another of Egypt associated with Seth. Had not Seth, in the guise of a black pig (p. 110) wounded the eye of Horus? Had not a wild boar, a near relative of the pig, killed Attis and Adonis? In all probability, there had been an old Egyptian legend that told of Osiris being slain by the same animal, thus rendering the pig as Seth's representative inimical to followers of Osiris.

Seth's oldest role was as the foe of Horus the Elder. Whereas Horus as Sun-God was regarded as the face of the sky by day and therefore as a god of light and sunshine, Seth was his opposite, the face of the sky at night and therefore a deity of darkness and terror. According to the Pyramid Texts, Seth, aided by the seven stars of the Great Bear, attacked Horus, the Sun God. This story was probably a relic of the time when the earliest Egyptian gods were regarded as stars and constellations: the attack of Seth on the sun probably represented for the Egyptians the 'attack' on the sun by showers of meteorites and shooting stars; or even an eclipse.

By the New Kingdom, Seth's relationship to the sun had changed. His ferocity, his reputation as a 'most valiant god', had earned him a place in the prow of the Barque of Re, where he defended the Sun God from attack by his enemies. As a god of Storm, Seth was himself regarded at times as a threat to the Barque of Re. But its greatest enemy was the serpent, Apopis (p. 64). Although by the Late Period, Seth had become identified with the monstrous serpent, in the New Kingdom he was thought to stand in the prow of the Barque warding off its attacks.

Chapter 39 of the Book of the Dead gives a graphic account of Seth's efforts to perform his task, enraged by Apopis' taunts. In a reference to an episode in Seth's long-drawn-out fight against Horus, in which Horus tears out Seth's testicles, Apopis jeers at him, saying:

'What was done to you was so terrible that you will suffer from it for ever. You will never go a-wooing, you will never make love!'

Seth overcomes Apopis, only to be driven away from the Barque by its divine crew, ostensibly for boasting but in reality for fear least he himself harm it. Obviously, even when being valiantly helpful, Seth was not trusted!

Seth's most famous role was as the implacable enemy of Horus, son of Osiris. One legend relates that Geb decided to divide Egypt between Horus and Seth, in equal halves. Horus ruled wisely and well, but Seth proved to be an unjust king. Geb was so displeased that he deposed Seth and handed over his throne to Horus. Thus began the great quarrel between the two gods.

Later versions of the quarrel, influenced by the popularity of the cult of Osiris, give as the cause of the quarrel the murder of Osiris by Seth, exacerbated by Seth's attempts to prevent Osiris' son, Horus, inheriting the throne of his father. The most entertaining version of the quarrel is found in the Contendings of Horus and Seth (p. 102), although Seth is not shown to great advantage in this account, being wont to appear slightly stupid and blundering, easily tricked by both Isis and Horus.

In a letter to the Tribunal of the Gods, Neit recommends that Horus should be confirmed in the office of kingship, whilst Seth is fobbed off with an increase in his possessions and the gift of the two erotic goddesses, Anath and Astarte—a move obviously calculated to appeal to Seth's lecherous nature. Seth's lust for women enabled Isis to trick him by disguising herself as a beautiful young girl (p. 95); but he was equally capable of an act of homosexual rape.

This episode in the Contendings of Horus and Seth is told in a frank manner. Until quite recently, scholars would have translated into Latin what were to them offensive parts of the text, preferring, like Gibbon, that their English version should be 'chaste and all licentious passages . . . left in the decent obscurity of a learned language'— presumably to ensure that their womenfolk and their servants would not be able to read and be corrupted by such indecency! The Egyptians, however, would not have understood such a convention, being an earthy people not at all inhibited or prudish about sexual matters.

Having been commanded by Re-Horakhty to stop quarrelling day after day and to let him have some peace, Seth invited Horus to his house, and, in all innocence, Horus accepted the invitation.

When night came, a bed was made up for them, and the two gods lay down together. And in the night, Seth made his penis become stiff; and he put it between the thighs of Horus. Thereupon, Horus put both his hands between his thighs and caught Seth's semen in one of them.

Alarmed, Horus ran to his mother, crying, 'Help me, Isis, my mother! Come and see what Seth has done to me!' When he opened his hand and showed Seth's semen to Isis, she was horrified, and, seizing her knife, she cut off his hand and threw it into the nearest water.

Isis then made Horus a new hand to replace the one that had been defiled by Seth's semen. Next, she took a little sweet ointment and rubbed Horus' penis with it until the penis became stiff. Then she inserted it into a jar and Horus made his semen drip into the vessel.

Early next morning, Isis went to Seth's garden carrying the jar with Horus' semen in it. There, she asked the gardener which was Seth's favourite vegetable and was told that he only ever ate lettuces, the vegetable that the Egyptians thought had aphrodisiacal qualities. Isis put Horus' semen on the lettuces so that when Seth arrived and consumed his daily portion of the vegetable he 'became pregnant with the seed of Horus'.

Shortly after this, Seth challenged Horus to come before the Tribunal of the Gods again, confident that this time he would win his case, for he knew that to subject an enemy to an act of homosexuality was considered by the Egyptians to be the worst indignity a conqueror could inflict upon his foe. He was sure that once his attack upon Horus became known, Horus would become an object of scorn.

Sure enough, when Seth stood up in the Tribunal and pointed to his victim, saying: 'As to Horus, this creature who is standing here, I have performed a sexual act against him!', the Ennead uttered a loud cry and spat and belched in Horus' face.

Undismayed, Horus laughed at them and swore that Seth was lying. He demanded that the semen of Seth be summoned so that everyone could see from whence it answered.

Then Thoth laid his hand upon Horus' shoulder and cried:

'Come forth, O semen of Seth!'

And it answered him from the water into which Isis had thrown it.

Then Thoth laid his hand upon Seth's shoulder and cried: 'Come forth, O semen of Horus!' And it said to him: 'Whence shall I come forth?' And Thoth said to it: 'Come forth from his ear!' But the semen said to Thoth: 'Is it from his ear that I should come forth seeing that I am a divine essence?' And so Thoth said to it: 'Come forth from his forehead!' And it came forth as a golden disk upon Seth's brow.

Seth was exceedingly angry and stretched out his hand to seize the golden disk. Before he could do so, Thoth took it away from him and set it upon his own head. Then the Ennead gave their judgement:

'Horus is right, Seth is wrong.'

Seth, furious at being tricked, issued one more challenge, this time to a race using boats made of stone. Horus accepted the challenge, but, instead of making a boat out of stone, he fashioned one of cedarwood, coated with gypsum, which he launched at night when there was not a soul around to see the boat close-to. When Seth looked at Horus' boat, he was taken in by the gypsum coating, which made the boat look as though it were made of stone as had been agreed. Accordingly, he sliced off a mountain peak and used it to make for himself a boat '138 cubits long'.

And then the two contestants boarded their boats in the presence of the entire Ennead. Horus' boat, being made of wood, floated beautifully: Seth's boat sank like the stone it was. Immediately, Seth transformed himself into a hippopotamus and overturned Horus' boat. But this was his final fling. Before long, the Tribunal had exchanged letters with Osiris (p. 103) and found that Horus' case was proved.

Atum commanded that Isis should fetch Seth into the Tribunal tightly bound in a wooden collar. Isis took great delight in obeying the command and the hapless Seth was brought in as a prisoner. When Atum charged him with being unwilling to accept the Judgement of the gods that the office of kingship should be given to

Horus, Seth made no further attempt at bravado but cravenly denied the charge, saying:

> 'Not so, my good lord. Let Horus, son of Isis, be summoned and let the office of his father, Osiris, be given to him.'

In the midst of the general rejoicing and relief that at long last the case was over, Ptah asked what was to be done with Seth; and Re-Horakhty decreed that he should live with him as his son. Horus was set upon the Throne of Egypt: and Seth was set to thunder in the sky and put fear into the hearts of men.

In the Late Period, the unpopularity of Seth grew: from about 700 BC, hymns were composed celebrating his defeat by Horus. During the Ptolemaic period, Seth came to symbolise the Macedonian Greeks who ruled Egypt, and in the Temple of Horus at Edfu in particular (p. 104), he was reviled both as the enemy of Horus, who was the symbol of Egyptian nationalism, and as the representative of the despised conquerors of Egypt. Late in Egyptian history, Seth's name and image were often cut out of ancient monuments; his statues were remodelled by having the characteristic long ears of the Seth-animal cut off and replaced by ram's horns so that the statues were transformed into representations of Amun.

In spite of this, compromise could still be reached, with the most famous example being the temple that was built some 170km south of the earliest centre of the cult of Seth, *Nebet*, which the Greeks called Ombos. The new site was also called Ombos after the god of the ancient city—who was, of course, Seth, the Ombite. Kom Ombo (the Mound of Ombos), as this temple is now called, was begun by Ptolemy V (203–181 BC) and decorated in the reigns of several Roman emperors, Tiberius, Domitian and Caracalla amongst them. The decorations are some of the best examples of Ptolemaic art.

Kom Ombo is unique among Egyptian temples because it is dedicated jointly to two deities: Haroeris, or Horus the Elder; and Suchos, or Sobek, the crocodile god, who was worshipped at many places in Egypt but especially at Gebelein and in the Fayum. At Kom Ombo, the temple stands on a stretch of river that was infested with crocodiles until the latter half of the nineteenth century AD. Evidently the people of the district felt that Sobek was a god to be placated.

Sobek, however, was a form of Sutekh, the Semitic name for Seth, whilst Haroeris was a form of Horus. In spite of the fact that only a short distance away at Edfu, Horus was worshipped as the vanquisher of Seth, and was even depicted in some reliefs on the walls of the temple in the act of slaying crocodiles, at Kom Ombo the two adversaries share a temple, the left-hand side of which is dedicated to

Haroeris, his wife, Hathor-ta-sent-nefert (Hathor-the-good-sister) and their son, Panebtawy (the Lord of the Two Lands); and the right-hand side to Sobek, who is not accompanied at Kom Ombo by his usual consort, the cobra-goddess, Renenutet, but by Hathor, who is normally the wife of Horus, with Khonsu, son of Atum and Mut, being allotted the role of their son.

Although Kom Ombo temple was not dedicated to Seth under his own name, the fact that a form of Seth could still be worshipped there proves that he was not entirely out of favour. There were probably two separate priesthoods in the temple who worshipped their respective gods in perfect amity. However, in many places in Egypt, the worship of this turbulent deity had for a long time been proscribed; and by the Christian era, Seth had been demoted from ancient and powerful god to a mere evil demon.

NEPHTHYS

The goddess commonly known as Nephthys figures only in the Heliopolitan myths: she was one of the five children born to Nut on the extra days she won from Thoth (p. 49). Although Nephthys was the wife of Seth, at all times she was loyal to her siblings, Osiris and Isis. She helped Isis collect together the pieces of Osiris' dismembered body and then to wrap them in bandages; with Isis, she was chief mourner for Osiris as the two sisters wailed for the dead god.

Nephthys' participation in the protection and resurrection of Osiris, and her mourning for her dead brother, was later extended to the protection of the dead in general: she is one of the four protector-goddesses of Canopic jars (p. 101); and was carved on the corners of sarcophagi and shrines for the protection of their contents, in which position she was often equipped with the wings of a kite like her sister, Isis (pp. 80, 95).

An ancient legend tells of how Nephthys was enamoured of Osiris and went to him at night. In the darkness, Osiris mistook her for Isis and made love to her. The result of their adulterous union was Anubis.

Nephthys was normally depicted as a woman with no special attributes except for the hieroglyphs which form her name worn as a headdress. Her name, in Egyptian *Nebet-hoot*, ☐, means 'Lady of the House': which house or to whom it belongs is not known. Neither is anything known of Nephthys before she became a part of the Heliopolitan myths. She seems never to have been the object of a cult; and no temple or shrine has yet been discovered that is dedicated to her alone.

HATHOR

In an agricultural society such as Egypt, it was natural that the cow should become a sacred animal: worship of a cow-goddess, therefore, was found throughout Egypt from a very early date.

In predynastic Egypt, the cow represented fertility: she was the great mother. Statuettes of naked women with arms upraised in imitation of a cow's horns have been found in graves of the period, placed there presumably because they had been used as votive offerings to the mother-goddess, perhaps in supplication for a child. A fetish of the fertility-goddess was found in a tomb at Naqada dating to the fourth millenium BC. It is in the shape of a vase, the exterior of which is decorated with a relief of a human head flanked by cow's horns; and a pair of arms holding breasts.

Other predynastic vases are painted with arms holding breasts; or figures of women dancing with their arms held up and curved towards their heads. Such a 'cow-dance' is performed to this day by the women of the Dinka and Shilluk tribes of the southern Sudan.

On many of the vases, the fertility-goddess is accompanied by a representation of a young man with twigs or feathers in his hair, performing a ritual dance. He is the son or lover of the goddess who, in later times, was called the *Ka-mutef*, or Bull of his Mother, and impersonated in temple ceremonies by a priest. On one vase, the goddess and her lover are shown in a boat standing together under an awning: the first representation of the sacred marriage of the fertility-goddess.

The most famous cow-goddess was Hathor. She was not only a symbol of fertility but also a sky-goddess, regarded as the Eye of the Sun God, Re; and as the personification of the sky itself. The Egyptians thought of her as a gigantic cow which straddled the earth, her legs marking the four cardinal points. Between her horns she carried the sun's disk; her belly was the sky, her hide and udders were the stars and planets. The iconography of Hathor as cow- and sky-goddess is not dissimilar from that of Nut (p. 57) but Hathor was by far the more pervasive and popular of the two goddesses.

In dynastic times, Hathor could be depicted as an actual cow; or as a woman with a cow's head; or as a woman wearing upon her head a sun-disk set between a pair of cow's horns. The earliest certain representation of Hathor is on the great ceremonial palette that was found at Hierakonpolis, the ancient capital of Upper Egypt: the Narmer Palette, now in Cairo Museum. Palettes, often made of slate, as is the Narmer Palette, were used by predynastic Egyptians as surfaces upon which to grind their cosmetics, especially the malachite that was used as a protective eyeliner. Towards the end of the predynastic period, the palettes were often used not as utilitarian objects but as decorations; the Narmer Palette was designed to commemorate the union of Upper and Lower Egypt, and was probably made as a votive offering for the local shrine of Hathor.

3 *The Narmer Palette (recto): the top edge is carved with the head of Hathor in the form of a cow with a woman's face. (Height of palette 64cm)*

At the top of each of the two sides of the Narmer Palette are carved two heads of Hathor, showing her with a cow's horns and ears but with a human face. This depiction of the head of Hathor was perhaps based on her fetish, the form in which she was worshipped in predynastic shrines and which probably was composed of a wooden post or pillar topped by the skull of a cow. In the dynastic period, this was stylised into the *Bat*-symbol (☥) of Hathor (p. 127).

Hathor's head as shown on the Narmer Palette was later developed so that whenever the Egyptians used her head alone in decoration, she could be shown as what at first glance seems to be a woman with a round, somewhat flattened, face, wearing a wig which falls into two thick ringlets on either side of her head. Only on closer inspection can it be seen that the ears of the goddess, protruding from beneath the wig, are not human ears but those of a cow.

This depiction of Hathor broke the normal conventions of Egyptian art which decreed that the human head should be shown in profile; indeed, Hathor is the only goddess ever to be shown full-face in reliefs, and in her shrines and temples use was made of this special form of Hathor's head in the decoration of the capitals of columns. These capitals are four-sided, with each side bearing the face of Hathor.

Hathor was a goddess of many attributes and functions. The story of how Re sent his Eye in the form of Hathor the cow to destroy mankind has already been told (p. 62) and illustrates that Hathor had a fierce aspect as an agent of destruction.

The most popular conception of Hathor, however, was not as an angry, vengeful goddess, only pacified because she became drunk, but as a beautiful young woman who brought joy and happiness not only to mankind but also to gods, even, as an indelicate episode from the Contendings of Horus and Seth relates, to the Lord of the Universe himself. The story goes that Re, having been insulted by one of the lesser gods, retired to his booth to sulk. And Hathor came and stood before him and uncovered her vagina in front of his face; an act that cheered up the Lord of the Universe so much that he laughed and rejoined his Company of gods.

Hathor was often described as the Beautiful One, the Golden One, the Lady of drunkenness, of song and of myrrh, Mistress of maidens who gives a husband to she whom she loves. The Greeks chose to equate her not with the age-old Mother Goddess, who for them was Artemis, but with their goddess of love and beauty, Aphrodite.

The ceremonies performed in Hathor's temples laid great emphasis on the presentation of wine, and of the beer that had become especially sacred to her because of the part it had played in saving mankind from destruction; and on music and movement: the king himself sang and danced before the goddess.

Music played an important part in all Egyptian temple rituals: one instrument much used in them was the sistrum, a kind of rattle that was sacred to Hathor. Sistra were made of metal or faience and formed in the shape of a Hathor-head or *Bat*-symbol, with horns bent round to form a loop. Three thin metal rods were threaded through holes and passed across the loop from one side to the other. The rods were either threaded with metal beads or left loose in their sockets so that when the sistrum was shaken they rattled.

The sistrum-player *par excellence* was Ihy, the son of Hathor. He is always depicted as a young boy whose head is shaven except for one long lock of hair (the so-called side-lock of youth). In his hands he holds a sistrum which he shakes in honour of his mother.

Hathor was especially revered by women. As the goddess of love and beauty, she looked after the interests of unmarried girls. In an association of ideas, she is often found on the handles of the mirrors that women used to inspect their beauty. The mirrors themselves could be made of disks of polished copper, bronze or silver (there were no silvered glass mirrors in Ancient Egypt), a reminder of the disk that Hathor sometimes supported on her head.

As a fertility-goddess, Hathor was clearly associated with childbirth: she protected pregnant women and helped them during their labour, aided by her son, Ihy, who soothed them with his music; and by Bes.

Bes was a very ancient god, possibly of Sudanese origin. He is usually depicted as a squat male figure—a dwarf, or perhaps a pygmy—with a large head, a lion's mane, protruding ears, flat nose, bow-legs, a tail and a long penis. He sometimes wears a panther skin wrapped round his body and a crown of feathers on his head. His ugliness, and the fact that he was shown pulling tongues at his beholders, made people laugh and frightened away demons. He also killed snakes and other harmful animals.

Women looked upon Bes as their protector in childbirth: children looked upon him as their particular friend. Even queens might turn to the ugly little god for comfort during labour: in a relief in the mortuary temple of Hatshepsut at Deir el-Bahri, for instance, he is shown attending the queen's mother, Ahmose, at the birth of Hatshepsut. Goddesses, also, did not scorn the comforting presence of Bes during their travail, as the carvings of him in the Birth Houses of many temples demonstrate.

Bes was allotted a partner in the shape of a pregnant female hippopotamus: Ta-weret. Hippopotami in general were not popular with an agricultural people such as the Egyptians. Although these ungainly animals are not vicious by nature, they do have the habit of invading carefully tended fields and trampling on anything that they do not actually eat. Male hippopotami were identified with Seth and regarded as symbols of evil. Females, however, with their broad flanks, were considered to be symbols of fecundity and were worshipped under names such as 'the White One' or 'the Great One'. The hippopotamus-goddess of Luxor (p. 142) was Ipet or 'She-of-the-Harem'; and she was identical in form with Bes' consort, Ta-weret (Thoueris), 'the Great One', who helped every woman, whether divine, royal or ordinary mortal, in labour.

The concern of Hathor with childbirth did not, in the case of royal babies, end with the birth of the child, for she was his nurse, also, and in her cow form, she suckled the king. Special attention to this aspect of Hathor was paid at Deir el-Bahri, the locality traditionally connected with the cult of the cow-goddess as practised in Western Thebes. Here, in Hatshepsut's mortuary temple, a shrine was dedicated to Hathor, and in reliefs on its walls, Hatshepsut and her stepson, Thothmes III, are shown crouched under figures of the cow-goddess, drinking from her udders.

This theme is taken up in the magnificent statue of the Hathor-cow and Thothmes III that was found at Deir el-Bahri during Naville's excavations of AD 1903 still standing in its chapel of painted sandstone; both statue and chapel are now in Cairo Museum. The 'Seven Hathors' were analagous to the Greek *moirai* (Fates); or to the Good Fairy who attended the christening of the Sleeping Beauty: they were a group of goddesses, all of whom were forms of Hathor, who had the power to foretell the fate of a new-born child. Thus, they are found in stories such as the Tale of the Two Brothers,[7] where they prophesy that the beautiful maiden who has been created to be the wife of the younger brother, Bata, will meet a violent death—as she does. In another story written down in Dynasty XIX, the Doomed Prince,[8] they decree that the prince shall die either by a crocodile, or by a snake, or by a dog. Unfortunately, the papyrus is damaged, so we do not have the end of the story and perhaps will never know whether the prince evaded his Fate.

Hathor offered help to the deceased as well as to the living. From Dynasty XVIII onwards, she served as the patron deity of the Theban necropolis, and as such she is often depicted as a cow standing partially concealed in a papyrus thicket at the foot of the Western Mountain of Thebes; only her head is visible through the reeds. The gilded head of a cow with lyriform horns found in Tutankhamun's tomb, and now in Luxor Museum, was probably meant to represent this aspect of Hathor.

The equipment with which Tutankhamun was furnished for his journey to the Afterlife shows that Hathor played an important part in his protection, either under her own name, or under the name of Mehet-weret. Apart from the gilded head, he was provided with three giant funerary couches, one of which has sides shaped like two long, slender cows, each of which carries a sun's disk between her horns.

An inscription on the bed places Tutankhamun under the protection of Isis-Meht (Meht probably being an abbreviation of Mehet-weret). Mehet-weret, whose name means 'the Great Flood', a reference both to the primaeval ocean and also to the celestial ocean across which Re was thought to sail in his barque every day, was second only to Hathor as a cow-goddess; at an early date, the two were merged so that she became another form of the great Hathor.

Just as Re journeyed to heaven on the back of the goddess Nut, who had assumed the form of a cow for the purpose (p. 63), so Tutankhamun must have believed that he, too, would journey to heaven reclining on this bed shaped like Mehet-weret.

Even before his death, Tutankhamun was protected by Hathor. The seat of his so-called Ecclesiastical Throne is inlaid with ivory and ebony in imitation of a cow's hide, inferring not only that real cow-hide was often used for chair seats but also that by sitting on the imitation cow-hide seat of his throne, Tutankhamun associated himself with the goddess. It was thought that, in the Afterlife, Hathor had her abode in a sacred sycamore tree. The deceased found refuge under its branches whilst Hathor leaned out to offer him food and drink. One of her epithets was Lady of the Sycamore, and at Memphis in particular she was worshipped as a tree-goddess.

Temples dedicated to Hathor were built at many places in Egypt. One of the oldest centres of her cult was the town that the Greeks called Diospolis Parva, the capital of the 7th Upper Egyptian Nome. In predynastic times, its Nome standard consisted of the skull of a cow suspended from the top of a pole. Later, probably during the Middle Kingdom, the emblem of a cow's skull was replaced by the head of Hathor as a woman, surmounted by a sistrum—the *Bat*-symbol—which was evidently felt to be a less crude motif than the original skull. The local temple of Hathor, which was called the *Hoot Sekhem* (meaning the Mansion of the Sistrum) gave its name to the whole town. By the Coptic period, *Hoot Sekhem* had been abbreviated to *Hoo*, which today has become Hiw.

At Gebelein, a temple of Hathor first built in Dynasty III was still functioning in the Graeco-Roman period. The name of this temple, *Per Hathor* (the House of Hathor), which the Greeks pronounced Pathyris, caused them to call the locality Aphroditopolis (City of Aphrodite). Other major temples of Hathor were built at Atfih (also called Aphroditopolis by the Greeks) and Cusae; and at Deir el-Medina, Western Thebes.

Here, a village was built to house the workmen who constructed the tombs of the Theban necropolis during the New Kingdom. Just outside the village, a sanctuary was built for use by the workmen and dedicated to Hathor, who was a particularly popular deity with the men because of her status as goddess of the Western Mountain of Thebes. During the reign of Ptolemy IV, a new temple was built on the site of the old: this was dedicated to Hathor, and to Imhotep (p. 167) and Amenhotep, son of Hapu, the Vizier and Master Builder of Tutankhamun's father, Amenhotep III—a very unusual dedication since temples normally belonged to gods and kings.

The Egyptians made Hathor the goddess of foreign lands such as Punt (Somaliland) and Byblos in the Lebanon. She was worshipped in places as far apart as the Sinai Peninsula and Nubia. From Dynasty III until the end of the New Kingdom, the Egyptians mined in the Sinai for turquoise, copper and malachite, and, at Serâbit el-Khâdim, they built a temple for her in which she was worshipped as 'the Lady of Turquoise'.

Nubia was the land from which the Egyptians obtained their gold, the metal sacred to Hathor who was herself the 'Gold of the Gods'. In Dynasty XIX, Ramesses II built a temple there for his favourite wife, Nefertari, next to his own temple at Abu Simbel; and dedicated the temple to Nefertari and, in a graceful compliment to his queen, to Hathor, goddess of love and beauty.

The temple was cut into a cliff-face and its façade is formed from six colossal statues, each about 10 metres high, two of the queen and four of the king. The main hall of the temple contains six square pillars; the front of each of them is decorated with the typical Hathor head surmounted by a sistrum. In the sanctuary, a recess holds a figure of the Hathor-cow protecting the king.

The most famous of Hathor's temples is that at Denderah, dedicated to the triad of Hathor, Horus of Edfu and their son, Harsomtus. Here, she was worshipped in her most important role, that of wife to the falcon-god, Horus. Her name, *Hat-Hor*, means 'Mansion of Horus', a reference to the fact that she was the sky in which the falcon flew. The hieroglyphs which represent her name, 𓉡, show a house or temple with a hawk inside it. Denderah, which lies some 60km north of Luxor, was the ancient capital of the 6th Nome of Upper Egypt. The antiquity of the site is shown by the existence of an ancient necropolis there, and its connection with Hathor by the number of cow-burials in this cemetery. In predynastic times, the fetish of Hathor worshipped at Denderah was a pillar, giving Hathor the epithet 'She-of-the-Pillar' (in Egyptian, *Iunet*); thus, the earliest name of the place was *Iunet*. The modern name, Denderah, is derived from a reference to Hathor as 'the Goddess', which in Egyptian was *Ta-neteret*; in Greek, this became Tentyris, in Arabic, Denderah.

The predynastic shrine of Hathor was rebuilt in Dynasty IV by Khufu and dedicated to Hathor, Lady of the Pillar, and to her son, the musician god, Ihy. The temple was refurbished and embellished at various times over the next thousand years or so, notably during the reigns of Mentuhotep III (Dynasty XI) and Thothmes III (Dynasty XVIII).

The temple at Denderah as it stands today dates from the Ptolemaic and Roman periods; most of it was built between 116 BC and AD 34. It is the most imposing and elaborately decorated structure of its period, rivalled only by the Temple of Horus at Edfu. The roof of the great hall of the temple is supported by twenty-four cylindrical columns, some 15 metres high, with a diameter of close-on 2 metres; their capitals are four-sided and each side is decorated with a head of Hathor. The outstanding features of the temple are the thirty-two long, narrow chambers built into the thickness of the walls and under the floors, whose entrances were covered by slabs of stone. Such 'crypts' are to be found in other temples, but only at Denderah are they decorated. Although some of them may have been used for the secret rituals of the goddess, most of them, prosaically enough, were used as storage places for temple equipment.

The roof of the temple is flat, and on it are several shrines or kiosks. One of these is formed from twelve Hathor-headed columns joined together at the top by stone architraves. The usual practice would have been to fill in the spaces between the architraves with slabs of stone to form a roof, but in this instance the shrine has been left open to the sky. It was here that the New Year ceremony was performed, the culminating point of which occurred when the sun shone upon the face of the statue of Hathor which had been carried up from her sanctuary within the temple expressly for this purpose of 'Uniting with the Sun's Disk'.

Denderah was one of the many places which laid claim to being the site of Osiris' burial (p. 80); and it was for the celebrations of his resurrection that the other roof chapels were intended. The ceiling of one of these chapels was decorated with a map of the sky, the so-called Denderah Zodiac, with its thirty-six decans, the constellations that enabled the Egyptians to tell the time at night. Each decan was visible on the horizon for about ten days at a time: its point in the sky determining the hour according to a set of rules worked out by priests.

Only a plaster copy now remains in the temple: the original 'Zodiac' is in the Louvre in Paris.

Outside the temple proper are subsidiary buildings: to the south, a small temple in which was celebrated the Birth of Isis, built by Octavian (Caesar Augustus) within a few metres of the rear wall of the main temple which is decorated with a relief showing his vanquished enemy, Cleopatra, with her son by Julius Caesar, Caesarion. To the west of the temple lies a mud-brick 'sanatorium' and two Birth Houses. The 'sanatorium' was used by the sick as a place in which to sleep in the hope of having a healing dream sent by Hathor; or as a place in which to bathe in water that had been blessed by the goddess or run over statues inscribed with magical texts, a process that was thought to impregnate the water with the magic inherent in the texts so that the bather would be imbued with its potency.

One of the Birth Houses was built by Nectanebo I (380–362 BC) and renewed by the Ptolemies. Reliefs in it show the divine birth of Nectanebo, his mother being Hathor and his father, Amun of Thebes, a reminder of the old tradition of theogamy (p. 36). The other Birth House was built by Augustus: it shows the birth of a divine child, in this instance not the king but the young Ihy.

The birth of the Divine Child of Denderah, Harsomtus, was a result of one of the great events in the Festival Calendar of both Denderah and Edfu temples. This was the Sacred Marriage of Hathor and Horus, an annual event which took place at Edfu Temple during the third month of Summer (May) on the night of the New Moon.

Fourteen days before the New Moon, the statue of Hathor was carried out of her temple at Denderah in a great procession that wended its way down to the Nile, where the goddess was placed in her state barge, after which the barge, accompanied by a flotilla of lesser boats bearing priests and notables of Denderah, was towed up-river towards Edfu, a journey of some 70km.

The journey was a slow one. Not only was Hathor's progress impeded by numerous pilgrims who joined her glittering cavalcade along its route, but she delayed her journey by stopping at several places along the way to visit local deities. At Thebes, for instance, she was taken ashore to visit the goddess Mut at Karnak; at Hierakonpolis, she greeted the local form of Horus. At each place she visited, more boats were added to her ever-growing procession, all crammed with local dignitaries and enthusiastic devotees of the goddess.

Eventually, on the afternoon of the day of the New Moon, Hathor reached Edfu, where she was met at the quayside by Horus and his retinue. For the rest of the afternoon, Horus and Hathor were carried to each of the sacred sites outwith Edfu Temple for the performance of certain rituals until the time came for them to enter the temple itself. There, the rites celebrating their marriage were enacted. Finally, they were led to the Birth House and there they spent their wedding night.

For the next fourteen days, the city and district of Edfu, crowded with visitors from all over Egypt, especially from the area between Denderah to the north and Elephantine (Aswan) to the south, rejoiced, and celebrated the sacred marriage with the food and drink supplied free to them by the temple staff. An inscription in the temple describes the scenes of festivity and celebration, and tells us that countless provisions were available—all kinds of bread in loaves numerous as grains of sand; oxen abounding like locusts; roast fowl, roasts of gazelle, oryx and ibex; free-flowing wine. The whole city was festive:

> Its youths are drunk, its citizens are glad, its young maidens are beautiful to behold; rejoicing is all around it and festivity is in all its quarters. There is no sleep to be had in it until dawn.

On the fourth day of the Festival, the son of Hathor and Horus was conceived. Before then, however, the nature of the Festival had undergone a subtle change: it was no longer just a sacred marriage but a fourteen-day festival called the 'Festival of *Behdet*', a great ancestral ritual combined with a harvest festival.

On the last day of the Festival of *Behdet*, the day of the Full Moon, the time came for Hathor to return home. She was escorted to the quayside by Horus and his followers, and set sail for Denderah, where, in due course, she gave birth to Horus' son, Harsomtus or *Hor-sma-tawy* (Horus-who-unites-the-Two-Lands i.e. Egypt).

In every large town in Egypt there was a shrine in which Hathor was worshipped; in many of them she was regarded as a form of the indigenous goddess. Thus, at Elephantine she was identified with Sothis; at Thebes, with Mut; at Buto, with Edjo. She was identified with Isis in so many places — Coptos, Panopolis, Aphroditopolis and Kanopus amongst them—that by the Late Period these two greatest of Egyptian female deities were inextricably mixed together.

Throughout Egyptian history, Hathor was given a place of honour in every company of gods: Hathor, the Golden One of the gods, the joyous goddess of love, music and intoxication, the bringer of happiness.

EDJO

Edjo was the goddess who in predynastic times was worshipped in the form of a cobra at *Dep*, a town in the north west Delta. Close by *Dep* was *Pe* (whose name is the same as that for 'seat' or 'throne'), where the Residence of the Kings of Lower Egypt is believed to have been situated. *Pe* and *Dep* merged gradually, so that by the New Kingdom they had become one city, named after its chief temple which was dedicated to Edjo and called *Per-Wadjet* (the House of *Wadjet* (Edjo)), rendered by the Greeks as Buto and known today as Tell el-Fara'in (the Mound of the Pharaohs). Edjo herself is known to us by a variety of different names: she is sometimes called Buto; and in older books her name is spelled variously as Wadjet, Wadjit or Uadjit. Since we do not know how Ancient Egyptian was pronounced, it is not possible to be dogmatic about the form her name takes. Its meaning is more clear: in hieroglyphic script, her name is written using the symbol of Lower Egypt, the papyrus plant 𝄼 : it means 'She-of-the-Papyrus'.

'The Souls of *Pe* and *Dep*' was a term often applied to the falcon-headed figures in reliefs and inscriptions which are thought to be representations of the early kings of Lower Egypt. Just as Nekhbet became the principal goddess of the South by virtue of the proximity of her cult-centre to the ancient capital of Upper Egypt, so Edjo became tutelary goddess of the North because her city was close to the place where the early kings of Lower Egypt resided.

The crown most closely associated with her was, naturally, the diadem of Lower Egypt, the Red Crown, which she is usually seen wearing. Reliefs in many temples show the coronation of the King. An important part of the coronation ritual was the crowning of the ruler first with the Red Crown of Lower Egypt, an act undertaken by Edjo, who is depicted in such reliefs in human female form; then with the White Crown of Upper Egypt by Nekhbet, also in the shape of a woman.

Apart from Coronation scenes, Edjo, like Nekhbet, was seldom depicted in human form: she was usually represented as a cobra. From the earliest times, the Egyptians considered the cobra to be a sign of royalty and sovereignty, presumably because the cobra-goddess was so closely connected with kings. The sun disk of Re was usually depicted with a cobra coiled round it as a symbol of his kingship, a convention which led to the cobra being thought of as the Eye of Re, which could spit fire against his enemies, and those of the king.

Representations made of gold of Edjo, the royal cobra, sometimes alone, sometimes accompanied by Nekhbet in her own vulture-form or in the guise of a cobra, made up the special emblem, the Uraeus, that was borne by kings and gods. The Uraeus (a word which comes from the Greek for cobra, *ouraios*) was worn on the brow, attached to crowns or fillets, and both protected its wearer and indicated that he had dominion over the whole land, with Edjo symbolising sovereignty over Lower Egypt and Nekhbet over Upper Egypt. Outstanding examples of Uraei were found in the tomb of Tutankhamun, those on his gold funerary mask and on his fillet being particularly fine. The most interesting were perhaps the two Uraei made of gold and faience beads embroidered onto the linen skull-cap that covered the king's mummified head.

Legend says that Edjo guarded the infant Horus, son of Isis and Osiris, after his birth on the island of Chemmis, near *Dep*. Later, it was her task to guard every king of Egypt who was regarded as the Living Horus on the Throne of Egypt.

The cobra was a popular form of deity throughout Egypt, for cobras are found all over the land; hence the popularity of the cobra-goddesses such as Renenutet (p. 97) and Mertseger (p. 35). Edjo, however, was the Royal Cobra. It is fitting that the last Queen of Egypt, Cleopatra, should have chosen to kill herself with the bite of what the Greeks called an 'asp', but which was probably a cobra. Thus Edjo, by helping 'Egypt' to die with dignity rather than to walk in a Roman Triumph, extended her protection of the rulers of Egypt to the end.

NEKHBET

Nekhbet was the local goddess of the ancient city of *Nekheb* whom the Egyptians worshipped in the form of *Vultur auricularis*, the Sociable Vulture, which today is fairly common in southern Egypt but hardly ever seen in the north. *Nekheb*, which is on the east bank of the Nile some 80km south of Luxor, was one of the oldest settlements in Upper Egypt, dating back to at least 6000 BC. Because of its geographical position, it had a great strategic importance in that it had control over the western outlets of the routes which led through the Wadi Abbad and the Wadi Mia to the Red Sea, and to the areas of the eastern desert that were exploited for flint, and for metals such as lead, tin and gold.

On the western bank of the Nile opposite *Nekheb* lay the earliest capital of Upper Egypt, *Nekhen* (to the Greeks, Hierakonpolis; modern name, Kom el-Ahmar). Because of the proximity of *Nekheb* to *Nekhen*, and because of the importance of *Nekheb* itself, Nekhbet, its goddess (whose name means 'She-of-*Nekheb*'), became the principal goddess of Upper Egypt during the predynastic period.

In dynastic times, Nekhbet was elevated to the role of protectress of the King of Upper Egypt. Her northern counterpart as tutelary-goddess was the cobra-goddess, Edjo. When Menes united Upper and Lower Egypt, he symbolised the event by adopting a title which identified him with the two deities: the *nebty*-name, which in hieroglyphic script is written showing a vulture and a cobra sitting on baskets—the Two Ladies (*nebty*), Nekhbet and Edjo. From thenceforward, the *nebty*-name formed part of the titulary of every King of Egypt.

Nekhbet's role of protectress is reflected in the design of royal jewellery: the broad collars and pectorals which were worn on the chests of kings, for instance, were often made of gold and semi-precious stones shaped to represent vultures. Outstanding examples of these vulture-collars were found at Thebes in the tombs of Smenkare and his brother, Tutankhamun. As far as queens were concerned, it was the custom of the principal wife of the king to wear a headdress fashioned in the form of a vulture. Although no actual example of this type of headdress has been found, it seems clear from the many reliefs depicting queens wearing it that it was made of small plates of gold wired together to make a flexible covering for the top of the head.

Whenever Nekhbet was used as a motif in jewellery, she held in her claws the hieroglyphic sign ☋ which means *shen* 'to encircle', and denotes that Nekhbet offers the King sovereignty over all that the sun encircles. Even the cobra-goddess, Edjo, could sometimes be equipped with claws in which to hold a *shen*-sign so that she, too, might offer the King mastery over the world.

Nekhbet was particularly concerned with the crown of Upper Egypt: as the embodiment of this, the White Crown, she was often called 'the White One of *Nekhen*', and she was normally shown wearing the diadem. She could appear on the head of the King, not only as the White Crown, but also in vulture, or even in cobra, form, as part of the Uraeus (p. 135) which he wore on his brow attached to his headdress.

On monuments, Nekhbet is usually shown with wings outstretched, hovering protectively over the figure of the King. She was also depicted attending royal births, an aspect of the goddess which caused the Greeks to identify her with their own Eileithya or 'She-who-comes-to-the-aid-of-women-in-childbed', and to call her city of *Nekheb* Eileithyiaspolis.

During the New Kingdom, *Nekheb* was the capital of the 3rd Nome of Upper Egypt. From predynastic times until the Roman era, kings built or renewed shrines and temples there and dedicated them to Nekhbet. Occasionally, Hathor, with whom she was sometimes equated, was honoured alongside her, as in the temple built in Dynasty XVIII by Thothmes IV and Amenhotep III for Nekhbet and Hathor, Mistress of the Entrance to the (Nile) Valley.

Nekheb suffered considerable damage over the centuries. Today, little remains to be seen of this once great city. El-Kab, as it is now called, is of interest mainly because of the biographical texts in the tombs of men such as Ahmose-Pennekhbet (Pennekhebet meaning 'the-man-who-belongs-to-Nekhbet'); and Ahmose, son of Abana, who fought against the Hyksos, and in Nubia, Syria and Palestine in the early part of Dynasty XVIII. However, the traveller who passes by the site, whether by train or by boat, cannot but be impressed by what remains of the massive mud-brick ramparts which once surrounded the city of *Nekheb*.

AMUN

The oldest god known by the name Amun was one of the eight deities who made up the Ogdoad of Hermopolis, the head of which was Thoth. The name Amun means 'Hidden-' or 'Invisible-one'; and he was a god of the air.

At the end of the First Intermediate Period, a god named Amun appeared in the 4th Nome of Upper Egypt, the *Waset* or Sceptre Nome. Whether this Amun is to be identified with the Hermopolitan Amun is not certain. What is certain is that within a matter of 150 years, Amun had displaced the indigenous god of the Sceptre Nome, Montu, and had begun the rise to power that was to make him King of the Gods.

A particular kind of sheep, found nowhere else in Egypt, was native to the area of the Sceptre Nome. This sheep belongs to the fat-tailed species (*Ovis platyura aegyptiaca*), the ram of which has a characteristic peculiar to it in that its horns are particularly large, curved and down-turned. It is possible that the original deity of the Sceptre Nome, older even than Montu, was a ram of this type. Amun not only displaced Montu, but he adopted the ram with down-turned horns as his own symbol.

Although the ram, famed like Amun himself for its virility and pugnacity, was Amun's sacred animal, Amun was never depicted in the form of a ram, or as a man with a ram's head. He was always portrayed in human shape wearing a cap surmounted by two tall plumes and a sun's disk. The mysterious, hidden part of his nature, implicit in his name, was expressed by the custom of covering the shrine that held his statue with a shroud. The soul of Amun was supposed to be enshrined in a serpent-shaped sceptre known as *Kem-at-ef* (He-who-has-finished-his-moment) which was perhaps his original fetish. The virility and fecundity of Amun was manifest not only in the ram but also in the bird associated with him, the goose.

At least as early as the Middle Kingdom, a temple was built for Amun in the Sceptre Nome, at *Waset*, the town named after the Nome

138

although not then its capital, which was further to the south at Armant (p. 190). Very little is known of the early history of *Waset*, the town, except that it had strategic importance due to its geographical position: it lay on both banks of the Nile, close to the deserts, with their natural resources; and not too far away from Nubia which supplied the Egyptians with men and gold. After the arrival of Amun, *Waset* grew ever more important and Amun flourished.

Eventually, *Waset* became known as 'the City of Amun' or just as 'The City'—named in the Bible as No Amon (Nahum iii 8) and No (Ezekiel xxx 16). The Greeks equated Amun with Zeus and so called *Waset* Diospolis. Earlier on, Homer had described it as

'Proud Thebes . . .
That spreads her conquests o'er a thousand states
And pours her heroes through a hundred gates.'[9]

Why Homer called *Waset* Thebes we do not know, unless he was complimenting his own Greek city of the same name. It is, however, convenient for us to call the City of Amun Thebes, although today it is usually known by the names of the two famous temples on its eastern bank, Karnak and Luxor (p. 142).

A century or so after Amun arrived in Thebes, the kings of Dynasty XI who were natives of the Sceptre Nome and adherents of its chief god, Montu, made Thebes the capital of Egypt, a position that it held for some fifty years. Then, in 1999 BC, the last king of Dynasty XI, Mentuhotep IV, was overthrown by his chief minister, himself a follower of Amun.

The new King of Egypt, the founder of Dynasty XII, called himself Amenemhat, 'Amun is Supreme', a practice followed by three of his successors; and not only honoured Amun by including him in his name, but began to build for him a temple at Thebes which he called *Ipet-esut*, a name which means 'the Most Select of Places'. Today, the site of this temple is known as Karnak.

Karnak was enlarged and embellished over the succeeding centuries, up to and including the Roman period. From the fourth century AD, the temple, abandoned by its priests, was used as a dwelling place by local villagers and their animals. Gradually, it was buried under their debris until eventually only the tops of the windows in the main hall were visible, earning for it the Arabic name, Karnak—'the town of the windows'.

Amenemhat decided that Egypt could not easily be governed from Thebes and so he built a new capital on the boundary between Upper and Lower Egypt, some 30km south of Memphis, which he called *Itj-tawy*, 'the Seizer of the Two Lands [Egypt]', better known today as

Lisht. Thebes, however, remained the administrative centre for the South.

In Dynasty XIII, the capital was shifted to Memphis. However, in 1674 BC, Memphis fell to the invading Hyksos (p. 144). Thebes fell into obscurity until 1650 BC or thereabouts, when the descendants of the Theban rulers of Dynasty XIII, having made the city into a rallying point for Egyptian resistance to the Hyksos, formed themselves into what Manetho later designated Dynasty XVII.

The Hyksos were finally driven from Egypt in about 1550 BC by the Theban king, Ahmose, the founder of Dynasty XVIII. Ahmose chose Thebes to be the capital of the newly-unified Egypt; and, as the glory of Thebes grew, so did the glory of her chief god, Amun, who became state god of Egypt. Under Thothmes III, Thebes became the capital of the mighty empire that he won for Egypt in the Near East; and Amun was given sovereignty over the deities of the countries that were subjugated. Amun thus became the supreme god of the then known world and was given the title 'King of the Gods'; he himself was thought of above all as a god of war who brought victory to the kings of Egypt.

Amun, and his city of Thebes, achieved their greatest importance in Dynasties XVIII and XIX, especially during the reigns of the warrior kings Thothmes III and Ramesses II, each of whom made great conquests in the Near East and Nubia and donated much of the wealth gained therefrom to Amun of Thebes. Thothmes III was a particular devotee of Amun, and with good reason. He was the son of Thothmes II and a concubine named Ese. Several years after he came to the throne, he recorded in an inscription at Karnak that when he was a mere child serving as an acolyte in the Temple of Amun at Thebes, his father the King came to make offerings to the God. Thothmes was standing in the hall outside the Sanctuary as his father's procession passed by; and the God (presumably the statue of Amun, carried by priests in a portable shrine with carrying poles) began to search for him:

> On recognizing me, lo, he halted . . . I threw myself on the pavement, I prostrated myself in his presence. He set me before him and I was placed at the Station of the King [i.e. the place usually occupied by the Ruler].

And so, by means of a divine oracle, the young boy was chosen to be crown prince. The oracle, of course, must have been worked by the priests of Amun, who had marked out the young Thothmes and were prepared to back his claim to the throne.

When Thothmes II died, his wife, Thothmes III's stepmother,

Hatshepsut, ruled Egypt, first as Regent for the young Thothmes III, then as King (note, not Queen) in her own right, for twenty-two years. She, too, favoured and was favoured by, Amun, claiming him as her heavenly father in the scenes in her mortuary temple at Deir el-Bahri showing her divine birth; and erecting obelisks for him within his temple at Karnak. Eventually, however, Thothmes came to the throne as undisputed King, ready to show his gratitude to Amun.

The Tuthmoside kings of Dynasty XVIII attributed their successes at home and abroad to the favour of Amun; they even claimed their rights to the Throne of Egypt by virtue of the fact that each of them was the son of 'his father, Amun'.

For over one hundred and fifty years, Amun reigned unchallenged. Throughout Egypt, new shrines and temples were built to him, often replacing those of other deities. Small chapels dedicated to these deities were erected within the precincts of Amun's own vast temple at Karnak, thus emphasizing their subordination to Amun. The titles of High Priest of Re and High Priest of Ptah were included amongst the titles of the High Priest of Amun, who claimed jurisdiction over all other priesthoods. The dead as well as the living came under the jurisdiction of Amun's priesthood, for it governed not only the east bank at Thebes where the temples were situated but also the west bank where the great necropolis of the city lay. They had charge not only of the royal tombs belonging to the kings of the New Kingdom, but of those of their queens and nobles also; and they ran the mortuary temples which stretched along the western bank of the Nile for over 7km. The size and number of the temples and tombs of the Theban necropolis as seen today never fails to impress a visitor with the immensity of the task.

From about 1412 BC, the character of Amun began to change. He no longer claimed to be just a god of war. Instead, he usurped some of the functions of Tatanen of Memphis and Re of Heliopolis. His priests claimed that he was a cosmic creator-god, self-engendered, who 'had no mother or father but shaped his own egg, mingled his seed with his body to make his egg come into being and took the form of Tanen to give birth to the gods'. It was claimed that Thebes was the birthplace of the whole universe, where the never-sleeping Amun ruled as 'Lord of Time who makes the years, rules the months, ordains nights and days'.

Eventually, the priests added Re's name to that of Amun, so that he was thenceforward known as Amen-Re, King of the Gods (*Amen-Re-Nesu-Neteru*), which the Greeks rendered as Amonrasonther. The power of Amun was such that it proved oppressive: and before the end of Dynasty XVIII there was a religious revolution (p. 152).

The eclipse of Amun that followed was short-lived. Within a few years, he was reinstated by the last kings of Dynasty XVIII, and by Dynasty XIX had regained his supremacy. In the papyrus now known as the Great Harris and preserved in the British Museum, Ramesses IV (Dynasty XX) records that in the reign of his father, Ramesses III, the practice of flooding the coffers of Amun continued until the estate of the God owned:

> 86,486 serfs, 421,362 head of cattle, 433 gardens and orchards, 691,334 acres of land, 83 ships, 46 workshops, 65 cities and towns, plus gold, silver, incense and other valuables in unmeasured amounts.

By the end of the reign of Ramesses III, all the temples of Egypt, not just those of Amun, owned vast amounts of property. It has been calculated that one fifth of the inhabitants of the country and about one third of the cultivable land belonged to the temples: and that some three quarters of all this wealth was owned by Amen-Re of Thebes. It is not surprising that the possession of such wealth gave the High Priest of Amun an enormous amount of power and influence not only in Thebes itself but throughout Egypt.

During the New Kingdom, with the exception of the Amarna Period (p. 149), Thebes flourished as the centre of the cult of Amun. Numerous shrines were built for him: on the west bank he was worshipped in the mortuary temples of the kings; on the east bank, his temples at Karnak and Luxor were enlarged year by year.

Karnak Temple does not consist of a single shrine: it is, instead, a vast complex of religious buildings in which at least twenty major shrines have been identified. The sacred enclosure covers an area of some $1\frac{1}{4}$ sq. km, in comparison to which the main temple in its final phase, measured at least $1\frac{1}{2}$ km long. Karnak Temple, which Champollion called a 'gigantic wonder', was for more than 2,000 years built, rebuilt, enlarged and embellished by numerous rulers of Egypt.

Luxor Temple lies just over 2 km away down to the south of the main temple at Karnak. At Luxor, Amun was worshipped in ithyphallic form in the guise of the fertility-god, Min. The Ancient Egyptians called the temple *Ipet-resyt*, or the Southern Harem. Today, the temple is called Luxor, from the Arabic el-Qusur, meaning 'The Castles', the name given to the village that grew up on the accumulated debris of centuries and encroached upon the site of the great temple. As seen today, that temple is largely the work of two kings, Amenhotep III, who built the sanctuary and its forecourt, and a processional colonnade; and Ramesses II who added a peristyle court.

Once a year, during the second month of the Inundation Season, the cult statue of Amun was carried in procession from its home at Karnak to spend a holiday with his *alter ego* at Luxor; and to celebrate his union with his divine consort, Mut, during the Beautiful Festival of the Harem (*Ipet*, often called *Opet* in books on Egypt).

During the reign of Nectanebo I (380–362 BC), Luxor was linked with Karnak by an avenue of human-headed sphinxes, the last-known embellishment of the temple by a native Egyptian king. At Karnak itself, avenues of sphinxes were used for the approach to the Temple of Amun; and to link that building with the Temple of Mut. These sphinxes, however, do not have human heads but have instead heads of the sacred rams of Amun.

The sanctuary of Luxor Temple was eventually transformed into a Christian church; and in the thirteenth century AD, a small mosque dedicated to Abu el-Haggag, a noted pilgrim to Mecca, was built on top of the debris that by then filled the forecourt that Ramesses II had built. To this day, a boat which is kept in the mosque is carried annually in procession round the town in unconscious imitation of the ancient days when Amun was carried out in his sacred barque to visit his Southern Harem.

The last kings of Dynasty XX were weak; little by little, the High Priests of Amun usurped their power in Upper Egypt until finally, during the reign of Ramesses XI, a military man named Herihor became High Priest of Amun. Herihor had himself portrayed as a king and founded a 'dynasty' of priest-kings at Thebes which ruled the Theban district if not most of Upper Egypt during the period when Dynasty XXI of Egyptian kings proper ruled from Tanis in the north-east Delta. Relations between Tanis and Thebes during this Dynasty were friendly. The Theban Triad of Amun, Mut and Khonsu were worshipped in Tanis where they displaced the old deities Sutekh and Anath. Princesses were sent from Tanis to Thebes to become wives of the High Priests of Amun.

The last king of Dynasty XXI, Psusennes II (959–945 BC) was also High Priest of Amun; he claimed the Throne of Egypt through descent from these princesses, and thus united both Thebes and Tanis.

When Psusennes II died, the line of Tanite kings ended simultaneously with the line of High Priests of Amun. The first king, Shoshenq, of the new Dynasty (XXII), reigned from Bubastis in the north; and Thebes was never again to be the capital of Egypt. Although Shoshenq installed his son in Thebes as High Priest of Amun, it took another three hundred years before Thebes became a fully integrated part of Egypt.

During Dynasty XXI, a custom arose that a daughter of the reigning king should be consecrated to Amun to be his wife. The Divine Wife of Amun, who was also called 'the Hand of the God', a reference to an ancient belief that the Creation was achieved through an act of masturbation (p. 46), was required to be a virgin: hence the device of adoption was resorted to.

Each Divine Wife adopted a daughter to succeed her; and successive kings in their capital cities of Tanis, Bubastis and Sais, and even the kings of Dynasty XXV who were of Sudanese origin, ensured that it was one of their own daughters who travelled to Thebes to become the heiress of the Divine Wife of Amun. Thus, Shepenupet, daughter of Osorkon III of Dynasty XXII, Amenirdis, daughter of Kashta of Dynasty XXV and Nitocris, daughter of Psammetichus I of Dynasty XXVI, and others less well-known, reigned in Thebes at least, not as Queen but as High Priestess of Amun, with a court of her own, surrounded by the concubines of Amun, the owner of vast estates with the privilege of making offerings in the temple. Having wielded great power in her lifetime, the Divine Wife of Amun, when she died, was buried in the same manner as a King of Egypt, usually on the west bank of Thebes at Medinet Habu, the great mortuary temple of Ramesses III.

Despite the fact that Amun was King of the Gods, and a very close associate of the kings of Egypt, his priests were at pains to encourage Egyptians to see him as a compassionate deity, one to whom they could turn when they were in trouble. Therefore, they built at Karnak a small temple called 'the Temple of Amun-who-hears-prayers' where the 'ordinary' Egyptian could petition Amun by leaving a small stele at the gate. Thus Amun, whose very name has given us our word Mammon with its connotations of wealth as an influence for evil, was to many Egyptians a kind god who protected the weak, succoured orphans, defended the oppressed and healed the sick. As was customary in Egyptian religion, he formed part of a triad or holy family, playing the role of husband and father to Mut and Khonsu respectively.

In 663 BC, Assurbanipal the Assyrian sacked Thebes and carried away to Niniveh a vast amount of treasure looted from its temples. Thebes never recovered from the blow, although Amun himself continued to receive attentions from the rulers of Egypt at Thebes and elsewhere. Proof that his power remained undiminished is provided by the behaviour towards him of Alexander the Great. In October, 332 BC, Alexander conquered Egypt without having to strike a blow, welcomed by the Egyptians as their deliverer from the hated Persians, who had ruled them intermittently since 525 BC. As was his usual

practice, Alexander took care to observe local religious suscepti-
bilities. Some three months after his arrival in Egypt, he took the
trouble to make a three-week journey across a distance of 500km
of burning Libyan desert in order to visit the Temple of Amun at the
Siwah Oasis, and to consult the oracle of Zeus-Ammon.

When Alexander emerged from the consultation, all he would
disclose about what the oracle had said to him was: 'I have been told
what my heart desires'. He was recognized and accepted by the
Egyptians, and more importantly by the Egyptian priesthood, as the
son of Amun and therefore the rightful ruler of Egypt. From
thenceforward, Alexander was depicted, on coins especially, wearing
the distinctive ram's horns of Amun.

The Greeks continued the worship of Amun under the name of
Zeus-Ammon; and later, the Romans honoured him as Jupiter-
Ammon. And Amun has left to us a legacy of words: ammonia is so
called because the ammoniac salt found at Siwah was, erroneously,
thought to have been formed from the dung dropped by camels used
by visitors to the temple; and the fossil ammonites owe their name to a
resemblance to the ram's horns of Amun.

MUT

Mut was possibly the original deity of Thebes. Although she is always shown on existing monuments in completely human form, she was probably worshipped in predynastic times in the form of a griffin vulture (*Gyps fulvus*). Her name, Mut, which is written using the hieroglyph depicting this vulture, is thought to have been old Egyptian for 'vulture', a word that was replaced in the Egyptian language of later times by another meaning vulture, *neret*, leaving *mut* as the name of the goddess.

The word *mut* also means 'mother', and so Mut is considered to be a mother-goddess. This concept was reinforced by the universal symbolism of the mother-bird with wings outspread protectively over her fledglings: since, in Egypt, vultures are the birds with the largest wing-span, vulture-goddesses such as Mut and Nekhbet became symbols of maternal love and protection.

When Amun arrived in Thebes, around 2170 BC, Mut was incorporated into his cult as his wife. Her temple stands within the precincts of Karnak, in the quarter known as Asher. The major part of this temple was built under Amenhotep III, but later kings, especially the Ptolemies, also delighted in honouring Mut, the Great Mother.

KHONSU

Khonsu was the son of Amun and Mut. He was depicted as a mummified youth holding in his hands a crook, a flail and a *waas*-sceptre (1). Like Ptah, he wears a *menat*-necklace; and on his head he wears the side-lock of youth, and a crescent and full moon, for he was a moon-god and as such rivalled only by Thoth.

It used to be thought that Khonsu's name derived from the words for placenta (*kh*, pronunciation unknown) and king (*nesu*) and that he was the personification of the royal placenta, which was preserved after the birth of the king, wrapped in a cloth and fixed to the top of a pole, to become one of the four standards that were carried in procession before the king. This idea is now generally rejected in favour of the interpretation that Khonsu's name is derived from the verb 'to cross over', thus giving his name the meaning 'He-who-traverses-(the-sky)', which seems an appropriate appellation for a moon-god.

As a moon-god, Khonsu helped Thoth to reckon time, and under his influence, 'women conceived and cattle multiplied their young'. He was also a god of healing. Although Khonsu had many sanctuaries throughout Egypt, his cult-centre and principal place of worship was at Thebes, where he had a temple within the precincts of the Temple of Amun at Karnak.

Khonsu's fame as a god of healing is recorded on a stele that was found in his temple at Thebes, and which is now in the Bibliothèque Nationale in Paris. The stele purports to have been erected in the reign of Ramesses II but was probably set up over two hundred years later in Dynasty XXI. The story on the stele tells of how Ramesses II marched into Naharin (which lay between the Tigris and the Euphrates) on his annual tour of inspection of the Empire. The prince of Bekhten brought his daughter and presented her to the king who was so pleased with the maiden that he made her his wife and gave her the Egyptian name of Neferu-Re.

In the fifteenth year of his reign, Ramesses went to Thebes to celebrate the Festival of *Ipet* (p. 143). Whilst he was there, a messenger came from Bekhten to say that the younger sister of Queen Neferu-Re, Bentresh, was ill. And so His Majesty sent one of his most learned men, Dehuty-em-heb, to Bekhten, to see what was wrong with Bentresh. Dehuty-em-heb discovered that the princess was possessed by an evil spirit and that he was powerless to help her.

In the twenty-sixth year of Ramesses' reign, a second envoy arrived from Bekhten, seeking help for the ailing princess. This time, Ramesses commanded that the statue of Khonsu, which normally lived in his temple at Karnak, should be sent to Bentresh. Accordingly, Khonsu was sent in a large ship which had five boats as escort, and equipped with a state chariot and numerous horses, so that he might make the journey to Bekhten by sea and by land.

Khonsu arrived in Bekhten after a journey of one year and five months. He was taken straight to the princess; and she was healed immediately. On seeing this, the prince of Bekhten resolved to keep Khonsu with him in Bekhten, and Khonsu was detained there for three years and nine months! However, the prince was frightened one night by a dream in which Khonsu appeared as a golden hawk and flew away to Egypt. And so he allowed Khonsu to return to Thebes, where he was welcomed home amidst great rejoicing.

Khonsu's fame as a healer lasted until the Ptolemaic period. When Ptolemy IV was afflicted with a serious illness, he appealed to Khonsu of Thebes, who intervened (although in what way we do not know) and cured His Majesty, who everafter called himself 'Beloved of Khonsu who protects His Majesty and drives away evil spirits'.

ATEN

Aten, or 'the Sun's Disk', is inextricably bound up with King Akhenaten who ruled Egypt for seventeen years or so in the fourteenth century BC, during what has become known as the 'Amarna Period', which is now a byword for both religious revolution and a distinctive style in art.

No other ruler of Ancient Egypt, and few rulers in the entire ancient world, have elicited as much attention as Akhenaten. On the surface, he is a figure sympathetic to modern man; indeed, James Henry Breasted, the founder of American Egyptology, hailed him as the 'first individual in history', a man whose appeal stretches over the millenia. The reason for this is not difficult to find. The kings of Egypt, in their own time, were presented to the world as giants among men, great conquerors who trampled on their enemies, the chosen of the gods with whom they communed. If they had any physical imperfections or human failings, these were never mentioned. For only a brief period, during Dynasty XII, were sculptors allowed to portray the ruler suffering the burden of office, the stresses of which can be seen in the lined, weary expression on the royal face. At all other times, the king was portrayed as the god he was believed to be, confident, untouched by human cares or even feelings, superhuman.

Akhenaten, however, broke with the traditions of more than 1,000 years. He allowed himself to be portrayed kissing his wife in public or chucking her under the chin; sitting her on his lap; dandling his children (and those children daughters rather than the usually preferred sons) on his knee. He is seen in numerous scenes of family intimacy playing the part of a loving husband and doting father, a dutiful son.

Not least of the aspects of Akhenaten that have caught the imagination of modern men is the fact that the wife with whom he apparently shared a life of conjugal bliss was Nefertiti, whose timeless beauty has transcended the ages through the celebrated portrait-bust of her now in Berlin Museum. Akhenaten is credited with having written poems in praise of Aten, the most famous of which is the Great Hymn to Aten which has been compared to Psalm 104. He is said to have inspired a new style in art which ignored old conventions in favour of 'truth' and a new honesty in revealing the deformities of its originator. Above all, Akhenaten is admired by those who do not feel comfortable with Egypt's polytheism for having replaced the many gods of his land with one god, monotheism being more acceptable to many people today, and even more so to the many influential Egyptologists of the last century who were committed Christians.

Many scholars have viewed Akhenaten as a great mystic, the first monotheist in history. Freud maintained that he was the inspiration for the monotheism of Moses. Breasted claimed that he was

> such a spirit as the world had never seen before, a brave soul . . . stepping out from the long line of conventional and colorless Pharaohs that he might disseminate ideas far beyond and above the capacity of his age to understand.

Arthur Weigall, whose publications in the early years of the present century helped to popularize Akhenaten, wrote:

> For once we may look right into the mind of a King of Egypt and may see something of its working and all that is there observed is worthy of admiration.

Others have not been so enthusiastic. To some, Akhenaten, far from being a man in advance of his time, a forerunner of Christ, was a fanatic (A.H. Gardiner); or a religious maniac (J. Pendlebury); and, as a king, deserving of nothing but censure (S.R.K. Glanville).

Even allowing for the modern fashion of debunking heroes, there is evidence enough to show that Akhenaten was not such a revolutionary or inspired figure as previous generations have believed, although such evidence as there is has not been easily come by. The ancient records of Akhenaten's reign are scanty and even more ambiguous than is the case with some other periods of Egyptian history, and are subject to much and varied interpretation.

Whether or not Akhenaten 'invented' the Amarna style of art, or whether this genuinely distinctive style was largely a natural development of traditional Egyptian art, perhaps showing some Cretan influence, it is nevertheless an extremely attractive, sometimes exquisite, genre. At first glance, it seems to be original in its realism and naturalness. However, all the old Egyptian principles and conventions of art are still there, especially in the canon of proportion employed in the drawing of the human figure, and in the convention that the most important person in any group should be depicted larger in scale than the others. The figure of the king himself is shown with all its deformities—the prognathous jaw, the protruding belly, the bulbous hips; and they are often reproduced in depictions of his family or his courtiers, presumably in obsequious deference to the King. This may be 'realism', at least in the case of Akhenaten himself, or 'naturalism'; equally, it may be said to be just a different convention. Akhenaten may not have invented the Amarna style, but at the least he permitted it.

As far as Akhenaten's family life is concerned, that, too, may not have been as idyllic as at first appears. For many people today, the fact that he married his own daughter, Meritaten, had a child by her, passed her on to Smenkare (who was probably his own brother and therefore her uncle), married his daughter, Ankhesenpaaten, and had a daughter by her, tarnishes Akhenaten's image as the devoted husband of the beautiful Nefertiti, although the marriage between father and daughter, when that father was the king, was quite normal to the Ancient Egyptians.

Above all, it is Akhenaten's reputation as the inventor of the one god, Aten, that suffers most when the evidence is examined.

The word *aten* had been in use since at least the Middle Kingdom, with the earliest reference so far discovered being in one of the Coffin Texts. Examples of it are found in the great narrative text of the Middle Kingdom known as the Story of Sinuhe, in which a king is described as dying and 'being united with the sun'; and which gives the text of a letter that Sinuhe sends to his king in which he says: 'the sun rises at your pleasure'. In both cases, the word used for 'sun' is *aten* rather than the more usual *re*. The chief source for the Story of Sinuhe, Papyrus Berlin 10499, uses the word *aten* in the first example with the sign for god, ⌐ , appended to it; a secondary source, an ostracon in the Ashmolean Museum in Oxford, uses the god sign for the second example also.

It seems certain, therefore, that the Egyptians had a sun-god called 'Aten' in the Middle Kingdom if not before. In Dynasty XVIII, more is heard of Aten. He probably became a member of the Egyptian pantheon some time during the reign of Thothmes III, or perhaps of his son, Amenhotep II. Thothmes III's grandson, Thothmes IV, issued a commemorative scarab on which Aten appears as a war-god who goes in front of the king to give him victory. In the reign of Amenhotep III, Aten was further honoured. One of the epithets of the king himself was *Tekhen-Aten*, 'Radiance of Aten', a term found also as the name of a company of the Royal Bodyguard; a town; a lake; the

King's State Barge. Amenhotep III seems to have favoured the worship of Aten. It was left to his son, Amenhotep IV (Akhenaten; p. 150), however, to develop the worship of the god.

The so-called revolution of Akhenaten is now generally thought to have been a political rather than a religious movement, a reaction to events outside Egypt. Thothmes III and Amenhotep II were great warriors who were able to take advantage of conditions in the Near East during their reigns, when many countries and petty states in the region were weak and ripe for conquest. Only Mitanni, which lay between the Tigris and the Euphrates, posed a problem for Egypt.

Thothmes III and his successors poured much of the booty brought back from their Near Eastern campaigns into the coffers of Amun (p. 140); and the resulting growth in the power and wealth of his priesthood eventually weakened the monarchy. At the same time, foreign influences were brought into Egypt from her new 'Empire', and also from further afield, from places such as Crete; more especially, 'new men' from the countries invaded by Egypt were given positions at Court.

When Amenhotep III came to the throne, the situation in the Near East had changed. Mitanni was no longer a threat to Egypt but rather her ally, being threatened by the rise of the Assyrians. Egypt's chief enemies were the Hittites. Although their land lay far to the north of Egypt (in what is now Turkey), the Hittites fomented rebellion amongst the princes of Egypt's Empire in the Near East. The existence of that Empire was threatened unless Egypt were prepared to fight for it. Unfortunately, Amenhotep III and his son were not much given to the pursuit of war, and were prepared to let the Empire fend for itself.

From the very beginning of his reign, Amenhotep III had flouted tradition. Before his time, it had been the custom for a son of the reigning king to marry the king's eldest daughter, who was the royal heiress and through whom the royal line was carried. This royal heiress was called the God's Wife of Amun (not to be confused with the later Divine Wife, p. 144) and by marriage with her a prince legitimised his claim to the throne. Amenhotep III did not marry the Royal Heiress; instead, he married Tiy, a noblewoman, and from that time on, the position of God's Wife of Amun fell into disuse, for Amenhotep III's son, Amenhotep IV, did not marry the royal heiress either.

Although the King of Egypt was thought to be a god, he was not usually worshipped as one until after his death. Amenhotep III was actively deified in his own lifetime, not in Egypt proper but in Nubia, where at Soleb he built a temple dedicated to himself as 'Lord of

Nubia', and in which he can be seen in reliefs making offerings to his deified self.

Amenhotep III's son went even further than his father in his challenge to the established gods of Egypt. He chose to deal with the threat posed to his throne, by Amun especially, by favouring a rival god. And, in a reversal of the age-old device employed by a ruler with problems at home, that is, the distraction of his people by means of a war against a foreign enemy, Amenhotep IV (Akhenaten) distracted attention from trouble in the Empire by initiating action at home against the gods of Egypt.

His choice of weapon for this action was the sun. The cult of the sun was a very ancient one in Egypt: its symbolism could be understood by everybody even if the remoteness of the sun did not endear its cult to all. There had always been an incipient monotheism in Egypt, for the Egyptians were accustomed to having local gods who syncretised with others from time to time. Because every local god in Egypt was identified in the minds of his followers with the state god, in essence this meant that each Egyptian could chose to worship one god made up of his own local god and whichever deity was the state god at the time. In practice, this did not happen, for the Egyptians tended to allot different functions to different gods. However, in Dynasty XVIII, the theoretically possible 'one god' was Re, the sun-god, for by that time it had become the custom for lesser deities to syncretise with Re: even the powerful Amun was known as Amen-Re (p. 141).

The sun-god chosen by Amenhotep IV, however, was not Re but Aten. Aten represented the physical power of the sun's disk, the life-giving properties of the sun, which were omnipresent. It had been the custom to depict the Aten as a man with the head of a falcon surmounted by a sun's disk—not dissimilar from Re-Horakhty. Early in Amenhotep IV's reign, however, the iconography of Aten underwent a change.

The inspiration for this change perhaps dates back to the reign of Amenhotep II. On the stele he erected in front of the Sphinx at Giza (p. 111), the sun is depicted with two arms descending from its disk to embrace the royal cartouche. The Aten of Amenhotep IV is depicted as a solar disk with many rays depending from it, each ray terminating in a hand, with some of the hands holding *ankh*-signs (☥), symbolizing the giving of life.

For the first four years of his reign, Amenhotep made no untoward move. Then, in his fifth year, the King changed his name from Amenhotep (Amun-is-satisfied) to Akh-en-aten, which is often translated as 'Beneficial-to-the-Aten', although a better rendering of the name might be 'Glorious-Spirit-of-Aten'.

4 Part of a limestone relief, now in Cairo Museum, from the Great Temple at Amarna showing Akhenaten and Nefertiti worshipping the Aten. The rays descending from the disk of the Aten terminate in hands, some of which hold the symbol ankh *(life)*

From the fifth year of Akhenaten's reign, the didactic name of Aten, that is, the name which elaborates on the basic appellation Aten in order to reflect what was perceived to be the true character of the god, was divided into two parts, with each part inscribed inside a cartouche, as though Aten were an earthly king. Aten is given regnal years which are identical with those of Akhenaten. And together, the two kings, Akhenaten and Aten; or the two gods, Aten and Akhenaten, celebrate their joint jubilee. From then on, great emphasis was placed on the kingship of Aten. Year five also saw the naturalistic style of Amarna art taken to extremes. The figures of Akhenaten became grotesque, almost caricatures. This was perhaps done to emphasise the break with the past.

An even more effective break was achieved in the following year, when Akhenaten moved his capital to the new city which he had had built between Memphis and Thebes, on a site that was virgin and therefore not contaminated by any of Aten's rival gods. This site is now known as Tell el-Amarna: it is not a tell, which is a mound, but the term was used in the past because of a confusion with the name of the local village, Et Till. El-Amarna is derived from the name of a local tribe, the Beni Amran. Akhenaten named his new city *Akhet-Aten*, 'Horizon-of-Aten'.

After the move to *Akhet-Aten*, Aten was supreme: Akhenaten even began to build a temple to Aten in Thebes, in the precincts of the Temple of Amun itself, although he had not yet proscribed Amun or the other gods.

In the ninth year of his reign, Akhenaten made a change in the didactic name of Aten. The earlier form of the name reads

> *Long live Re-Horakhty who rejoices in the horizon*
> followed by
> *In his name of Shu who is Aten.*
> The later form of the name reads
> *Long live Re ruler of the Two Horizons who rejoices in the horizon*
> and
> *In his name of Re the father who has come as Aten.*

The later name reflects a tightening-up of the religion. Shu and Re-Horakhty are dropped from the name and replaced by Re alone, Re being considered to be a more pure form of the sun who was Aten. Amun was a casualty of the tightening-up: his temples were closed down.

Even before the move to *Akhet-Aten*, Aten had become a trinity consisting of Re—the primordial god, the demi-urge—as the father; Aten—visible to man in the form of the sun's disk—as the physical expression of the father; and Akhenaten, the physical manifestation on earth of both Re and Aten. Akhenaten was the son of Re, the son of Aten; but at the same time, he was the father of both; and further, he *was* both Re and Aten.

This trinity which was at the same time a unity was worshipped in the Temple of the Aten. There, the High Priest was called the High Priest of Akhenaten, indicating that the King himself was worshipped. Atenism was a very exclusive religion. Only the King and the royal family were ever depicted worshipping him, and it is to them alone that Aten ever holds out the sign of life. The ordinary Egyptian was expected to worship Aten through the medium of the King; and to accept Akhenaten as his personal god.

But Egyptians had always found comfort in their own local gods; and, for a long time, had believed that Osiris offered them the hope of a better life to come. Akhenaten swept away Osiris and the other gods from the official state religion and put nothing in their place. It is not

155

surprising, therefore, that the worship of Aten held no appeal for the ordinary Egyptian; and that it was only at *Akhet-Aten* that Aten held sway with any conviction.

Even before Akhenaten died (probably in the seventeenth year of his reign), Atenism was dying. His successor, Smenkare, made no attempt to perpetuate the cult: he abandoned *Akhet-Aten* in favour of Thebes, leaving the city of Aten to crumble away, and made his peace with the old religion and with Amun in particular. Scarcely had he done so than he, too, was dead: and his successor, Tutankhamun, having changed his name from Tut-ankh-Aten (Living-image-of-Aten) to Tut-ankh-Amun (Living-image-of-Amun), issued the decree that reinstated Amun in all his glory, thus completing the triumph of Amun over Aten.

Tutankhamun spent the remaining nine years of his short reign restoring the temples of the old gods throughout Egypt, but paying particular attention to Thebes; he was the king who 'spent his life making images of the gods'. However, he did not forget Aten entirely; and on the back of the great golden State Throne that was found in his tomb there is a relief which shows Aten holding out his rays to the young king and his wife, who was none other than Ankhesenpaaten (She-lives-in-the-Aten), the daughter and wife of Akhenaten, who had changed her name to Ankhesenamun (She-lives-in-Amun) on her marriage to Tutankhamun.

Akhenaten's reign was disastrous for Egypt's Empire. Although Aten was supposed to shine in his beneficence on all mankind, Akhenaten ignored the people of his Empire and left them to their fate at the hands of the Hittites and their allies. Akhenaten became known as 'the Heretic'; and when Horemheb came to the throne some fifteen years after Akhenaten's death, he dated his reign from the last year of Amenhotep III with the intention of expunging from Egyptian annals all memory of the Heretic King and his successors, whom he considered to be tainted with the Atenist heresy.

In spite of the work that has been undertaken at Amarna since it was first visited by Sir John Wilkinson in AD 1824, work that is still going on under the aegis of the Egypt Exploration Society, there are still many unresolved problems concerning the Amarna Period, not least the puzzle of the cause of Akhenaten's seeming deformities; the date of his death, and that of Nefertiti; the place of their burial; his relationship to Tutankhamun. These, and other vexing questions about this perenially fascinating yet tantalizingly ill-documented period may never be answered.

Even the nature of Aten himself, as envisaged by Akhenaten, is not entirely clear. The fullest statement of what Akhenaten thought about his god is found at Amarna in the tomb constructed for Ay, later to be King and actually buried at Thebes: it is the beautiful poem known as the Great Hymn to Aten, a work that goes some way towards explaining the appeal of the Amarna Period:

How beautiful is your appearance on the horizon of heaven,
O Living Aten who creates life.
When you rise on the eastern horizon
You fill every land with your beauty.
You are beautiful and great, gleaming high over every land.
Your rays, they embrace the earth
To the furthest limits of what you have created.
You are Re; you conquer them all,
Making them subject to your beloved son.
You are far away yet your rays are upon earth;
You are on the faces of men yet your paths are unknown.

When you set on the western horizon
The earth is in darkness in the manner of the dead
Who sleep in their chambers,
Their heads covered
And no eye seeing its fellow.
All their possessions could be stolen, even though they are under
    their heads,
And they would know it not.
Every lion comes forth from its den
And all snakes are ready to bite,
For darkness is the only illumination
And the earth is silent,
For he who created it rests in his horizon.

Day dawns when you rise on the horizon,
You shine by day as Aten
Who dispels the darkness.
When you send forth your sunbeams
The Two Lands are festive,
The people awake and rise to their feet
For you have roused them.
Their bodies are washed
And they don their clothing;
Their arms are upraised in adoration at your appearance.

The whole world goes about its work;
All cattle rest in their pastures;
Trees and vegetation are verdant;
Birds fly up from their nests, their wings raised in adoration of your
    Ka;

Goats all jump on their feet and
Everything that flys and flutters lives when you shine upon it.
Boats sail upstream, and downstream likewise,
And all roads are open because you have arisen.
The fish in the river leap before your face,
And your rays are in the midst of the sea.

You are the one who causes women to be fecund,
Who makes seed in men,
Who gives life to a son in his mother's womb,
Who soothes him with whatever dries his tears
By acting as his nurse even in the womb,
Who gives the breath of life to everything that he has made.

When he emerges from the womb
To breathe on the day of his birth,
You open his mouth wide and supply what it needs.
The chick in the egg cheeps whilst still in the shell
For you have given it breath therein so that it might live.
You make for it the strength
With which it breaks it, namely the egg,
And it emerges from the egg at the appointed hour
To cheep and run on its feet as soon as it issues therefrom.

How legion are your works
That are hidden from the face of men.
O Sole God, who is like none other,
You made the earth according to your will, alone,
Men, cattle and all beasts,
Everything on earth that walks upon feet,
Everything above that flies with its wings,
Foreign lands, Syria, Kush
And the land of Egypt.

You set every man in his place and supply his needs,
Everyone has his provisions
And his allotted life-span.
Their tongues are diverse in speech
And their appearance likewise;
Their skins are different for you have differentiated the peoples.

It is in the Underworld that you make the Nile
And bring it forth at your will
So that Mankind might live:
For you have made them for yourself,

O Lord of them all, who grows weary on their behalf,
O Lord of every land, who shines upon them.

All distant lands, you make whatever they need to live on.
You have set a Nile in the sky
So that it may descend for them
And make waves upon the mountains like the sea,
So that their fields may be watered in their townships.

How marvellous are your schemes, O Lord of Eternity.
The heavenly Nile is what you have created for foreign peoples
And for all the game in the desert that walk upon feet;
But the (real) Nile comes forth from the Underworld for Egypt.

Your rays nourish every field
And when you rise, they live and flourish for you.
It is in order to sustain all that you have created that you have
made the seasons:
Winter to cool them
And the heat (of Summer) so that they may taste you.
You have made the sky afar off in order to shine therein
And to see all that you have made,
You alone, rising in your form of the living Aten,
Appearing and shining,
Far off, yet close at hand.
From out of yourself alone you have made myriad forms—
Cities, towns, fields, roads and river.
All eyes see you before them,
For you are Aten the daylight over the earth.
Even when you are done, your eye (still) exists
For you have created their forms.
If you did not see (damaged)

You are in my heart,
There is none other that knows you
Except your son Nefer-kheperu-re Wa-en-re (i.e. Akhenaten),
Whom you have acquainted with your plans and your power.
The earth exists in your hand, just as you have made it.
When you rise, it lives:
When you set, it dies.
You yourself are Lifetime
And it is by you that men live.
Eyes gaze upon your beauty until you set,
But when you set in the west, all work is laid aside.
When you rise again, you make .... grow for the king.

Movement has been in every leg
Since you founded the earth.
You have raised up (its inhabitants)
For your son who came forth from your flesh—
The King of Upper and Lower Egypt, who lives on Truth,
The Lord of the Two Lands, *Nefer-kheperu-re Wa-en-re* (Beautiful-
   are-the-Forms-of-Re, Sole-One-of-Re);
The Son of Re, who lives on Truth,
Lord of Diadems, Akhenaten, whose life is long;
And for the Great Royal Wife, his beloved,
The Mistress of the Two Lands, *Nefer-neferu-Aten* (Glorious-are-
   the-Beauties-of-Aten),
Nefertiti, may she live and grow young for ever and ever.

PTAH

Ptah was one of the oldest deities of Egypt. In prehistoric times, he was probably worshipped as a fetish in the district that Menes eventually chose to be the site of the first capital of Egypt, Memphis. The earliest deities to be worshipped at Memphis were Ta-tanen, an earth-god, and Sokar, a god of the dead. When Ptah was first established in Memphis, he coalesced with Ta-tanen and Sokar, thus becoming an earth-god with funerary associations.

The standard depiction of Ptah shows him in human form, shrouded like a mummy. His hands, projecting through the mummy-wrappings, are clasped round *waas-* (⌙ : meaning dominion) and *djed-* (⌘ : meaning stability) signs held in front of his body; and sometimes they hold the traditional symbols of kingship, the crook and the flail, or the so-called 'keys of life', *ankh-* (⚲) signs, also. He has a wedge-shaped beard and a close-shaven head upon which he sometimes wears a disk set between two feathers. This feathered disk resembles the crown that Osiris borrowed from Andjety (p. 74). Ptah's shoulders are covered with a broad collar with a counterpoise made of the fertility amulet, *menat* (⟋), hanging from the base of his neck. He often stands upon a plinth shaped like ⟋ which is the hieroglyph for *maat*, Truth, and also a representation of the measuring rod used by workmen.

The original Memphite deity, the earth-god, Ta-tanen, whose name means the Risen Land, was, so his priests claimed, the personification of the Primaeval Mound that rose out of the waters of the Nun. This was presumably an attempt to claim a greater antiquity for their god over Atum of On, since the concept of the Primaeval Mound was first introduced by his priests. At Memphis, Ptah was considered to be the supreme Creator God who came into existence before both the Nun and the Primaeval Mound: hence, he was given the names Ptah-Nun and Ptah-Ta-tanen.

The story of the creation of the world told at Memphis is remarkable in that its concept of the theogony of Ptah is a highly spiritual one, unlike the grosser acts of creation attributed to Ptah's contemporary, Atum. Ptah created the world by thought and tongue whereas Atum created it by masturbation or expectoration.

The Memphite Doctrine was probably determined right at the beginning of Egyptian history. When, in 3100 BC, Menes made Memphis the capital of his newly-united land, he determined that his new city should become the religious as well as the political centre of Egypt, and saw that one of the means to this end was to promote Ptah as chief god of Memphis and Egypt, and rival of Re-Atum of Heliopolis.

Although the Memphite Doctrine was one of the oldest in Egypt, our version of it is a relatively late one, dating to the eighth century BC rather than to the end of the fourth millenium, and is to be found inscribed on a large slab of black basalt that was discovered in the nineteenth century AD in the centre of Cairo, being used as a millstone. This basalt slab, or stele, was presented to the British Museum in 1805 by Earl Spencer: it is known today as the Shabaka Stone, after the twenty-fifth Dynasty king who ordered it to be made.

The inscription on the Shabaka Stone is badly worn but enough remains to give a clear idea of Memphite theology. The opening lines on the stele state that it was copied from an old inscription, written on papyrus (or perhaps wood), which had become worm-eaten. King Shabaka (716–702 BC) decreed that a fair copy of this ancient text should be cut on a large slab of black stone so that it could be erected as an offering to Ptah in his temple at Memphis.

The vocabulary and script of the text on the Shabaka stone is archaic; the grammar, however, is not. There is no evidence that in the Archaic Period, the period to which the original of the text on the Stone purports to date, the Egyptians could do more than write short, simple, unconnected sentences. It was only by Dynasty IV that they had developed the ability to write using a more complex grammar. It is doubtful, therefore, whether the text on the Shabaka Stone, which does employ fairly complex sentence constructions and verb-forms, could have been copied from a document composed as early as the Archaic Period; and it is more probable that it was written towards the end of the Old Kingdom as a form of propaganda against Ptah's then rival, Re.

The Shabaka Stone inscription says that in the beginning, chaos reigned. Then Ptah appeared on the Primaeval Mound as a god in whom were embodied several forms: Ptah-Nun; Ptah-Ta-tanen; Ptah-Nefertem and five more, the names of which have been lost.

By the effort of his heart and mind, Ptah created Nun and his female counterpart, Nunet. In their turn, Nun and Nunet brought forth Atum, who became the Thought of Ptah. Then Thoth came into being as the Tongue of Ptah. Thus did the priests of Ptah give their god an ascendency over his two chief rivals—he had existed before they did, and, indeed, was their creator, just as he was the creator and mover of the innermost being of every living thing:

> And it came to pass that Heart and Tongue gained power over every other member, teaching that he, Ptah, was the heart in every breast and the tongue in every mouth of gods as well as of men, of cattle and of all living things.

Memphite Theology teaches that Ptah's Company of Gods form part of him as his teeth and lips. The teeth correspond to the seed of Atum and the lips to his hands. But whereas the priests of Heliopolis taught that the world was created through masturbation or spitting, those of Memphis insisted on a far more intellectual concept: Ptah's teeth and lips are part of that great mouth which gave all things their names:

> Every divine word came into being through that which the Heart of Ptah thought and the Tongue of Ptah commanded. Thus every kind of work and every handicraft, and everything done with the arms, and every motion of the legs and every action of all the limbs takes place through this command, which is conceived by the heart [or mind: the Egyptians thought that the heart was the seat of man's being and of his intelligence] and brought about by the tongue.

The Memphite Theology was an intellectual concept rather than a warmly-felt belief. It holds a great appeal for modern theologians but never made a real impact on the ordinary Egyptian, who preferred his religion to have a more concrete expression.

Ptah was more than a creator-god. He was credited with the invention of crafts: and his High Priest was called 'Lord of the Master Craftsmen'. The Greeks identified Ptah with their own blacksmith god, the lame Hephaistos; and the Romans thought of him as Vulcan. Ptah was also the patron deity of kings. As such, he was closely connected with the ceremony which, in dynastic times, replaced the prehistoric ritual of the slaughter of the tribal chieftain whose powers were weakened with age. This ceremony, the *Heb-Sed* or Jubilee, was usually celebrated during the thirtieth year of a king's reign and then repeated at frequent intervals. It was designed to allow a king to renew his vital forces by magical means.

One of the rituals of the *Heb-Sed* was a symbolic 'race' run by the king around the walls of his capital city. During this 'race' the king took possession of his city; and incidentally proved that he was fit to rule. If he felt unable to complete the run himself, he was allowed to employ a runner! During Dynasty III, King Djoser built his tomb at Sakkara in the form of a six-stepped pyramid. The pyramid was at the centre of a complex of buildings and courtyards the whole of which was surrounded by a white limestone wall, some 10 metres high, with a peripheral length of about 1,600 metres, built in imitation of the white-painted mud-brick walls of his capital city, Memphis.

The space between the pyramid and its enclosure-wall was filled, on the southern and eastern sides, with the ceremonial buildings in which the King celebrated his Jubilee, in this world and the next. The culmination of the ceremony was reached when the King, or his substitute, ran round the enclosure-wall. Beneath the southern section of the wall lies a 'tomb' in which Djoser is depicted on blue faience tiles eternally running his *Heb-Sed* race.

Ptah was at the pinnacle of importance during the first three Dynasties of Egyptian history when the kings of Memphis, the site of his cult, flourished. From Dynasty IV, however, he began a period of decline which lasted until the New Kingdom, when he was again elevated to the status of a state god.

During the New Kingdom, the chief centre of the cult of Ptah was, as always, Memphis. But he was worshipped elsewhere also, particularly at Abydos and Thebes; and in Nubia. In Dynasty XIX, Ramesses II paid special attention to Ptah by building for him temples in Nubia at Gerf Hussein, El-Derr and Abu Simbel. These three temples were all affected during the last few years by the building of the High Dam at Aswan, with Gerf Hussein disappearing under the waters of Lake Nasser.

At Gerf Hussein, Ptah was worshipped alongside Ptah-Ta-tanen, Hathor and Ramesses II himself. At El-Derr, which was dismantled and reerected near Amada in AD 1964, he was worshipped together with Re-Horakhty, Amen-Re and Ramesses II. And at Abu Simbel, perhaps the most famous of the Nubian temples, which has been dismantled and reerected on high ground near the original site, he can still be seen in the restored temple as a statue sitting alongside images of Ramesses II, Amen-Re and Re-Horakhty within the innermost sanctuary.

The city of Memphis remained throughout Egyptian history the main home of Ptah. When Menes first built his new capital, he called it *Ineb-Hedj*, the White Wall, by which he probably meant the royal residence rather than the city wall. Ptah was often referred to as 'He-who-is-south-of-his-wall', and, indeed, his temple was built to the south of the White Wall.

During the Old Kingdom, kings built their pyramids near the White Wall. It is the name of one of these pyramids, *Men-nefer* ('the Established and Beautiful Pyramid'), built in Dynasty VI by Pepi I, that was adopted eventually as the name of the whole city. *Men-nefer*, which in Coptic was pronounced, and spelled, *Menfe*, was turned by the Greeks into Memphis.

Memphis lost its status as capital of Egypt when the Middle Kingdom kings chose Lisht as their capital; in the New Kingdom, Thebes enjoyed the position. Memphis, however, remained throughout Egyptian history one of the foremost cities of Egypt. It was always an administrative centre, and the seat of an important Royal Residence.

At Memphis, shrines and temples were erected for many deities; but it was always the Temple of Ptah which was considered to be the most important, worthy of enlargement and embellishment by successive generations of kings. It is the name given to the Temple of Ptah during the New Kingdom—the Mansion of the Soul of Ptah, which in Egyptian is *Hoot-Ka-Ptah*—that eventually was taken by the Greeks and applied to the whole land as far south as Aswan, thus giving rise to the name by which we call the country, Egypt. In the Late Period, *Hoot-Ka-Ptah* was probably pronounced 'Hi-Ku-Ptah', which the Greeks turned into 'Ai-gy-ptos'. Today, the Temple of Ptah, once one of the largest in Egypt, lies under the modern village of Mit-Rahina.

Ptah was worshipped in animal as well as in human form. The Egyptians regarded bulls as symbols of procreation and virility, and, since prehistoric times, a bull had been regarded as sacred in the district around Memphis. When Ptah became god of the city, the local sacred bull was associated with him: it became a manifestation of Ptah, his deputy, his 'blessed soul', and, as such, it was given the name *Hap* (now known by the Greek version of the name, Apis). According to Aelian,[12] the cult of Apis was established at Memphis by Menes and lasted until Graeco-Roman times.

The Apis Bull was black with distinctive markings on his hide: he had white spots on his neck and back, a white blaze in the shape of a triangle on his forehead. He was never depicted as a human-being but always retained his animal form.

Only one bull at a time was regarded as Apis rather than the whole species. The particular bull was kept in a sacred stall immediately south of the great Temple of Ptah at Memphis. He was equipped with a harem of cows and often lived to a great age. People from all over the land came to bring him gifts and to consult his oracle.

When an Apis Bull died, an event which occurred on average once every fourteen years, the search was mounted for his replacement.

Just as the lamas of Tibet used to travel round their country seeking the boy destined to become Dalai Lama, so the priests of Apis travelled throughout Egypt searching for a black bull-calf whose hide bore the distinctive Apis markings. When the calf was found, he was taken back to Memphis amidst great rejoicing and installed as the new Apis. The calf's mother was cared for by priests until she died, when she was mummified and buried in a special gallery at Sakkara as 'Mother of the Apis'. The calf's owner was suitably rewarded.

Meanwhile, the dead Apis Bull had been taken to a special embalming house within the temple enclosure. The remains of one of these houses, built by Shoshenq I (945–924 BC), together with the great stone tables on which the dead bulls lay during the mummification process, can be seen today at Mit-Rahina. After mummification, the Apis Bull was taken to his tomb in the Royal Necropolis at Sakkara. The sites of these Apis tombs are known from about the reign of Amenhotep III (1402–1364 BC).

In Dynasty XIX, Ramesses II ordered the building of an underground gallery to house the mummified Apis Bulls. This gallery, known as the Lesser Vaults, is about 68 metres long. Large niches are carved into its walls, niches which once housed mummified Apis Bulls. The work of constructing the gallery was probably supervised by Khamwese, one of the sons of Ramesses II, in his capacity of High Priest of Ptah.

A second gallery, the Greater Vaults, was begun in Dynasty XXVI, and is 198 metres in length and cut at right angles to the earlier gallery. The first Apis to be buried there died in the 52nd year of the reign of Psammetichus I (612 BC). The gallery remained in use until the Graeco-Roman period, when it became especially popular during the reign of Ptolemy I who promoted the cult of Serapis (p. 87). Since Serapis was a composite deity formed from Osiris and Apis, naturally, the burial place of Apis became a place of pilgrimage for followers of the new god who lent his name to the Apis galleries so that they became known as the Serapeum.

In Dynasty XXX, Nectanebo I and Nectanebo II contributed an avenue of human-headed sphinxes to mark the path that led from Memphis to the Serapeum. It was one of these sphinxes, sticking up above the sand that had engulfed the Serapeum after it had fallen into disuse, that was supposed to have led Auguste Mariette to rediscover the site in AD 1850. When Mariette excavated the Serapeum, he found twenty-four basalt and granite sarcophagi still intact and in position: they had been emptied of their contents—mummified Apis Bulls—but their weight (up to seventy tons) had prevented their own removal.

Like many Egyptian gods, Ptah was given a wife and child. His vife was a goddess from the Eastern Delta, Sekhmet (p. 171), a lioness-goddess; and his son was Nefertem. Although in deference to his mother, Sekhmet, Nefertem was sometimes depicted as a man with a lion's head, he is more often shown in fully human form, as a youth seated upon a lotus blossom. On his head he wears either a crown composed of a lotus flanked by two plumes, with two *menat*-amulets suspended from them; or a lotus alone. The lotus links him with the sun (p. 59) and at Heliopolis he was regarded as the young sun. At Memphis, however, he was the son of Ptah and Sekhmet.

Ptah was thought to have another son by a woman called Khredu'ankh. This son was Imhotep, a real man who lived in Dynasty III and was a high official of King Djoser. Imhotep was a sage and magician; and, although his burial place is as yet undiscovered, he is almost certainly buried at Sakkara, near the Step Pyramid, the tomb that he is credited with having designed for his master, thus becoming the first named architect of stone buildings.

A statue base discovered near the entrance to the Step Pyramid enclosure, inscribed with Imhotep's name and titles, gives us some idea of the man's versatility:

> Chancellor of the King of Upper and Lower Egypt, the first after the King of Upper Egypt, administrator of the Great Palace, hereditary noble, High Priest of Heliopolis, Imhotep, the builder, the sculptor.

This statue base was also inscribed with one of Djoser's names: it is probably contemporaneous with the Step Pyramid.

Imhotep was traditionally supposed to have been the author of several books (long since disappeared) and was regarded as the patron of scribes. Typical statuettes of Imhotep show a shaven-headed man seated with a papyrus-roll spread open on his knees. It was the custom with scribes to sprinkle a few drops of water from their pots before they began work, in honour of Imhotep, the Sage, the Scribe.

A temple at Sakkara was dedicated to this most famous of scribes. It stood near the Serapeum and was especially popular as a place of pilgrimage in the Late Period. The Greeks called it the Aesculapion, an indication that they identified Imhotep (whom they called Imouthes) with their own great physician, Aesculapius. Imhotep's reputation as a god of healing brought sick people, especially cripples, from all over Egypt flocking to his temple at Sakkara, and shrines dedicated to him are found in temples such as Karnak, Deir el-Bahri, Deir el-Medina and Philae.

The cult of Ptah was popular only as long as the King of Egypt was his patron. The Memphite Theology held no great attraction for the ordinary Egyptian, who did not find the concept of the world being created by thought and tongue congenial, relying, as it does, on an effort of the imagination. By Dynasty IV, Re of Heliopolis had found favour with the king and had, therefore, become state god of Egypt. Meanwhile, Osiris was making headway in the affections of the Egyptians. By the end of the Old Kingdom, Ptah had been eclipsed.

There is some evidence, however, that the Egyptians continued to consider it worthwhile to make petition to him. At his temple in Memphis, a large number of votive tablets have been found, carved with representations of ears, or sometimes of eyes. Similar ear-tablets have been discovered in the temple at Deir el-Medina at Thebes. They are the ears of the god as Ptah-hearer-of-prayers, the stone ears of the god into which a petitioner could make his request for help in the confident expectation that Ptah was not inaccessible, that he would listen, something that the Egyptians did not normally expect a state god to do.

Ptah, although not the most popular of Egyptian deities, was never forgotten. It is perhaps appropriate, therefore, that Verdi, when he wrote '*Aida*' for the opening of the Suez Canal in AD 1871, should conclude the opera with the chorus: 'O mighty Ptah, life-giving spirit of the world, we invoke thee . . . O mighty Ptah!'

SOKAR

In prehistoric times, Sokar was probably worshipped somewhere in the area around Memphis in the form of a fetish. Later, he was considered to be incarnate in a species of hawk, possibly a peregrine falcon, and therefore took shape as a man with the head of a hawk. In the Old Kingdom, Sokar was normally represented sitting upon a throne holding the *waas*-sceptre and an *ankh*-sign in his hands. In the New Kingdom, he often appeared as a hawk-headed mummy holding a flail, a crook and a *waas*-sceptre.

The essential nature of Sokar is obscured by his early association with Ptah. However, the great annual festival celebrated in his honour took place in the fourth month of the seaon of *akhet*, that is, on the eve of the winter sowing. Two of the rituals performed during the festival were those of hoeing the earth and driving cattle, which would suggest that originally Sokar was an agricultural deity.

From the earliest times, Sokar was considered to be the guardian of the Memphite necropolis. It is ironic that a hawk-god should be connected with graves, since hawks are essentially creatures of light and air. However, the Memphite necropolis was in use for centuries before the city of Memphis was built, and Sokar's connection with it probably predates his manifestation as a hawk to a time when he was worshipped as a fetish. In addition, the Egyptians tended to bury their dead in the desert rather than in good, arable land, and hawks are often seen wheeling above the sand. Sokar, however, was not just a general necropolis-deity: he was more particularly associated with the darkness and decay of the tomb itself.

When Ptah became the principal god of Memphis, Sokar joined him there and fulfilled the role of funerary god to Ptah's creator-god. At the same time, he lost to Ptah one of his earliest functions as patron deity of artisans, and became more specifically the patron of goldsmiths.

Sokar had many sanctuaries in Lower Egypt, notably at *Restau* on the Giza necropolis and at *Pedjushe* on the Sakkara necropolis. In Dynasty XIX, he joined Ptah in Upper Egypt in the funerary temple that Seti I built at Abydos, the domain of the funerary-god *par excellence*, Osiris. The site of the chief shrine of Sokar, the *Shetayet*, is so far undiscovered. It was probably near the Temple of Ptah in Memphis; perhaps even within the precincts of that temple; and certainly close enough to it for the High Priest of Ptah to hold office in the Temple of Sokar also.

Early in the Old Kingdom, the proximity of the cult-centres of the two deities led Ptah's priests to claim that Ptah had created Sokar, and to link both gods under the compound name of Ptah-Sokar. By the end of the Old Kingdom, Ptah-Sokar had been eclipsed by another deity with funerary associations, Osiris. The similarity between the nature of Osiris and that of Sokar, both being agricultural deities who were connected with death, facilitated a link between them, and in the Middle Kingdom Ptah-Sokar became Ptah-Sokar-Osiris.

Ptah-Sokar-Osiris, whose popularity reached its height during the New Kingdom, was often represented as a squat male figure, rather like a pygmy, wearing a beetle on his head to indicate that he has creative powers similar to those of the god, Khepri. From the time that the city of Memphis was founded, a ceremony of 'going round the walls' of the city was enacted each year to mark the king's accession. This ritual was eventually incorporated into another ceremony in which Sokar was carried out of his temple to join the king in rites consisting of hoeing the earth and digging canals or ditches.

For this ceremony, the cultus statue of Sokar was placed in the portable shrine that was characteristic of Sokar, the *Henu*-barque. This boat was of a unique design: it had a high prow shaped like a horned, oryx-like animal; and a funerary chest, surmounted by a hawk, stood in the centre of it. The whole thing was set on the runners of a special sledge called the *mefekh*-sledge. Originally, it was dragged in procession on this sledge; eventually, however, the structure was placed upon carrying poles and transported on the shoulders of up to sixteen priests.

These two ceremonies eventually became the great Festival of Sokar, held annually on the 26th day of the fourth month of the *akhet* season from at least as far back as the early part of the Old Kingdom. The Festival took place not only in Memphis itself but also in the funerary temple of the king wherever that happened to be. In Dynasty XX, for instance, the Festival of Sokar was held in Ramesses III's mortuary temple of Medinet Habu in Western Thebes, where it was one of the most richly endowed of all the feasts celebrated in that temple.

By the Ptolemaic period, Sokar's festival had become assimilated with the Festival of Osiris; and Sokar himself had turned into little more than a variant of that ubiquitous god.

SEKHMET

Sekhmet, a leonine goddess whose name means 'the Powerful One', was worshipped wherever a wadi opened out at the desert edge, for, in Ancient Egypt, those were the places where lions might be found having come down from the desert to drink at water-holes on the edge of the cultivation; and to prey on cattle and sometimes on men. A late tradition held that the worship of Sekhmet was introduced into Egypt from the Sudan, where lions were more numerous. Her chief sanctuary, however, was at Memphis, where she was considered to be the wife of Ptah and the mother of Nefertem, thus taking her place in the Triad of Memphis.

Sekhmet, who was usually depicted as a woman with the head of a lioness, was believed to be a manifestation of the enraged Eye of Re who devoured the enemies of the Sun God. This fierce goddess was mistress of war and strife; she helped the king to slaughter his enemies against whom he was sometimes said to rage 'like Sekhmet'.

Paradoxically, she was also mistress of healing who drove away sickness. The bloodthirsty goddess who could kill could also cure. Just as this Lady of the Messengers of Death could visit them upon Egypt in the form of epidemics, so she could be persuaded to remove them through the performance of the rite of 'appeasing Sekhmet'. The title 'Priest of Sekhmet' came to mean 'doctor', possibly because her priests were entrusted with the task of driving out the evil spirits that the Ancient Egyptians thought were the causes of sickness; and who better to fight demons than the goddess of war.

Sekhmet was identified with several other goddesses, Hathor, Bastet, Mut and Pakhet (see below) among them. In the original version of how the Eye of Re destroyed his enemies, it was Hathor who played the role of Sekhmet (p. 62). Bastet was a more sympathetic form of Sekhmet in the shape of a cat. Mut was associated with Sekhmet when the worship of the Lioness was carried to Thebes; there, in the Temple of Mut at Karnak, Amenhotep III set up seated statues of Sekhmet, nearly six hundred of which are extant, thirty or so being in the British Museum: they are carved in grey diorite and average nearly two metres in height.

Pakhet was the local lioness-goddess of Beni Hasan, the necropolis of the Middle Kingdom nomarchs of the 16th Nome of Upper Egypt, the Oryx Nome, which lies on the east bank of the Nile some 23km south of el-Minya. In Dynasty XVIII, Hatshepsut built a temple just south of Beni Hasan which she dedicated to Pakhet, whose name means 'She-who-scratches'. The Greeks must have thought that Pakhet had more in common with the gentler Bastet than with the fierce Sekhmet for they called the place Speos Artemidos or 'the Cave of Artemis', the goddess they identified with Bastet.

In the Speos Artemidos, Pakhet was worshipped as the 'Goddess-of-the-mouth-of-the-wadi' and 'She-who-opens-the-ways-of-the-stormy-rains', epithets which could equally well be applied to the lioness-goddess *par excellence*, Sekhmet.

ANUBIS

Anubis was a very ancient Upper Egyptian god of the dead, who became identified at an early date with an even older deity, *Imy-wt*, 'He-who-is-in-his-mummy-wrappings'. The fetish of *Imy-wt*, consisting of a headless animal skin hanging from a pole, which held solutions for washing or embalming a dead body, became the fetish of Anubis.

Anubis was usually represented as a jackal-headed man. In southern Egypt, jackals are found to this day roaming the high ground at the desert edge, the very place where the Ancient Egyptians buried their dead. The jackal has a habit of prowling round the cemeteries, scavenging. What more natural, then, than that the Ancient Egyptians should associate him with death and go on from there to revere him out of fear that he might molest the dead in their graves.

Other jackal-gods such as Wepwawet (p. 81) were worshipped in Egypt; Anubis, however, was the most important of them. Although he was the totem deity of the 17th Upper Egyptian Nome (el-Qeis in Middle Egypt, which the Greeks called Cynopolis or City of the Dogs), from a very early date his worship extended throughout the whole of the land.

Before the advent of Osiris, Anubis was the great funerary-god and Judge of the Dead. In many Old Kingdom *mastaba*-tombs, the prayers for survival after death that were carved on the walls were addressed to Anubis in his capacity as the god who led the deceased to the Afterlife. When Osiris rose to prominence as chief mortuary-god, the priests of Heliopolis gave Anubis a place in their scheme of things as the bastard son of Osiris and Nephthys (p. 123) and the faithful protector of Isis. Anubis it was who embalmed the dead Osiris' body and wrapped him in bandages, thus making the first mummy.

At first, Anubis as mortuary-god was chiefly concerned with the king; gradually, however, he became the god of death for everyone. His four most important titles reflect his role: he was 'He-who-is-set-upon-his-mountain' (to guard the necropolis); 'Lord of the Necropolis'; 'Chief of the Divine Pavilion' (where mummification procedures were carried out); and 'He-who-is-in-his-mummy-wrappings'.

Because Anubis had prepared the mummy of Osiris, he became the patron of embalmers. In the necropolis of Memphis at Sakkara, the embalmers' quarters of at least the Late Period and the Ptolemaic era were specifically under the guardianship of Anubis, so much so that modern Egyptologists who have been excavating the area since the 1960s have named it the Anubieion.

It is thought that the priests in charge of preparing the body for burial wore jackal-headed masks in order to impersonate Anubis. Possibly the priests who conducted the burial ceremonies at the tomb also impersonated him, for on funerary papyri such as those belonging to Ani and Hunefer, Anubis is depicted holding the mummy of the deceased at the door of the tomb.

On arrival in the Afterlife, it was Anubis who guarded the scales in which the heart of the deceased was weighed at the Judgement of the Dead by Osiris. Anubis read the scales and the fate of the deceased depended upon his report, which was accepted without question by Osiris and the Assessor Gods.

Although Anubis is said to be a jackal-god, representations of him in wholly animal form sometimes show an animal that is more like a dog, a fox or a wolf. The Greek name for the city of the jackal-god, Wepwawet (p. 82), Lykopolis or Wolf City, illustrates the extent of the confusion that was felt.

Perhaps the most famous figure of Anubis was found at the entrance to the Treasury in the tomb of Tutankhamun, where a life-sized recumbent Anubis-animal, made of wood overlaid with black resin, lay upon a gilded shrine set upon four carrying poles. He was covered by a linen shirt dating to the seventh year of the reign of Akhenaten, under which a gossamer-thin linen shawl was tied at his throat, whilst around his neck, like a leash, was a linen scarf.

Tutankhamun's Anubis, like so many others, bears many features characteristic of a dog: long muzzle, eyes with round pupils, five-toed forefeet and four-toed hindfeet. But the tail, drooping down the side of the shrine, is long, straight; and club-shaped at the tip, more like the brush of a fox than the curved tail of a dog which is normally carried in an upright position rather than low down like that of a jackal or wolf or fox.

Howard Carter recorded[10] having seen two animals resembling this jackal-like dog, one in 1926, the other in 1928, but neither had the characteristic tail, a fact which led him to suppose that the original

Anubis-animal may have been a jackal crossed with a sub-genus of the canine family.

Whatever his origin, the ever-vigilant Anubis was deemed to be the lord of the necropolis who presided over burial rites and guarded the dead on their way to the Afterlife.

NEIT

Neit was a very ancient goddess whose cult-centre was at Sais in the Western Delta, on the right bank of the Rosetta branch of the Nile. The Ancient Egyptians probably pronounced her name 'Neet'; the Greeks later softened the final t to a th, and it is this pronunciation, 'Neeth', that is sometimes used today, with many writers spelling her name Neith. The standard depiction of the goddess shows her as a woman wearing the diadem associated with Lower Egypt, the Red Crown. The oldest name of this crown was 'Net' which leads one to suppose that Neit's name means 'She-of-the-Lower-Egyptian-Crown', making her the personification of the diadem.

There were two emblems sacred to Neit: one consisted of two arrows crossed in front of a shield; the other, ⤜⤛ , has often been said to be a shuttle, thus connecting Neit with weaving. However, the shape of the emblem is entirely wrong for it to have been a shuttle, which must surely taper at the ends to facilitate movement between the warp threads. Old Kingdom depictions of the object, which show it in detail, reveal that it represents two bows placed back-to-back in a case of some kind.

These ancient emblems of Neit, shield, arrows and bows, indicate that in predynastic times she must have been a goddess of hunting and warfare who only later became the personification of the Lower Egyptian Crown. Neit, however, had many aspects besides these.

She was a primaeval bisexual goddess who was said to have created the world and to be the virgin mother of the sun. A late version of how she accomplished this is found in the Temple of Khnum at Esna (p. 184). The Esna Creation Legend tells of how Neit emerged from the Primaeval Waters and brought into being the Primaeval Mound by uttering its name. She then rested on the mound, which later became the land upon which Esna was built. Next, Neit created light and the primordial gods, and prophesied the birth of a child, the sun. When this child appeared on the horizon, Neit was able to leave Esna and travel through Egypt to take her normal place at Sais in the Delta.

At an early date, the worship of Neit was widespread in the Delta and Lower Egypt, where she was regarded as the Great Mother Goddess, the patron of the North, with her crown, the *net*-crown, having been adopted as the symbol of sovereignty over Lower Egypt. When Menes united Upper and Lower Egypt, he adopted the title *nesu-bit*, which means, in effect, King of Upper and Lower Egypt, in other words, *nesu* 'He-who-belongs-to-the-reed' (symbol of Upper Egypt) and *bit* 'He-who-belongs-to-the-bee' (symbol of Lower Egypt). Why a reed and a bee should have been chosen as symbols of their respective halves of the country is not clear; however, in the case of the bee, it is known that the Temple of Neit at Sais was called 'the Mansion of the Bee' (*Hoot-bit*), and a connection between Neit and bees would have been ample reason for the bee to be chosen as the symbol of Lower Egypt. What this connection was between Neit and bees is as yet unknown—her sacred animal, kept in her temple at Sais, seems to have been a cat.

Menes married a princess of Lower Egypt named Neit-hotep (Neit-is-satisfied), one of the three queens in Dynasty I who had Neit as a component in their names, Her-neit (Pleasing-to-Neit) and Meryet-Neit (Beloved-of-Neit) being the other two. It is possible that the husbands of these demonstrably Lower Egyptian princesses married them in order to legitimize their rule in the North.

Menes' son, Hor-aha, built a temple for Neit at Sais, which is the oldest temple for which we have any direct evidence. The temple is recorded on an ivory label, found in AD 1900 by Petrie at Abydos, on which is engraved a stylised representation of a hut-shrine. The lattice-work hut is surrounded by a fence, also lattice; in front of the hut is a standard bearing the shield and arrows of Neit, and the entrance to the enclosure is marked by two masts with flags.

Neit's cult centre, Sais (*Sau* in Ancient Egyptian; today called Sa el-Hagar), was the capital of the 5th Nome of Lower Egypt, the Nome standard of which consisted of her emblem of two arrows crossed over a shield. The city rose to political prominence at the end of the eighth century BC, when, around 730, a local prince, Tefnakhte, challenged the Nubian kings of Dynasty XXV for supremacy in Lower Egypt. In 664 BC, Tefnakhte's successors, whom Manetho grouped into Dynasty XXVI, became the kings of Egypt, and Sais, their native city, became the capital of the country, the great city in which were built the temples and palaces of the rulers of the so-called Saite Dynasty, who were buried in the precincts of the Temple of Neit, their patron goddess.

The first king of Dynasty XXVI, Psammetichus I, drove out invading Assyrians and Nubians from Egypt, and having restored the country to a unified state, began a period in which every aspect of life in Egypt flourished. As patron goddess of the Dynasty, Neit prospered. Her shrines were embellished; but so also were those of other deities, including Amun, whose temples at Thebes were left under the direction of the Divine Wives of Amun (p. 144).

The Saite Period was a mixture of looking back to the past for inspiration for artistic and intellectual achievements; and an opening up of the country to Greek commerce and of the written language to a new cursive script, Demotic, which made use of an entirely new vocabulary which is obviously derived from the dialect of Egyptian that was spoken in the Delta. The Persian invasion of Egypt in 525 BC put an end to the Saite Period, which had achieved a renaissance in art, architecture and literature.

Neit was associated with several other deities, chiefly with Khnum, whom she made her deputy as creator-god; with Sobek, the crocodile-god (p. 121) whose mother she was said to be; with Osiris, as one of the four goddesses who protected sarcophagi and Canopic jars (p. 101); and with Amunet, the primordial goddess of Hermopolis (p. 180).

Although Neit herself was a significant figure in the Egyptian pantheon at an early date, she achieved the height of her popularity only very late. This popularity lasted from the Saite Period, through the Persian occupation when Neit continued to receive attention not only from Egyptians but also from the Greeks who lived in Egypt, to the time of the Macedonian Greeks who drove out the Persians from the country in 332 BC. The Greeks paid Neit the compliment of identifying her with their goddess of wisdom, Athena.

THOTH

Thoth was a lunar god worshipped in the form of an ibis (*Ibis religiosa*, the sacred ibis) or a baboon, and usually portrayed in reliefs as a man with the head of an ibis, often holding a reed pen in his hand. His cult dates at least to Dynasty I, if not before, for his standard appears on slate palettes of the predynastic period. In hieroglyphs, his name was written ⲭ, *Djhuty*, and is thought to mean 'He of *Djhut*', *Djhut* presumably being his place of origin. The whereabouts of *Djhut* is unknown, but it was probably in the Delta.

Very little information has survived concerning the progenitor of Thoth. One ancient legend says that he was the son of Horus who emerged from the forehead of Seth whom Horus had succeeded in impregnating with his seed by tricking him into swallowing it hidden in some lettuces. A late version of the legend modified it by making the seed of Horus appear on Seth's forehead as a golden disk which was seized by the already existing Thoth who placed it on his own head as an ornament (p. 120).

From early dynastic times, the main cult-centre of Thoth was a town in Middle Egypt that the Egyptians called *Khemenu*, or 'the Town of the Eight'. When Thoth first arrived there, he found several ancient deities already installed: a hare, a baboon and the eight frog- and serpent-gods after whom the town was named.

Thoth rapidly absorbed or replaced the indigenous deities of *Khemenu*. The hare, a goddess named Wenet, survived as the name of the Nome of which *Khemenu* was the capital, the Hare Nome, the 15th Nome of Upper Egypt, although she is sometimes regarded as a demon of the Underworld. The baboon became a representation of the spirit of Thoth and was incorporated into his cult. The eight gods became his Company, or Ogdoad.

The Ogdoad, which means 'group of eight', is the name given to the four pairs of deities who, according to tradition at *Khemenu*, represented the elemental forces that were in play before the creation of the world. The male halves of these pairs were frog-headed, the female halves, serpent-headed, and their names were: Nun and Nunet, the male and female personifications of the Primaeval Waters; Heh and Hehet, the male and female personifications of infinite space or eternity; Kek and Keket—darkness; Amun and Amunet—invisibility. At *Khemenu*, they were said to be the oldest gods in the world, the fathers and mothers of the sun, for whom they created the sacred mound at *Khemenu* so that he could stand on it.

The Ogdoad of *Khemenu* was held in great regard at Thebes once Amun arrived there, for he had the same name as one of these primordial deities, whose partner, Amunet, was sometimes regarded at Thebes as the mother-goddess, the consort of Amun alongside Mut. Amun of *Khemenu* and Amun of Thebes may or may not have been the same god, but certainly during the Graeco-Roman period, the Ogdoad was paid particular attention, not least because the Eight Gods were believed to be buried under the temple at Medinet Habu, on the west bank at Thebes, where, every ten years, the last kings of Egypt came to offer libations to these, their primaeval ancestors.

Today, the name of the town in which the Ogdoad originated is a reminder of the one that it bore in honour of the Eight Primaeval Gods: the Arabic el-Eshmunein is derived from the Coptic Shmun, which in turn was derived from *Khemenu*. Thus is the Ogdoad commemorated.

Thoth was above all the god of wisdom, connected with everything that had to do with intellectual pursuits in both arts and sciences. He was the inventor of hieroglyphic writing, which was called *medoo-neter*, 'the words of the god'; and acted as scribe to the gods. Thoth was credited with having written with his own hand forty-two books containing all the wisdom of the world. Some of these books contained the laws of Egypt, of which Thoth was the guardian; others were books of magic, for Thoth was a great magician, rivalled only by Isis; yet others contained the annals of Egypt.

The female counterpart to Thoth, who was variously regarded as his wife or daughter, was the goddess of writing and books, the keeper of the Royal Annals, Seshat. Unlike Thoth, Seshat was never a deity of the people: she belonged to the king alone. It was Seshat who wrote the name of the king on the leaves of the *Ished* (Persea) Tree, each sacred leaf representing a year of the king's life as allotted to him by the gods. It was Seshat who helped the king to measure out the foundations of temples; and temple reliefs show her, dressed in a leopard-skin and wearing her fetish, a pair of cow's horns inverted over a flower, upon her head, helping the king to perform this task by 'stretching the cord' to measure and mark them out.

Thoth, also, was a royal god, who attended the coronation of the king, and, together with Horus, purified him before that and other ceremonies in the ritual known as 'the Baptism of Pharaoh', in which Thoth and Horus pour water over the king.

Thoth was the master of chronology and counting, and, since the moon was regarded as the natural measurer of time, he was a moon-god. As such, he was often depicted wearing a crescent moon on his head.

Thoth played an important role in the mythologies of several other gods. At Memphis, he was said to be the tongue of Ptah (p. 163); at Heliopolis, he was the mind and tongue of Re personified as Sia and Hu respectively; and also the messenger who brought back the Eye of Re and restored it to its rightful place (p. 53). In the Osiris legend, it was Thoth who taught Isis the spell for restoring Osiris' ability to procreate (p. 92) and helped her to reassemble the pieces of Osiris' dismembered body (p. 80); and it was Thoth who expelled poison from her son, Horus (p. 94).

In the Osirian version of the Judgement of the Dead, Thoth and his baboon play an important part. Vignettes of the Judgement scene in New Kingdom funerary papyri show Anubis weighing the heart of the deceased in the balance, supervised by the baboon, Thoth's *alter ego*. The baboon reports the result to Thoth who is standing by to record it.

Thoth was not only the scribe of the gods; he was also their messenger. Hence, the Greeks identified him with their own messenger of the gods, Hermes, and renamed his town of *Khemenu*, calling it Hermopolis (City of Hermes). During the Graeco-Roman period, Thoth was worshipped by both Greeks and Egyptians as Hermes Trismegistos (Thrice-great Hermes).

Some 7km west of Hermopolis lay the necropolis of the city, which dates from about the fifth century BC and is now known as Tuna el-Gebel. The necropolis is the site of an extensive underground gallery, the Ibeum, so-named because it is the place which housed the mummified bodies of thousands of ibises and baboons, many of them still in the pottery containers in which they were buried—testament to the great popularity of Thoth at that period. Nearby was a large artificial lake which was kept watered by means of a giant water-wheel. Palm trees were planted round the lake, making it into a place fit for the sacred ibises to live in.

Another huge burial place for the baboons and ibises sacred to Thoth is at Sakkara. Since 1964, excavations undertaken there by the Egypt Exploration Society have uncovered underground galleries for the burials of baboons, out of which lead further galleries crammed from floor to ceiling with mummified ibises in pottery containers. The exact size of these catacombs is as yet unknown, for the archaeologists are faced with the daunting task of removing thousands of ibises before exploring further.

Thoth's role as god of writing connected him closely with scribes. It was the custom for scribes to make a small libation to Thoth at the start of each day's work—they simply poured out a drop of water onto the ground from the pot in which they dipped their brushes. In a bureaucratic country such as Egypt, the scribe enjoyed a position of great power, and the immense popularity of Thoth at all times was due in no small measure to his role as their patron deity, the greatest scribe of all.

KHNUM

Khnum was one of the oldest gods of Egypt, revered since predynastic times in the area of the First Cataract on Egypt's southern border. His cult-centre was at *Abu*, capital of the First Nome of Upper Egypt, the *Abu* or Elephant Nome, which the Greeks called Elephantine. The town of *Abu* was on an island in the middle of the Nile opposite the modern town of Aswan.

Khnum was originally worshipped in the form of a flat-horned ram of the species *Ovis longipes palaeoaegypticus*, which became extinct somewhere around 2000 BC. He can appear as a ram or as a ram-headed man. Because the ram was valued for its procreative powers, Khnum was thought to be a creator of life. He was sometimes depicted as a ram-headed man moulding a human figure (usually a king) and his *ka* or double on a potter's turn-table; hence his appellation, 'the Potter God'. The most famous scene of Khnum in this role is found in the Mortuary Temple of Hatshepsut at Deir el-Bahri, where he is shown modelling the queen and her *ka* on his turn-table.

Each person modelled by Khnum was given an allotted life-span. This life-span was personified as Shay or 'that-which-is-ordained', and came to have the broader meaning of 'Fate', which the Greeks rendered as Agathodaimon and the Arabs as Kismet. As a deity, Shay was given two partners, the goddesses of fate, Meskhenet (p. 185) and Renenutet (p. 97).

Khnum was closely connected in the minds of the Egyptians with the Inundation, which was thought to start in a sacred pool on Elephant Island; and with the Nile, of whose mythological source at Biga (p. 80) he was the guardian. The cult of Khnum was widespread from an early date, and it is perhaps ironic that his most famous sanctuary should be the Temple of Khnum at Esna, which was built towards the end of Egyptian history. The temple, of which only the great twenty-four-column hypostyle hall, built by the Roman Emperors Claudius and Vespasian in the first century AD, stands today, was dedicated not only to Khnum but also to several other deities, including Neit.

It was the fish sacred to Neit, the Nile perch (*Latus niloticus*), that was the sacred animal of Esna, causing the Greeks to name the town Latopolis (the City of the Perch). The Arabic name of the town, Esna, was derived from the Ancient Egyptian (*Ta*)-*sny*. Because of its position, on the left bank of the Nile some 50km south of Luxor, at a place where the routes across the desert to the Sudan meet, Esna was an important town from at least the Middle Kingdom.

There are numerous ritual and religious texts carved on the walls of the temple, the last dating to the reign of Decius (AD 249–251). They tell us, for instance, that the Creation of the World was performed by Neit, who, after her initial creative work, departed for her own city of Sais, leaving Khnum to continue the task which he did by fashioning living things on his potter's turn-table.

The Esna theories of the origin of life are exceptionally interesting: once beings had been created, it was necessary to animate them and fill them with the breath of life. There were two elements—water and air—which, in certain conditions and when mixed in given propor-

5 Part of a limestone relief from the Dynasty XVIII *Mortuary Temple of Queen Hatshepsut at Deir el-Bahri, Thebes. The ram-headed god, Khnum, is shown fashioning Hatshepsut and her* ka *upon his potter's turn-table, with the frog-headed goddess, Heket, in attendance*

tions, allowed life to be born and to develop. This vital breath, which was in the possession of the god, was said to penetrate the egg to animate the chick before the breaking of the shell; to descend to the bottom of the waters to vivify the fish; to give colour to the leaves of the trees; and to cure the sick.

After many years of creating and maintaining life, Khnum became tired of the incessant effort. He therefore thought of a device to relieve him of his burden: he placed a potter's turn-table in the womb of all female creatures, thus transmitting to them his creative powers. From then on, he was able to concentrate on his task of maintaining the creation of the life-force.

Khnum had three consorts: Heket, Anukis and Satis. Heket was a primordial creator-goddess who took the form of a frog. The oldest centre of her cult was in the Elephant Nome where she was, for a long time, regarded as the wife of Khnum. Eventually, however, Heket's position in the Elephant Nome was usurped by Satis (see below); and the centre of her cult moved to the Fayum Oasis.

Heket helped Osiris rise from the dead, an activity which was later remembered by Egyptian Christians, for whom the frog was the symbol of Resurrection. Her chief function, however, was as goddess of childbirth: at royal births she acted as midwife.

A story[11] written on papyrus probably during the Hyksos period (*c.* 1674–1550 BC) and now in Berlin as Papyrus Westcar, illustrates Heket's role as divine midwife: the wife of a priest of Re, a woman named Reddjedet, was pregnant with three children belonging to Re, children who were destined to become kings of Egypt. And so Re decided to send a company of gods to help Reddjedet in her time of travail. He commanded that Isis, Nephthys, Meskhenet and Heket should go to the aid of Reddjedet, and so the four goddessess set out disguised as musicians; and Khnum went with them to carry their baggage!

They duly delivered Reddjedet: Isis and Nephthys supported her; Meskhenet, who was the personification of the birth-stool, stood by ready to act as the good fairy who predicted the future of the newly-born child. But it was Heket who brought each of Reddjedet's three children safely into the world.

Anukis, who was a concubine of Khnum, was goddess of the cataract on Egypt's southern border, where her chief shrine was on the island of Seheil. She is normally depicted as a woman wearing a headdress composed of what might be the feathers of a red parrot, perhaps indicating that her origins were in the Sudan, where such birds were found. The Greeks identified her with Hestia, goddess of the Hearth.

Satis, whom the Greeks identified with Hera, the wife of Zeus, was the daughter of Khnum and Anukis; she replaced Heket as the consort of her father, probably at a very early date because she herself was an ancient deity who is mentioned in the Pyramid Texts. She was depicted as a woman wearing the White Crown of Upper Egypt flanked by two gazelle horns, suggesting that originally she came from a region where gazelles proliferated—perhaps the Sudan. Her name seems to be derived from the word 'shoot' (arrows) or 'pour' (water), which probably means that she was a local goddess of hunting who became a goddess of the Inundation. Her cult-centre, like that of Anukis, was on the island of Seheil.

Satis became fused with Sothis, presumably because their names have a similar sound. Sothis was the Egyptian name for what we call Sirius, the Dog Star; and was thought to be the goddess responsible for the Inundation. She was depicted as a woman wearing on her head a five-pointed star.

In turn, Sothis was fused with Isis; and during the Late Period they were worshipped under the joint name of Isisothis.

Khnum, Anukis and Satis together formed the Great Triad of the Elephant Nome, where above all they played their parts as guardians and donors of the waters of the Nile, who 'dispensed the cool water coming from the Elephant Nome'.

MIN

Min was one of the most ancient Egyptian gods, a deity of fertility whose origins are lost in the mists of time but whose sacred object (p. 188) is often found on predynastic painted vases. The statues of Min discovered at Koptos by Petrie during his excavations of AD 1893–94 are probably predynastic in date and, at over four metres high, are considered to be the oldest examples of large-scale sculpture in Egypt. They are headless but show Min standing in what was later to become his typical pose. The legs of the statues are not separated but carved in one piece, suggesting the great antiquity of the figures since individual delineation of these limbs in sculpture in the round was not practised until well on in the Old Kingdom.

Min was usually depicted as a man standing upright wearing on his head a cap surmounted by two tall plumes. His legs are never seen, seemingly being wrapped in mummy bandages, but more probably copying the style of his predynastic statues. One arm, bent at the elbow, is raised and outstretched, its hand open; above it floats a flail. The other arm is tucked under his robe, from which projects his penis, huge and erect. Any area of skin not covered by a garment is painted black: in dynastic times, it was one of the duties of the High Priest of Min to make up the bituminous substance with which the cult statue of the god was ritually painted, black being the colour of the fertile soil of Egypt and therefore symbolic of regeneration.

The worship of Min was universal throughout Egyptian history; but two cities were particularly associated with him: *Gebtu* and *Khent-Min*.

Gebtu (called Koptos by the Greeks; now known as Qift) lies on the east bank of the Nile some 40km north of Luxor, at the terminus of the route which leads from the Red Sea to the Nile. It achieved great importance at an early date because of its geographical position: mining expeditions to the Eastern Desert and trading expeditions to the Red Sea had their starting point at *Gebtu*, which therefore became the obvious choice to become capital of the 5th Nome of Upper Egypt.

187

The original god of *Gebtu* seems to have been a phallic deity named Rahes or Aahes, who appears in the Pyramid Texts as 'Regent of the Land of the South'. Rahes and Min, depicted as falcons, formed the Nome standard, although later on, when Horus and Isis became popular in *Gebtu*, the two falcons of the Nome standard were identified with Horus and Min.

Min of *Gebtu* (Min of Koptos) was considered to be the tutelary deity of nomads, hunters, miners and travellers, for the Eastern Desert was his special domain. As a deity of the desert, Min was associated with the thunder that was thought to emanate therefrom. Thus, when the Canaanite-Phoenician god of thunder and war, Reshep, was introduced into Egypt during the New Kingdom, it was natural that he should be allied with Min. They were both given the Syrian goddess of love, Kadesh, as partner, with the three deities combining to form a triad of fertility, thunder and love!

Khent-Min (today called Akhmim) lies on the east bank of the Nile some 80km south of Assiut. Its name means 'the Shrine of Min' and it was once the capital of the 9th Nome of Upper Egypt. Since the Greeks equated Min with Pan, they called the city Panopolis. The emblem on the Nome standard was the fetish of Min, which consists of two fossil belemnites flanking a small circle ⟵⟶; this emblem also forms the hieroglyphic symbol for the god's name. The belemnite is an extinct cephalopod related to the cuttle-fish. Although a pre-dynastic green stone model of a cuttle-fish, now in the British Museum, can be taken as evidence that this mollusc had itself been the object of a cult, the belemnite was probably chosen as Min's fetish for symbolic reasons. It has been suggested that it represents a thunderbolt, which would link it to Min. Its cigar-like shape, however, could equally well be interpreted as a phallic symbol.

One of the most famous sons of *Khent-Min* was Yuya, the grandfather of Tutankhamun, who served Min as High Priest and Superintendent of Cattle. Yuya's daughter, Tiy, who was married to Amenhotep III, owned extensive estates in the *Khent-Min* region; and even had a lake constructed for her there by her husband (p. 71). During the reign of Yuya's son, Ay, who became King of Egypt after Tutankhamun, much attention was paid to *Khent-Min*, partly because it was Ay's family seat but much more importantly because during Dynasty XVIII, Min became associated with the most powerful god in Egypt, Amun.

At both *Gebtu* and *Khent-Min*, Min was worshipped in the form of a sacred white bull, a symbol of his virility. And wherever he was worshipped, lettuces were offered to him, for these vegetables, whose white sap is reminiscent of semen, were considered to have aphrodisiac qualities.

Thus Min was the god of fertility *par excellence*. His cult placed such great emphasis on procreation and fecundity that, in an agricultural country like Egypt, it was bound to be extremely popular. For many Egyptians, the highlight of the year occurred at the beginning of the harvest season, when Min's statues were brought out of their temples for the great 'Festival of the Coming Forth of Min'.

MONTU

Montu was a falcon-god who was usually depicted as a man with the head of a hawk wearing a sun's disk surmounted by two tall plumes. He originated in Upper Egypt, probably in *Iuny*, a town which lay on the west bank of the Nile some 20km south of modern-day Luxor.

Until Dynasty XVIII, *Iuny* was the capital of the 4th Nome of Upper Egypt, the Sceptre Nome. Because of the similarity of pronunciation with *Iunu*, or On, the city of Re (p. 44), *Iuny* was called *Iunu-Montu*, 'On-of-Montu', to avoid confusion with the Lower Egyptian city. Today, *Iuny* is called Armant, a name which is derived from *Iunu-Montu*, which the Copts pronounced Ermont, which was itself turned into Hermonthis by the Greeks.

The rulers of Dynasty XI probably came from *Iuny* (Armant). Although Montu's name is mentioned in the Pyramid Texts, and he appears in the decorations of Pepi II's funerary temple at Sakkara as one of the representative deities of Upper Egypt, he did not achieve great status until Dynasty XI when, as the patron god of the kings of that dynasty, he was elevated to the position of one of the major deities of Egypt; and, at about the same time, became particularly associated with war. The rulers of Dynasty XI showed their adherence to Montu not only by building temples to him but by including his name in their own: thus we have four rulers of Dynasty XI called *Montu-hotep* (Montu-is-satisfied).

Montu was often equated with Horus and called Horus-with-the-strong-arm; but by the early Middle Kingdom he seems to have been regarded as the Upper Egyptian counterpart of Re of Heliopolis and was merged with him under the name of Mont-Re. He was worshipped at several places in the Sceptre Nome either in the form of a falcon-headed man; or in the shape of a bull.

In his falcon form, Montu was the local god of *Djerty* (now called Tod), a town on the east bank of the Nile facing *Iuny* (Armant), which received much attention during the Middle Kingdom. Later, in Dynasty XVIII, Thothmes III built a shrine there for the barque of

Montu; and later still, other kings, Seti I and Ramesses III amongst them, carried out restoration work on the shrine. Ptolemy VIII built a temple at *Djerty* (by then called Tuphium); and further work was undertaken there during the Roman period.

At *Iuny* itself, Montu was worshipped in the form of a sacred bull, the *Bekh* or Buchis Bull. This animal was renowned for his strength and ferocity; he was probably black, although the colour of his hair was said to change every hour of the day; and Aelian[12], who reported that this bull was called Onuphis, also wrote that the hair on the animal grew and lay the contrary way to that of other animals.

The sacred Buchis Bull was buried on the edge of the desert just north of *Iuny* in a special catacomb known as the Bucheum. The earliest burial so far found dates to the reign of Nectanebo II (360–343 BC); and the latest to some six hundred and fifty years later in the reign of Diocletian. The Mothers of the Buchis Bulls were also accorded a special burial site near their sons.

Some 20km north of *Iuny*, on the east bank of the Nile, another shrine was built to Montu at *Madu* (Nag el-Medamud). The temple which stands there today was built during the Graeco-Roman period on the site of a temple that was begun during the Middle Kingdom and enlarged during the New Kingdom.

At Medamud, the local Buchis Bull was kept in a special building just behind the main temple. This sacred 'stable' seems to have consisted of two compartments where the Bull was allowed to roam at will.

Montu enjoyed the supremacy that the rulers of Dynasty XI gave him as chief god of the Sceptre Nome and mighty war-god of Egypt only briefly. In Dynasty XII, his position was usurped by Amun, although he never lost his appeal to warrior kings such as Thothmes III who on one occasion called himself 'beloved son of Montu who resides in *Iuny*'; or Thothmes' son, Amenhotep II, who was 'a hero like Montu' and 'like Montu in his might'.

BASTET

Bastet, the cat-goddess, was the benevolent counterpart of Sekhmet, the lioness. The Wild Cat (*felis vercata maniculata*) was native to Egypt, and it was probably this aggressive cat that was the prototype for the Cat of Heliopolis (p. 64); for the cat-goddess, Mafdet; and even for the early forms of Bastet herself. In later manifestations, however, Bastet was the domesticated cat, which was introduced into Egypt, according to some authorities, from the west and the south perhaps around 2100 BC.

From the Middle Kingdom, pictures of cats are found in tombs where they are sometimes shown sitting under chairs at feasts, but are more often depicted out hunting in the marshes with their owners. The domesticated cat of Ancient Egypt was not just a catcher of mice, the inspiration of the advice given in medical papyri: 'To prevent mice from coming near things—put cat-grease on everything'. It was a hunter, a killer of the snakes feared by Egyptians, although it could be trained, if reliefs in tombs are to be believed, as a retriever, trusted to bring back birds brought down by the throwsticks of its master. In Ancient Egyptian, the word for domesticated cat was *miw*; and little girls were often given the nickname *miw-sheri*, 'Little Cat' or 'pussy-cat'.

Bastet may originally have been a lioness; however, her worshippers preferred her in the form of the less fierce, more charming, domestic cat. Hence, from at least the Middle Kingdom onwards, she was worshipped as a woman with a cat's head; or in the form of a queen cat, of the type familiar from the numerous statuettes found in museums the world over.

The cult-centre of Bastet was at *Bast*, which lies some 60km to the north-east of Cairo; and the name, Bastet, means 'She-of-*Bast*'. In hieroglyphs, the word *Bast* was written using a picture of a sealed oil-jar 𓎯; it is possible, therefore, that the fetish originally worshipped at *Bast* bore a resemblance to an oil-jar.

At *Bast*, the main temple was called *Per-Bastet* (The House of

Bastet), and gave its name to the town in the Greek period when it was called Bubastis, the Greek pronunciation of *Per-Bastet*; today, it is called Tell Basta. *Bast* controlled the routes from Memphis to Sinai, which in turn led to Asia; hence, it was strategically important. During Dynasty xxII, it became politically important also, for the kings of that Dynasty originated in *Bast*. In the Late Period, it became the capital of the 18th Nome of Lower Egypt.

Herodotus visited *Bast*, which he, of course, being Greek, called Bubastis, in the fifth century BC. In his opinion, there was no temple in Egypt that was a greater pleasure to look at than that of Bastet.[13] In Herodotus' time, the temple stood in the centre of the city, and, since the level of the surrounding buildings had been raised over the years since the temple was first built, one could look down and enjoy a fine view of it.

It was surrounded by a low wall, and the entrance was approached by a stone-paved road about 120 metres wide, lined on both sides with 'immense trees — so tall that they seem to touch the sky'. The main gateway was 18 metres high; and more tall trees stood about the actual shrine, which contained a statue of Bastet. Two canals, each 30 metres or so wide, had been led from the Nile to sweep round the temple, one on each side as far as the entrance, where they stopped short without meeting. There were several temples at *Bast*, including one dedicated to Mihos, a lion-god who was said to be the son of Bastet. Large cemeteries of sacred cats have also been found there.

It seems that these sacred cats from the Temple of Bastet were not the only ones accorded burial in the cat necropolis of *Bast*/Bubastis. Herodotus maintained[14] that the Egyptians were so fond of all cats that, whenever one of the animals died, they were deeply distressed: they shaved their eyebrows and took the cat to Bubastis, where it was embalmed and buried in a sacred receptacle.

The popularity of Bastet was such that, again according to Herodotus, the most important and best-attended festival was the one held at Bubastis in honour of Bastet, whom the Greeks identified with Artemis. The animal sacred to Artemis was the she-bear, not the cat; hence the Greeks could not have associated Artemis with Bastet because of any identity between sacred animals. They were both, however, virgin-goddesses (Bastet in spite of being the mother of Mihos!), although their worship was orgiastic, and in Bastet's case included ritual frenzies.

The evidence of the numerous statuettes, made in the Late Period especially, of beautifully observed cats, lissom, muscular and dignified, testifies to the popularity of Bastet, which never abated from the time when she rose to importance as the local deity of the kings of

Dynasty XXII to the Graeco-Roman period. The Romans carried her worship to Italy, to Rome, Ostia, Pompeii; and to Nemi, where she was provided with 'a robe of silk, purple and turquoise-green; a shirt of purple linen with two girdles, one gilt; two mantles, a tunic and a white dress'.

Notes on the text

1 HERODOTUS *The Histories*, trans. A. de Sélincourt, Harmondsworth 1954, p. 130

2 HOCH, E. 'Reflections on Prehistoric Life at Umm an-Nar (Trucial Oman) based on Faunal Remains from the Third Mellenium BC', *South Asian Archaeology*, 1977, p. 626ff.

3 GRIFFITH, F.L. *The Antiquities of Tell el-Yahûdîyah*, London 1890.

4 GOLENISHEFF, W. *Die Metternichstele*, Leipzig 1899. For a translation see BUDGE E.A.W. *Egyptian Literature, Legends and the Gods*, London 1912, p. 142ff.

5 GARDINER, A.H. *Description of a Hieratic Papyrus*, London 1931 and *Later Egyptian Stories*, Brussels 1932

6 FAIRMAN, H.W., ed. *The Triumph of Horus*, London 1974

7 ERMAN, A. *The Ancient Egyptians: a Sourcebook of their Writings*, trans. A.M. Blackman, New York 1966, p. 150.

8 as above, p. 161.

9 HOMER *The Iliad*, Book 9, trans. Alexander Pope, The World's Classics, Oxford University Press

10 CARTER, H. *The Tomb of Tutankhamun*, London 1972, p. 164

11 ERMAN, as above, p. 44.

12 AELIAN *On the Characteristics of Animals*, XI, 10, Loeb Classical Library

13 HERODOTUS as above, p. 156

14 as above, p. 128

Further reading

ALDRED, C. *Akhenaten, Pharaoh of Egypt*, London 1968

ALLEN, T.G. *The Egyptian Book of the Dead*, Chicago 1960

BAINES, J. & MÁLEK, J. *Atlas of Ancient Egypt*, Oxford 1980

BOYLAN, P. *Thoth, the Hermes of Egypt*, Oxford 1922

BREASTED, J.H. *Development of Religion and Thought in Ancient Egypt*, New York 1959

BUDGE, E.A.W. *From Fetish to God in Ancient Egypt*, Oxford 1934

ČERNY, J. *Ancient Egyptian Religion*, London 1952

CLARK, R.T. RUNDLE. *Myth and Symbol in Ancient Egypt*, London 1959, reprinted 1978

ERMAN, A. *A handbook of Egyptian Religion*, trans. A.M. Blackman, London 1907

FAULKNER, R.O. *The Ancient Egyptian Coffin Texts*, Warminster 1973

FAULKNER, R.O. *The Ancient Egyptian Pyramid Texts*, Oxford 1969

FRANKFORT, H. *Ancient Egyptian Religion*, New York 1961

GREEN, R.L. *Tales of Ancient Egypt*, Harmondsworth 1967

GRIFFITHS, J.G. *The Conflict of Horus and Seth*, Liverpool 1960

GRIFFITHS, J.G. *The Origins of Osiris*, Berlin 1966

HOLMBERG, M. SANDMAN *The God Ptah*, Lund 1946

JAMES, T.G.H. *Myths and Legends of Ancient Egypt*, London 1969

JENKINS, N. *The Boat Beneath the Pyramids*, London 1980

JUNKER, H. 'Die Onurislegende', *Denkschrift der Wiener Akademie*, 59 (i), Vienna 1917

LURKER, M. *The Gods and Symbols of Ancient Egypt*, 2nd ed. rev. and enlarged by P.A. Clayton, London 1981

MORENZ, S. *Egyptian Religion*, trans. A. Keep, London 1973

OTTO, E. *Egyptian Art and the Cults of Osiris and Amon*, London 1968

POSENER, G. *A Dictionary of Egyptian Civilization*, London 1962

SAUNERON, S. *The Priests of Ancient Egypt*, London 1960

WEIGALL, A. *The Life and Times of Akhenaten*, London 1922

Index

Numerals in italics refer to figure numbers of photographs between pages 80 and 81.